Defeating the Hacker

Defeating the Hacker

A non-technical guide to computer security

Robert Schifreen

John Wiley & Sons, Ltd

Copyright © 2006   John Wiley & Sons Ltd, The Atrium, Southern Gate, Chichester,
                       West Sussex PO19 8SQ, England

                       Telephone (+44) 1243 779777

Email (for orders and customer service enquiries): cs-books@wiley.co.uk
Visit our Home Page on www.wiley.com

Other Wiley Editorial Offices

John Wiley & Sons Inc., 111 River Street, Hoboken, NJ 07030, USA

Jossey-Bass, 989 Market Street, San Francisco, CA 94103-1741, USA

Wiley-VCH Verlag GmbH, Boschstr. 12, D-69469 Weinheim, Germany

John Wiley & Sons Australia Ltd, 42 McDougall Street, Milton, Queensland 4064, Australia

John Wiley & Sons (Asia) Pte Ltd, 2 Clementi Loop #02-01, Jin Xing Distripark, Singapore 129809

John Wiley & Sons Canada Ltd, 22 Worcester Road, Etobicoke, Ontario, Canada M9W 1L1

Wiley also publishes its books in a variety of electronic formats. Some content that appears
in print may not be available in electronic books.

Library of Congress Cataloging-in-Publication Data

Schifreen, Robert.
    Defeating the hacker : a non-technical introduction to computer security / Robert Schifreen.
        p. cm.
    Includes bibliographical references and index.
    ISBN-13: 978-0-470-02555-0
    ISBN-10: 0-470-02555-7 (cloth : alk. paper)
    1.   Computer security.   I.   Title.
    QA76.9.A25S343 2006
    005.8 – dc22
                                                                 2005033916

British Library Cataloguing in Publication Data

A catalogue record for this book is available from the British Library

ISBN-13: 978-0-470-02555-0
ISBN-10: 0-470-02555-7

Typeset in 11/13pt Bembo by Laserwords Private Limited, Chennai, India
Printed and bound in Great Britain by Antony Rowe Ltd, Chippenham, Wiltshire
This book is printed on acid-free paper responsibly manufactured from sustainable forestry
in which at least two trees are planted for each one used for paper production.

Contents

1

Introduction

This is a book about hackers, crackers, phishing, pharming, spammers, scammers, virus-writers, Trojan horses, malware and spyware, and how to keep them out of your company's computer systems. By which I mean the private computers on your employees' desks in the office and at home, and the servers which look after your company's email, file storage and Web site.

Your email and Web servers may be your own machines, housed either on your premises or off-site in what's known as a 'co-location facility'. Or, as is very common, you may be renting space on someone else's servers. The precise arrangements don't matter – if these computers are handling your own information then you need to give consideration to their security, and this book will tell you how. Equally, whether your employees store their document files on their own desktop PCs or on your networked file server, this book will tell you how to keep the hackers away.

All the advice which follows is straightforward, and anyone with a reasonable knowledge of computers and Windows should be able to follow it. I've deliberately avoided recommending procedures or solutions which are complex or expensive.

If you've never read a book such as this before, what took you so long? You owe it to yourself and your company to ensure that your computer systems don't fall victim to an attack, and this book will tell you what you need to know.

If you've read lots of security books and you're wondering what makes this one different, the answer is that I used to be a hacker. So you're getting advice from someone who knows just how exhilarating it would be to break into someone else's computers, and who has, in the past, been prepared to invest large amounts of time attempting to do so. If you want to learn how to protect your systems, I reckon that it makes sense to take advice from someone who knows what he's talking about.

In case you're wary about taking advice from a practising criminal, I should point out that my hacking career happened way back in the 1980s, and is long since over. I never broke any anti-hacking laws because, at the time, there weren't any. I was arrested after freely admitting what I'd done and bragging about it on TV. I was charged with forgery, because the police reckoned that they could convince a jury that my typing someone else's password into a computer was no different to signing their name on a cheque or other legal document. The courts disagreed, and my ultimate acquittal on all charges led to a change in the law in the UK, where the Computer Misuse Act 1990 now outlaws hacking. And before you ask, no I don't hack any more. I had my 15 minutes of infamy – it would be pointless and stupid to try again.

The British legal process is fascinating, but incredibly slow and expensive. It has been estimated that my legal costs, thankfully covered in full by the state rather than myself, amounted to almost £2 million. The whole episode dragged on for three years and involved 10 different judges, a couple of QCs (senior barristers), two standard barristers, a couple of solicitors, some members of the House of Lords, not to mention the services of a jury. All of whom had to decide simply whether section 1 of the 1981 Forgery and Counterfeiting Act was intended to apply solely to permanent marks on paper, or whether it should also extend to electronic impulses stored temporarily in a computer chip while the system attempted to decide if they represented a valid password.

Most authors dream of writing a book that readers can't put down. But this book is different. My hope is that you'll keep putting it down in order to fix, or at least consider, security problems in your company's IT systems of which you were previously unaware. If you get to the end without having had a single panic attack or a 'gotta-fix-this-right-now' moment, I will be hugely impressed, yet slightly disappointed.

A Journey

I guess I should begin by explaining how I got here. My credentials, if you like. After all, if you're going to take advice on such a serious subject then it's only fair that I spell out why you should trust me.

First, I like to think that an ex-hacker is the best person to explain the risks that hackers pose, and the tricks that they use.

Second, I have no vested interests other than the desire for you to buy this book and, hopefully, recommend it to others. I don't sell security products, or get paid for those that I recommend. The advice contained in these pages is given because I believe it to be the truth. Which, you may be surprised to know, isn't always the case when you read product reviews in magazines. These publications are funded by advertising, so the subjects they cover and the type of products they review (and, very occasionally, the opinions of the reviewers) are dictated by the list of advertisers that the magazine wishes to attract.

You may also have seen adverts in the computer press which show pictures of a stressed IT manager or security guy relaxing on a beach somewhere, safe in the knowledge that product X, which he's just purchased, is taking care of security, and he doesn't have to worry about it any more. I hate to tell you this, but the real world really isn't like that. Despite what the glossy adverts tell you, you can't buy peace of mind. You still need to worry. But at least this book will help you to prioritize your worrying, and to direct your efforts into fixing the most important problems first.

Ideally, you already have a dedicated IT security person on your payroll and he or she will know all about the topics which follow. But my experience is that most small and medium companies don't have any in-house IT security staff at all, and the responsibility is given to someone who already has another role and doesn't really have time to do both. So security only gets his attention when something goes wrong. If this is the case in your company, then this book is for you. My hope is that it will help to answer most of your questions about where the risks lie and what to do about them.

This is not a book aimed at users or administrators on one particular hardware platform, but more a collection of useful advice that is applicable to information security in all environments. In a nutshell – if you use computers to store or process information then this book will help you prevent that information from falling into the wrong hands or being tampered with. Because most small and medium companies don't have domain-based networks, most of this book is designed for people looking after networks that don't use domains.

Like all facets of the IT world, security is a constantly changing subject. There's a continual cat-and-mouse tussle between the good guys and the bad guys. In an ideal world, the good guys would always be one step ahead of the baddies, and thus our computers would always be secure. But sadly it doesn't work like that. Most of the time, the IT security industry (and especially those involved in producing antivirus software) is playing catch-up, fixing holes and blocking viruses that have already been exploited and unleashed. This means that the dedicated IT security manager can never afford to stand still and glory in the knowledge that the battle has finally been won. It will never be won. The best we can do is to hold the attackers at bay, but even this cannot be achieved without constant expenditure of both time and money.

And yet, despite what the sales departments of security companies will tell you, it's perfectly possible to improve your company's IT security without throwing huge amounts of money at the problem. In many cases, knowledge and procedures are what's required, rather than expensive hardware or software or annual maintenance agreements. Hopefully this book will help you.

Because things change so quickly in this field, use the Web to keep yourself up to date with developments. One useful online resource is www.itsecurity.com, which publishes useful free advice, and also allows you to put questions to the resident panel of security specialists (including myself). It's free of charge, too. There are many other great sites too, which I shall point out as we go along.

This book has its own presence on the Web at www.defeating thehacker.com. There you'll find a clickable collection of all the links mentioned in the pages that follow, plus a discussion forum where you can seek advice and opinions from fellow participants including the author.

In my 20 years as a writer and commentator on IT security issues, on both sides of the fence, I've accumulated thousands of tips and dozens of anecdotes. I've tried to include as many of them as possible within these pages, but there is no implication that you must take every piece of advice on board right away. To do so will take you many years, and lots of it won't be relevant to your organization or financially viable. But by reading the book there will, I hope, be many topics which ring particular alarm bells for you and which will alert you to a problem within your own company that needs to be solved sooner rather than later. To help you, each chapter ends with a set of five action points – I call them the Fundamental Five. If you do nothing else, at least consider these as demanding your immediate attention. In most cases, it will simply be a case of you saying 'yes, we've got that in hand'.

Diversions Everywhere

As you walk through your local shopping street or mall, you have probably seen signs warning you that 'pickpockets operate in this area'. Most people assume that such signs drive the pickpockets away. In reality it actually attracts them, because most shoppers subconsciously reach to touch their wallet or purse when they see the sign. Which tells the pickpocket everything he needs to know.

Information security is a fast-moving field, and the hackers' desire to find new methods of attack never wanes. Whatever you put in their way, they will use to their advantage. To outwit them and to beat them at their own game you need to think as they do, because traditional defences simply don't work any more. Which is, I sincerely hope, where this book will help you.

2

A Hacker is Made

By profession, I work as an IT journalist. I've done it almost continually since leaving school in 1982 at the age of 18. I've done it as a full-time writer on one particular magazine, and as a freelancer writing for any magazine or newspaper which is interested in the story idea that I am trying to sell them at the time.

In addition I often speak at IT security seminars and conferences in the UK (where I live), and throughout the rest of Europe and the USA. Sometimes these events are commercial – people pay to listen to myself and others scare them into taking IT security seriously. Mostly, though, the events are sales conferences put on by vendors of security products. I tell things from a hacker's point of view, and show just how easy it is to break into a computer. The host company then rolls out its senior management who take great delight in explaining to the assembled audience that, if they buy the product which the organizers just happen to be launching today, they don't have to worry any more over the grave dangers about which I previously spoke. If you've ever attended one of my talks and wished that the organizers had allowed me more than 35 minutes to explain everything you need to know about IT security, this book is dedicated to you.

Mostly I speak alone, but occasionally I share the stage with a retired Detective Inspector from London's Metropolitan Police called John Austen. Some 22 years ago, John helped set up the Met's Computer Crime Unit, and our first encounter was in 1985 when he came to my house to arrest me.

Like many other children of the 1960s, I became interested in computers while at school. During my final couple of years at secondary school, in the very early 1980s, the school received its first microcomputers. These were very low-tech by today's standards, including a terminal that was linked by 300-baud modem to a mainframe at the local Town Hall.

The terminal was slow. Very slow. When we needed to print out a very long program listing there were two options. One was to start the thing running before morning assembly at 9am and hope that it would have finished printing by the time school broke for lunch some three hours later. The other was to issue a command that would print the listing on the much faster line printer at the Town Hall, and for our computer science teacher to drive (or sometimes cycle) the eight miles to collect it. Try telling that to the educators of today.

Shortly after I left school, I got a job on a computer games magazine, and progressed rapidly from resident geek and troubleshooter to full-blown journalist. Around that time, an online service called Micronet 800 was launched. Micronet was rather like a precursor to today's Web. Lots of pages of information, stored on a network of mainframe computers that you could access via a modem from your home micro if you paid the monthly subscription.

Micronet was part of a larger system called Prestel, run by British Telecom. While other parts of the Prestel system held information that was of interest to farmers, travel agents and the financial services community, Micronet was aimed at home computer users. They could read news stories, download software for their home microcomputers, send letters for publication, and exchange emails with fellow subscribers. Needless to say, the concept of Micronet and modems attracted my attention, and I subscribed as soon as the service went live.

Shortly after I started work on the computer games magazine, I discovered that Micronet was actually owned by the same company which published the magazine, and that Micronet's editorial offices were in the basement of the building in which I was working. It wasn't long before I had introduced myself to the staff and was contributing the occasional news story for publication on the system.

With my standard user account I could view the Micronet content, but not much else, and I certainly couldn't publish information onto the system. But if I entered the ID and password that I was given for use in the Micronet offices when writing stories, I was able not just to view information but to create pages too.

It gradually started to occur to me that the mainframes held much more information than I was being allowed to see, even using a Micronet staff account. Presumably there were other usernames and passwords, even more powerful than the ones I knew. Passwords which would allow me to publish information on other areas of Prestel rather than just the Micronet pages. Passwords which might permit access to the management system, used by Prestel staff to create new accounts or monitor existing ones.

The Micronet staff had made occasional mention of 'page 99', which was the system management menu for the Prestel network on which Micronet's pages resided. Although they knew of its existence, no one within the Micronet organisation had sufficient privileges to access it. Although it crossed my mind that it might be fun to see this secret page, it was merely a curiosity rather than an obsession or a real goal.

But one evening, everything changed.

I was working late at Micronet's offices in London, writing some news stories and publishing them onto the system. Having finished my work, and with some time to kill before my next train home was due to depart, I decided to try setting up a new modem that had recently arrived in the office. I connected it to a computer and programmed it to dial the Prestel mainframe's telephone number. After a while, the familiar screen appeared which asked me to enter my 10–digit user id.

At this point I really didn't care about the user ID I was enter-ing – I was merely testing a modem. I reached for a handy key on the keyboard and pressed it 10 times in quick succession. To my surprise, the system accepted 2222222222 as valid and asked me for the accompanying

4-character password. My curiosity aroused, I went for the obvious 2222 and it was instantly rejected. I decided to try once more. My second guess, 1234, was accepted. "Good morning Mr G Reynolds, Welcome to Prestel" said the welcome screen. It was clearly later than I thought, so this new hacker headed home.

Mr Reynolds, I later discovered, was a Prestel employee, and I'd stumbled across a Prestel internal account. Despite being mostly a demo account with a very guessable ID and password, it had access to a closed area on the system which held the telephone numbers of various test computers that were not part of the public Prestel mainframe network. Still curious, and still keen to learn as much as I could about the way that Prestel worked, I dialled these numbers occasionally over a period of around 10 months, but got no further than the "Please enter your user ID and password" screen.

And then one evening, everything changed. Again.

I dialled the test computer as normal and the familiar authentication screen appeared. But underneath the main text were two sets of 14 digits, each on a separate line. One line was preceded by the letters SMAN, and the other by SED. It transpired that SMAN was shorthand for System Manager and SED stood for System Editor. These were the two most powerful accounts on the test computer, and someone had left the details on the welcome screen. I guessed that it had been done by a programmer who wanted them to hand, and who felt safe in doing so because no members of the public knew the telephone number of the test computer. In court it was subsequently confirmed that my guess was correct.

To cut a long story short, I logged into the test computer as System Manager and immediately tried to go to the legendary Page 99 management menu. Success. I now possessed absolute power. Among the options available on the management menu were facilities to shut down the entire Prestel network or to look up the password of a subscriber. Neither of which, in my opinion and in the opinion of various expert witnesses, should ever be permitted to any remote user of any computer system. But that is the way that Prestel had chosen to implement their system, and the password I chose to request was that of His Royal Highness the Duke of Edinburgh, husband of the Queen.

Confident that I was not breaking any law, I never made any secret of my hacking. I mentioned it to a member of Micronet's staff the following day and she immediately called Prestel HQ to report it. But instead of accepting my offer of explaining what I'd done and how they could prevent others from doing the same, they called in John Austen's new Computer Crime Unit and so began my prosecution. After a legal battle, which ultimately ended in the House of Lords (the supreme court in the UK), I was acquitted of all charges.

Having tried unsuccessfully to have the law regard hackers as forgers, the judiciary was now able to approach Parliament and ask for what they'd wanted all along, and which they knew would be denied unless they could prove that they'd exhausted all the other possibilities – a specific law to criminalize computer hacking.

This is the story of how I became a hacker. But people get into hacking for all sorts of reasons, and it is essential to understand the different motives if you want to protect your systems from abuse and attack. Some people are born hackers. Others, like myself, have hackerdom thrust upon them. Some are criminals who decide to give hacking a go because they're bored with armed robbery. Some are curious college students who pick targets at random. Some are political activists who deliberately set out to disrupt the computers belonging to companies that they dislike, such as those in the arms or fur or tobacco trades. Some are employees of the target company who simply want to play a joke on their boss, or find out how much their colleagues earn. Some are simply mad, and think nothing of breaking into the computer in a hospital cancer ward and changing patients' drug doses.

The fact that people hack for so many reasons is important to understand. Because protecting your systems from a disgruntled employee requires different actions than protecting it from political 'hacktivists' or a bored teenager. And because you never know which type of hacker is targeting your computers, the only safe option is to ensure that the defences you put in place can protect you from them all. It's a tall order. You can never take your eye off the ball. But that's the way you have to play the game if you are to have a hope of succeeding.

In the days when I was an active hacker, very few companies had any serious dependence on computers. All the important corporate data was on paper in filing cabinets. A day-long loss of all computing facilities would probably not even have been noticed by the majority of employees or customers. Nowadays it's quite different. Just how long could your company survive in business, and retain the trust of its customers, if you lost all computing and network facilities?

Preparation and Planning

Risk analysis, or risk assessment, is a key component of any IT security strategy. There are a number of formal methodologies for analysing risk. See www.cramm.com, for example. You can also buy detailed textbooks which contain all the complex formulas. But for now we'll keep things simple.

Risk analysis allows you to prioritize your efforts and expenditure by focusing resources where they will have the greatest effect. There's little point in adding to your network server's workload by encrypting non-confidential information such as tomorrow's canteen menu, or spending £1000 on a product which will prevent casual thieves from walking off with some kit that cost £1500 when it was purchased three years ago.

Sometimes the figures aren't quite as easy. If you reckon that losses from fraud by employees could be reduced by £40,000 per year if you switch to fingerprint recognition instead of password security for the tills in your shops, it's clearly not worth spending more than £40,000 per year on the implementation project. But what if the trade press gets hold of the story and you start to lose sales because customers lose confidence in your company? Do you simply reduce the threshold at which the project becomes viable by the amount of the lost business, or do you also factor in the goodwill and the adverse publicity?

There is no simple answer to all of these questions, except to give careful consideration to the sorts of damage that hackers, viruses and other security breaches can wreak in your company, and to decide how much it is worth spending to reduce your exposure to these risks. Remember, too, that few risks can be completely eliminated. For example, while the law of diminishing returns will make it impossibly expensive to reduce casual misuse of the internet by staff to 0%, a relatively painless expenditure might be all that's required to halve it. And half a risk is better than all of a risk, even if it's not quite as satisfying as removing that risk entirely.

Getting Started

Basic risk assessment/analysis involves compiling a list of all your company's electronic resources and then deciding which ones are the most deserving of your time and money. Electronic resources include, but are not limited to, staff workstations, your public Web site, the intranet server, email facilities, network hardware such as routers and firewalls, accounting systems, internet connectivity for staff, data backups, and so on.

Compiling such a list is rarely as easy as it might seem because, in most companies, not all systems are properly documented or accounted for. There are probably some systems that you're not even aware of, even though it might be your job to know about them. The IT manager of a large New York hospital once told me about the time that he'd received a call from the radiology department to request some technical advice about the minicomputer on which they were storing patients' x-ray images. This IT manager was shocked, to say the least, because no one had told him that radiology had ever bought such a machine. It later transpired that they had purchased it and connected it to the hospital's central network without going through the official channels, resulting in confidential patient data being managed by unqualified staff on a machine that wasn't included in the central weekly backup strategy.

Although you can make great inroads into the compilation of your assets list by referring to existing documentation and sending out email requests to anyone who might be able to help, that's not the end of the story. You will also need to do some detective work yourself to ensure that your list is as comprehensive as it can be.

Having assembled the list, it's a relatively straightforward job to consider the impact on the business if a certain resource were rendered unavailable for a period of time. Your job is to decide what amount of time is acceptable, and how much you're willing to spend to stop the risk becoming reality.

There's often a temptation to consider each risk separately. For example, when considering the safety of the purchase ledger system, you might consider the impact upon that system of a virus, a hacker, a hardware fault, theft of data, and so on. However, during the initial risk assessment phase your task is merely to decide how important something is, and how much effort you are willing to expend in order to keep it safe. The precise risks to which it might be exposed aren't important yet, so don't get into the minutiae of viruses, hardware faults and so on. Such detail can wait for the final phase of the risk analysis, in which you work down your list of resources in order of their importance and then plan precisely how you're going to protect them from all possible threats.

Those threats that might be relevant will, of course, depend upon the nature of the resource. The subsequent chapters of this book will, I hope, provide you with the information you need to decide which of your resources are at risk from which threats. A hardware-based firewall, for example, is unlikely to be infected by a computer virus, whereas a computer situated on the reception desk in an office that isn't manned 100% of the time is probably more in danger of being stolen than being infested with spyware. And while the company can certainly manage without a PC on the reception desk for a day while someone pops down to the nearest shop in order to replace it, a computer in such a location needs to be devoid of any confidential information unless it's encrypted and the passwords are not written down in full view of every passing visitor.

The Risk Register

Large organizations often compile and maintain something called a risk register, because legal or regulatory bodies decree that they have to do so. Even if your company is small enough not to have to maintain such a dossier, it's still a very useful exercise.

A risk register is simply a document, often laid out as a table, which identifies each risk, the person responsible for managing it, how it might become reality, the effects of it becoming a reality, what you're doing to prevent it becoming a reality, and how you'll be able to detect if it does ever become a reality. You should review and update the document every few months to ensure that it contains current information. A separate document (known as a Disaster Recovery Plan or Business Continuity Plan) will cover the details of how to deal with the situation when risk becomes reality, and this is covered in Chapter 40.

You don't need any special software to produce a risk register. A simple Word or Excel file will suffice, and a Web search for 'risk register examples' will show you how it needs to look. You can also download some free Word and Excel templates from **www.method123.com** that will make your life even easier.

Risks should include things that happen unexpectedly and things that fail to happen. For example, a hacker who corrupts your payroll database is a risk, but so is a six-month delay in the current project to replace your Web server with a faster model. So each time a major project begins, add it to the risk register.

It Couldn't Happen Here

It's tempting, during a risk assessment, to start thinking that you're wasting your time. That it couldn't happen to you because no one would be interested in hacking your particular company. Or sometimes you might be keen to do a proper risk analysis, only to be told by senior management that the risks are actually tiny and you're wasting everyone's time by spending money protecting the organization from non-existent threats.

The truth is, every company is at risk from electronic attack. Some more than others, for sure, but no one is totally immune, and any degree of complacency is very dangerous.

The precise nature of an attack will depend upon the type of company being attacked. If you're in the vivisection or arms trade, expect your firewalls to be frequently probed by so-called hacktivists who want to disrupt your company because they don't believe with its motives. Similarly, if your company has recently announced embarrassingly high levels of profit. If, on the other hand, your systems contain secrets such as Government intelligence or the recipe for the world's most famous brand of cola, hackers are more likely to be considering blackmail than mere irritation. If you're a small backstreet company that does no one any harm, and which most people have probably never even heard of, don't assume that you are immune from the hackers' attention, because many of them simply pick targets at random.

When Microsoft releases a new security patch which fixes a loophole in Windows, hackers all over the world spring into action with automatic software that will scan the entire internet in search of computers that have not yet been patched. When they find one, it's simply a case of referring to Microsoft's own documentation to find out about the flaw and how to exploit it. Those who don't quite understand how to do this, but still want to do a little recreational hacking, simply download some software and follow instructions posted in hackers' forums on the Web. So never assume that the only companies who get hacked are the likes of CNN and Amazon. It could, and almost certainly will, happen to you. The trick is to know what to do when it does.

Insiders

Risks to your computers and information don't just come from anonymous hackers over the internet. In fact, contrary to the impression that the media and Hollywood like to portray, such attacks make up a small minority. In practice, if someone hacks into your company's computers, it's more likely to be perpetrated from the inside by staff than from the outside by the sort of person that you might imagine a hacker to be. Experts reckon that this is the case in around 70% of computer misuse. It's important to understand this, because protecting your systems from hackers doesn't just mean installing firewalls to keep outsiders out. Staff who have legitimate access to your computers will not be noticed by your firewall, and are thus much harder to detect.

For this reason, insiders are an ideal ally for any hacker who needs to penetrate an otherwise impenetrable system. I'm often asked, during media interviews, how I'd go about breaking into a top-secret computer such as that of a bank, police force, Government department, and so on. Conventional hacking doesn't work in these cases, because such organizations are generally on the ball when it comes to protecting their systems. Those who want to break into such systems, such as tabloid journalists and private investigators, generally find that the easiest way is to hang around the local pubs or restaurants near the establishment, get talking to a poorly-paid employee or two, and offer them a bundle of cash if they'll abuse their access privileges by looking up information and handing over some printouts. All of which will go unnoticed by even the most efficient firewall.

Hacking is almost always illegal, even if it's committed by insiders. In the summer of 2005 a director of an Internet Service Provider in the UK received a six month jail sentence, suspended for two years, after he admitted spying on the email of a fellow director with whom he was currently involved in a boardroom power struggle. The culprit had programmed his email servers so that all emails to or from the fellow director were copied to a safe external Hotmail account from where they could be read in comfort. The most worrying aspect of such activity is that there's no easy automated way of finding out whether it's happening in your company. It all comes down to vigilance and good management.

Even if you go to great lengths to install all the necessary technology to prevent attack, such as firewalls and antivirus software and intrusion detection/prevention tools, there is one more potential point of ingress for attackers, namely ignorant or untrained staff who inadvertently become the weakest link in your security chain. While your firewall will block attempts by hackers to circumvent your security, it won't block incoming email messages that contain a newly-invented virus carrying an attachment which, if clicked on by an unsuspecting staff member, can run with impunity inside the firewall and send all your confidential files back to the hackers via email. Avoiding this risk is where security awareness training comes in, and this is discussed in Chapter 7.

Just How Real are the Risks?

Just how likely is it that your company will suffer some form of electronic mishap over the next 12 months? Although it's impossible to predict the future, events of the past give us some pretty useful information.

A survey by IBM in 2005 looked at 237 million security attacks that occurred against companies within a six-month period (the vast majority of these were port-scans that were stopped by a firewall and were therefore unsuccessful, hence the high numbers). Of those 237 million attacks, 54 million were aimed at organizations in the areas of government, 36 million in manufacturing, 34 million in financial services and 17 million in healthcare. IBM published the figures alongside some commentary suggesting that this indicates that hackers are clearly targeting these four particular areas rather than simply acting indiscriminately and with random opportunism. Whether or not you believe this to be the case, the fact that 237 million attempts were made to break into systems in just six months illustrates the scale of the problem. To ignore it, or pretend that it won't affect you, is foolhardy to say the least.

Of the various surveys that are carried out into the extent of computer crime, one of the most respected is undertaken every two years by the Department of Trade and Industry in the UK. It's actually produced by PriceWaterhouseCoopers, a firm of management consultants and accountants, and is sponsored by big names such as Computer Associates, Entrust and Microsoft. The results for 2004, downloadable free of charge from **www.security-survey.gov.uk**, make fascinating yet worrying reading. For example:

- 68% of UK businesses had a premeditated or malicious incident, compared with just under 50% in the previous 2002 survey.

- A quarter of companies experienced a significant incident involving accidental systems failure or data corruption.

- The average UK business has around one security breach a month. For larger companies it was around one per week.

■ The average cost of a company's most serious breach was around £1000. For large companies it was £120,000.

■ Only half of all wireless networks have security controls in place.

■ Most companies spend around 3% of their IT budget on security, up from 2% in the previous survey. In large companies it's now 4%.

■ Of the incidents suffered by large companies, 68% had suffered virus infections, 64% had detected unauthorized use of systems by staff, 39% had been hacked by outsiders, 49% had experienced losses due to computer-related theft or fraud, and 42% had suffered from systems failure or data corruption.

While such surveys make fascinating reading, it is impossible to know just how trustworthy their results are. Whenever I lecture senior managers about IT security, I always advise them never to divulge this type of information because it does not make business sense to do so. They generally nod in agreement at this point. Yet when I subsequently ask whether they trust the results of surveys, most say that they do. In the introduction to the 2004 DTI survey, the authors note that the response rate has gradually declined over the years because companies are understandably unwilling to reveal this type of information, even with a promise of anonymity.

My considered opinion from talking in person to senior managers and IT security personnel at seminars and presentations is that the figures mentioned above are broadly correct. Even if they're not, surveys of this kind have another benefit apart from just helping you appreciate the risks from hackers, viruses and so on. What Managing Director or CEO could possibly resist increasing your budget for security, faced with results such as these? Don't be afraid to frighten your bosses into giving you the funding you need to do your job properly. Sometimes it's the only way.

On the very first page of the survey report is a set of DTI recommendations, the first two of which make particularly good sense. Draw on the right expertise to understand the security threats you face and your legal responsibilities; and integrate security into normal business practice through a clear security policy and staff education. I couldn't put it better myself.

Honeynets

A fundamental intelligence-gathering technique that is used by spies all over the world is the old-fashioned honey trap, which involves using seduction and sex (or at least the promise of it) to persuade people to divulge secrets. The hi-tech equivalent involves connecting a relatively unprotected computer to the internet, filling it with documents which look important but which actually contain nothing of interest, and then waiting for it to be attacked. Observing the behaviour of the hackers, and the techniques and tools they use, can be hugely beneficial to the security community.

The honeynet project (`www.honeynet.org`) consists of a group of organizations that set up honey traps and make their findings freely available in a series of enlightening documents. The set of forensics-related documents, for example, provide a complete walk-through of precisely how a machine was attacked, why the attackers managed to succeed and, in some cases, how the attacker was tracked down through clues that he left.

More than any survey into computer misuse, the honeynet documents provide real insight into just how sophisticated, determined and indiscriminating today's hackers are.

Is it Already too Late?

We have assumed that your company's computers, or the information on them, might at some point come under attack and that you want to prevent this happening. The rest of this book will offer a range of advice to help you do that. But before you sit back and decide which computers and facilities need your immediate attention, there's something else to consider: have you already been hacked? Have Trojan Horse programs or keystroke loggers already been installed, which are recording your users' passwords as they connect to confidential systems such as payroll, personnel records and even your bank? Even if you connect to your online bank via a secure SSL link (complete with closed padlock symbol on the Web browser), a keystroke logger will intercept information before it has been encrypted.

If you don't routinely scan your firewall logs for evidence of attempted electronic breaking and entering, now might be a good time to do so. Equally, do you have records that indicate whether all company computers are running up-to-date antivirus software? If not, this needs doing right now. Are all company PCs fully patched against every security vulnerability that Microsoft has announced? If you're not sure, download the Microsoft Baseline Security Analyser from www.microsoft.com/security and find out. It's free.

▶ FUNDAMENTAL FIVE

Your action points for this chapter:

1. Carry out some basic risk assessment to identify where you should concentrate your efforts. ☐

2. Identify any resources, departments or other areas of the company that require immediate attention and decide what action is required. ☐

3. Check your firewall logs to ensure that your systems have not already been penetrated. ☐

4. Ensure that all company computers have up-to-date antivirus software installed. ☐

5. Ensure that all company computers are fully patched with all operating system and application patches. ☐

International Laws and Standards

4

Wherever your company operates, there is a host of legislation, directives and other rules that govern the way you must operate your computer systems. There may also be additional standards or guidelines which, whilst not law, might be advisable to follow for commercial reasons.

This chapter focuses primarily on the issues that apply in the UK and, more specifically, in England and Wales. If your company operates wholly or partly in the UK, you would be well advised to be aware of the existence of all of these. If your budgets or workloads preclude you from actually obtaining and reading all of the documents mentioned below, check out at least the Computer Misuse Act and BS7799 in greater detail.

Computer Misuse Act 1990

The most important piece of legislation that affects computer crime of all hues is the Computer Misuse Act 1990. Offences under this Act fall into one of its three main sections.

Section 1 of the Act refers to unauthorized access to computer material. This states that a person commits an offence if he causes a computer to perform any function with intent to secure unauthorized access to any program or data held in any computer. For a successful conviction under this part of the Act, the prosecution must prove that the access secured is unauthorized and that the suspect knew that this was the case. This section is designed to deal with common-or-garden hacking.

Section 2 of the Act deals with unauthorized access with intent to commit or facilitate the commission of further offences. An offence is committed under Section 2 if a Section 1 offence has been committed and there is the intention of committing or facilitating a further offence (any offence which attracts a custodial sentence of more than five years, not necessarily one covered by the Computer Misuse Act). Even if it is not possible to prove the intent to commit the further offence, the Section 1 offence is still committed.

Section 3 offences cover unauthorized modification of computer material, which generally means the creation and distribution of viruses. For a conviction to succeed there must have been the intent to cause the modification, and knowledge that the modification had not been authorized.

During the early years following the introduction of the CMA, experts expressed opinion that it was severely lacking in a couple of crucial areas. Most notably there were fears that it did not cover Denial of Service attacks, where a hacker programs one or more computers to crash a server by making legitimate requests to it (such as opening the home page of a Web site) in far greater numbers than would normally be experienced. Experts feared that requests for legitimate information could not be classed as hacking. However, these fears appear to have been unfounded.

As with all other offences in UK law, it's illegal to incite someone to commit an offence. So for example, anyone who includes links to computer hacking tools and techniques on their Web site is potentially guilty of incitement to commit an offence under the CMA. This is why very few books in print now explain how to hack without being seen to package the information as being of use to IT security professionals who wish to audit their own networks. Equally, TV documentary producers who telephone me and ask if I can show their viewers just how easy it is to download and deploy automated no-brainer hacking tools are sent packing.

In addition to allowing you to prosecute those who break into your company's networks, the CMA is also a handy deterrent. Ensure that your IT security policy makes it crystal clear to staff that any misuse of corporate information may render them liable to prosecution rather than internal disciplinary action or mere dismissal. However, ensure that fear of prosecution doesn't dissuade people from reporting incidents of computer crime or misuse. Someone who fears that they may have infected their PC with a virus by installing some software without permission is much better off coming clean straight away, rather than festering with fear of prosecution while the virus makes its way to all of your other staff and customers.

You can download the full text of the CMA from the Web at `www.opsi.gov.uk/acts/acts1990/Ukpga_19900018 _en_1.htm`

Most countries have legislation similar to the UK's Computer Misuse Act. Germany, for example, prosecuted the author of the infamous Sasser virus in 2004, finding him guilty of computer sabotage and illegally altering data. Sven Jaschen was just 17 when he wrote the program and was consequently charged as a minor, receiving a suspended 21-month jail sentence.

ISO 17799

Publication number 17799 of the International Standards Organisation, also known as publication 7799 of the British Standards Institution, is entitled 'A code of practice for information security management'. The latest version was published in June 2005. In 2007 it will change its name to ISO 27002.

Like the Computer Misuse Act, the Code of Practice is essential reading if you haven't already encountered it. You can buy it online from the BSI for around £50.

For large companies, familiarity with ISO 17799 is *de rigueur*. Various organizations offer training courses for technical staff and senior management in 17799 compliance, and it is possible to obtain official certification of such. Some 80,000 companies around the world are currently basking in official recognition that they are compliant and many more adhere to its principles in a less formal way. In a handful of industries, notably defence, companies which lack official certification rarely make it onto any shortlist of suppliers for goods or services.

Although the standard is not exactly light reading, its 100 pages contain a wealth of useful advice which was originally compiled with the assistance of major British commerce heavyweights such as the Nationwide Building Society, Shell, and Marks & Spencer. It is aimed at senior management rather than technical staff, with the intention that readers will make decisions and then delegate the required actions to those at the sharp end.

Among the major sections in the standard are those dealing with:

- how to draft and maintain a corporate information security policy;

- setting up an information security infrastructure and forum among senior managers;

- creating an asset control register and assigning control of assets;

- personnel security, confidentiality agreements, the need for security awareness training, and reporting of security breaches;

- physical and environmental security of people and equipment;

- communications and operations management;

- access control, user registration, password management, privilege management, monitoring system access and use;

- systems development, change control, covert channels and back doors, encryption and key management;

- business continuity management, writing and implementing plans, testing the disaster recovery plan;

- compliance with applicable legislation, data protection and privacy issues.

Early versions of the standard were heavily criticized for being light on practical advice, for instance recommending the use of encryption but not explaining how or why. The most recent revision is far better, and is essential reading for anyone with a professional involvement in IT security, regardless of location.

Additional Relevant UK Legislation

Among the other UK laws of which any practising IT security professional should have a passing knowledge are the following:

The Data Protection Act 1998 sets out rules for storing and processing information about people. Whether you have a simple mailing list for names and addresses of customers, or a detailed database containing highly personal data such as salary or sexuality information, you have to register with the Information Commissioner (`www.informationcommissioner.gov.uk`). It is illegal to use information for purposes other than those which been declared. Data subjects, i.e. those people on your lists, have a right to request a copy of the information that you hold about them for a nominal fee. The full text of the Act is at `www.opsi.gov.uk/acts/acts1998/19980029.htm`.

The full text of the Electronic Communications Act 2000 can be viewed online at `www.opsi.gov.uk/acts/acts2000/20000007.htm`. This Act sets out the legal standing of electronic signatures as opposed to written ones.

The Regulation of Investigatory Powers Act 2000 replaces the old Interception of Communications legislation and deals with, as you might expect, the interception of data and voice communications by private bodies and Government agencies. It covers, for example, the rules which apply if you need to monitor your employees' use of the internet. It also provides an exemption for cases of wide-scale interception that are required in order to keep a system running smoothly, such as programs which automatically scan the contents of email messages in search of viruses or banned content. The text of the Act is at `www.opsi.gov.uk/acts/acts2000/20000023.htm`.

The Protection of Children Act of 1978 covers, among other things, child pornography. Under this Act it is a criminal offence to take, permit to be taken, distribute, show, advertise or possess for distribution any indecent photograph or pseudo-photograph of a child who is, or appears to be, under the age of 16. Note the inclusion of pseudo-photographs, which encompasses the activities of those who use computer programs to put young heads on adults' naked bodies. When TV news reports talk about someone being convicted of 'making indecent images of children', this (rather than actually taking the pictures) is normally what is meant.

Unlike conventional pornography, child porn is also unique in that mere possession of the material is an offence. Hence the various police operations that have targeted those whose credit card numbers appear on the customer lists of Web sites selling such material.

Parts of this Act were modified by the Sex Offences Act 2003. For example, the age limit for the definition of a child was raised from 16 (as mentioned above) to 18.

Although it is illegal to actively seek out images (both still and moving) of child pornography on the Internet, it is not an offence to encounter such material unwittingly. For example, if you innocently click a link on a Web page and, without warning, are taken to a page containing child porn, you are committing no offence even though the image is on your screen and is saved in your Web cache directory on your computer. Similarly, if you suspect that one of your employees is using his computer at the office to view or download child pornography, you are permitted to view and store any material that you find in order to gather evidence for a subsequent appeal against dismissal and/or a prosecution. Furthermore, you can also forward it to the relevant authorities without fear of being accused of illegally transmitting such material.

Legislation and directives which set out ways in which companies can monitor staff use of email includes the Telecommunications Act 1984, the Privacy and Electronic Communications (EC Directive) Regulations 2003, and the Telecommunications (Lawful Business Practice) (Interception of Communications) Regulations 2000.

Email Law

In many countries, including the UK, a company is legally liable for the content of email that is sent from its systems, regardless of whether the message was sent for private or business-related purposes. This could lead to prosecution for the sender and for the company's directors if, for example, outgoing email was found to contain material that was pornographic, racist, or likely to incite someone to commit an act of terrorism. Furthermore, ignorance of the law is no defence. Because of these rules, it makes sense to keep archive copies of all outgoing mail if your systems permit this.

Incidentally, one fascinating fact that I learned during my brush with the legal system on hacking charges is that, while ignorance of the law is no defence, plain ignorance can be. In my case, I was charged under the Forgery and Counterfeiting Act with making a 'false instrument'. My barrister took great care to remind the jury that it is no defence to say "I didn't know that making a false instrument was illegal" yet it is a perfectly valid defence to say "I was not aware that my actions amounted to making a false instrument".

In the UK, the Data Protection Act states that all confidential information must be handled and transmitted securely. Therefore, if you send such information by email without taking steps to encrypt it you are committing a criminal offence. For example, if a new member of staff is employed and the personnel department sends details of their name, address and salary to another department by email over the internet, then this is highly likely to be illegal. Use a method other than email, encrypt it before sending, or don't send it at all.

Confidential data sent by email must also be held securely by the recipient, such as in encrypted form, and should be stored for no longer than is necessary. To comply with the law you should remind all staff of these facts.

Data Retention

In law there is a possible ambiguity regarding the retention of communications data. Such information might include copies of all outgoing mail messages as well as logs from firewalls, Web servers and even telephone switchboards. You might also keep logs of all Web sites visited by your employees. From a technical perspective it makes sense to retain such information for a fairly long period (at least a year). However, while the UK's Data Protection Act states that confidential information must not be kept for longer than is absolutely necessary, and not held for speculative purposes, US rules such as the Public Company Accounting Reform and Investor Protection Act (commonly known as Sarbanes-Oxley) decree that companies must retain accounting data in tamper-evident archives for long periods.

In addition, the UK's Freedom of Information Act says that someone is entitled to request a copy of all the information held about them by an organization in the public sector, and similar legislation allows consumers to request a copy of their file from credit reference agencies. So again, you need to balance the requirement to delete unnecessary data with the possible need to refer to that data in the future for purposes currently unknown.

Monitoring Staff Activity

Sometimes it is necessary to monitor the computer activity of a member of staff who is suspected of misusing the network or possibly committing criminal acts such as fraud or distributing racist material. The procedures and software for doing this are discussed in Chapter 39, but it's also important to understand the legal situation.

Monitoring of your network, including the content of email messages and other network traffic, is generally permitted if it's done to maintain the performance and security of the network and if you don't specifically target the email or traffic of a particular person. So, for example, scanning all incoming email messages for viruses or recording traffic levels generated by the sales department is not a problem. However, if you wish to monitor the activity of a particular person without their knowledge or consent, this is very much a grey area with respect to the law are you are strongly advised to consult a legal expert before doing so.

Summary

No one who has a professional involvement in IT security can avoid occasional dalliances with the confusing and complex mass of laws and regulations. If your personnel department keeps a database of staff addresses and salaries, there are rules as to how you must protect the information. If you are in the financial services industry, the rules governing accounting practices are strict. In a world where those fighting international terrorism rely more on telephone and email intercepts than on old-fashioned James Bond spying, the number of rules and laws will only increase in the future. Yet those rules can be a benefit too, such as acting as a useful deterrent to staff who are tempted to misuse their employers' computer systems. Getting to grips with the rules is a necessity and you ignore them at your peril.

FUNDAMENTAL FIVE

Your action points for this chapter:

1. Familiarize yourself with the laws that relate to IT and security in your country of business. ☐

2. Consider whether there are additional laws and regulations that cover your specific area of business. ☐

3. Investigate the ways that your company stores and processes information and ensure that everything is within the law. If you are in the UK, have you registered your systems under the Data Protection Act and, if so, are your original declarations as to the range of your systems still correct? ☐

4. Is your company doing anything that might be in a legal 'grey area' and of which your lawyers should be aware, such as monitoring personal email messages of staff? ☐

5. Examine your data retention policies. How long do you store log files for? Is this longer than the law allows? Is it long enough to be useful? ☐

Passwords and Beyond

5

In most organizations, the only method of authentication by which users identify themselves to computer systems is the password. The concept of passwords has been around for decades and, while not perfect, it's cheap to establish and easy to support.

To gain maximum security you need a company-wide password strategy. In practice this will be a mix of management, education and technology. Management and education techniques can be used to stress the importance of having a sensible password policy, and technology can be used to enforce it. Windows 2000 and XP, for example, have a Local Password Policy setting, which allows you to specify how often a user must change their password, the minimum length for the password, whether the password must be forced to meet complexity requirements, and how many previous passwords the system will remember to prevent users recycling them from a list rather than thinking of new ones each time. More details are in Chapter 9. If you select the option that requires passwords to meet complexity requirements, this causes Windows to ensure that a password selected by a user:

1. Is at least six characters long.

2. Contains characters from at least three of the following categories:
   - English uppercase characters A–Z
   - English lowercase characters (a–z)
   - Digits 0–9
   - Non-alphanumeric characters such as $, #, or %
   - Unicode characters

3. Does not contain three or more consecutive characters from the user's account name.

Whether to enforce complexity, and how often you should force users to change their passwords, is a complex decision. While frequent changes and complex passwords would at first glance appear to be more secure than passwords which rarely change and are easier to remember, human nature means that reality is quite different from the theory. The biggest problem with passwords is that users forget them. This causes difficulties for companies that rely on them, because technical support staff spend most of their time resetting forgotten passwords rather than helping people with real problems or doing long-term work to improve the system. The more complex a password, and the more often it changes, the more often it will be forgotten, and the more often it will be written down by users who are frightened of forgetting them. Beware, therefore, of making your password policy so complicated that you actually weaken security, because a password that's written down isn't really providing you with any security at all.

If you don't currently have a policy for dealing with people who claim to have forgotten their password, then this should be defined as part of your password policy. A common technique used by hackers, especially those well-versed in the art of social engineering (which we'll cover in Chapter 34), is to pass themselves off as a member of your staff who claims to have forgotten their password. So, your policy needs to ensure that:

1. Only a handful of duly authorized people are able to reset passwords.

2. A user is only ever advised of a reset password in writing to the address that you have on file, or in person. Never over the telephone.

3. A user who is given a new password in person must produce some form of identification if they are not known to the person who is handing out the password.

4. Someone who forgets their password is not criticized or penalized, or they'll start writing it down so as to prevent it happening again.

5. Administrator passwords should only ever be used when their additional functionality is required. At all other times, administrators should use their standard user–level passwords. This helps to avoid data loss caused by mistakes that would otherwise have been prevented, and reduces the amount of time available to a hacker who might be trying to intercept or otherwise discover the administrator's password.

6. Employees must never be allowed to use each others' passwords, even if both employees are afforded the same access privileges, because it is imperative that your log files can be relied upon to provide an accurate record of which actions have been taken by which person.

7. Ensure that passwords are not duplicated across systems. It's common for administrators to set themselves up with the same password on every machine they look after – this should be discouraged.

8. Change administrator passwords frequently. If an administrator leaves the company, all of the passwords to which he or she had access must be changed within an hour.

9. There must be no exceptions to these rules, ever.

New computer equipment, especially networking kit, is always supplied with one or more default passwords that are pre-programmed. These passwords are incredibly powerful as they are normally administrator or root level, yet they are also well known because the hardware manufacturer makes no attempt to protect them. Type 'default password' into your favourite Web search engine if you want to find out just how many of these there are, and how easily most of them can be discovered. Whenever you install or accept delivery of new computer networking equipment or software, make it your urgent priority to ensure that the default built-in passwords are changed as soon as possible, and definitely before the hardware or software goes live. Hackers are known to have software tools which automatically prowl the internet in search of routers and other devices which still accept the manufacturers' initial passwords, so don't allow your company to become a victim.

How Hackers Crack Passwords

When I was an active hacker, remote computers were protected by three layers of security. First, I had to find the computer's telephone number, because the pre-internet days meant that each system had its own connection to the outside world via modems, rather than being part of a large global network. Secondly, I needed a username. Thirdly, a password was required. With so many millions of computers now connected to the internet, the typical computer is secured by only two layers nowadays, namely a username and a password. That's a reduction of one-third in the number of hurdles between the hackers and your computers.

Hackers crack passwords in many ways. Often they simply guess them, and if your systems don't have security policies that lock out the account for a few minutes after every few incorrect guesses then a hacker can use a program that can automatically fire off thousands of guesses every minute. Another technique is to intercept the passwords as they travel across the wires of the internet or your network, or to install a password logging program on one of your company's computers to monitor passwords as they are typed and then to send them by email to the hacker. We'll discuss these in more detail later.

A common technique for cracking passwords is the dictionary attack. The existence of this technique is the reason why security experts always tell you never to choose a password that consists of a single word that could be found in a typical dictionary. The attack works as follows. First, the hacker retrieves the list of usernames and passwords from your server. This is often trivial because the list is not always strongly protected. Instead, the protection lies in the fact that the stored passwords are encrypted using a one-way algorithm, i.e. one for which there is no decryption function possible. An entry in the list for a username of robert and a password of hacker would appear as:

robert:jJMvAiwqcXI.6

If your Web server uses Basic HTTP authentication to provide password protection for certain directories (and most do), then your protection is probably based around this system. So how does a hacker turn jJMvAiwqcXI.6 back into 'hacker' if there's no decryption facility in existence? He acquires a list of hundreds of thousands of unique words, and encrypts each of them using the same publicly available algorithm that is used for encrypting passwords. The end result is a long table of words alongside their encrypted counterparts. Then he just looks down the table to find jJMvAiwqcXI.6 and reads off "hacker" from the opposite column.

In reality, the amount of effort required to do a dictionary crack on a password is zero. There are plenty of Web sites that contain pre-encrypted lists of millions of potential passwords, and which offer hackers the facility to enter an encrypted password for immediate lookup. Those lists of pre-encrypted passwords also include common transpositions, such as '**protect1On**' instead of '**protection**'. Anyone who suggests that you can avoid falling prey to a dictionary attack by changing the occasional letter to a lookalike digit is sadly mistaken.

Password Recovery Software

Software companies which offer password protection facilities always tell you that their protection mechanisms are 100% secure, and that, if you forget or lose your password, there's no way to recover it. If truth be told, this is not entirely accurate, as a Web search for 'password recovery' will show you. Whether your data is protected by Word or Excel, PKZIP or PowerPoint, Acrobat or Outlook, someone somewhere can sell you a program or a service which can recover the password or change it to something else. Even a Windows administrator password can be recovered, but only by someone with physical access to the server to run the recovery program. Which is good reason not to allow anyone to have such access.

To protect your most highly confidential files, encrypt them rather than merely password-protecting them. Then you can rest easy in the knowledge that no one can crack them. However, make sure you use a strong encryption algorithm (see Chapter 27 for more on this). Not all encryption systems are created equal. The one built into Microsoft Office, for example, can be cracked fairly easily – type Office Password Recovery into your Web search engine for the gory details.

One common mistake that companies make is inadequate control of the information that gets uploaded to their Web sites. For example, do you use a File Transfer Protocol (ftp) program to upload files to your Web server? If so, do you upload entire directories to the server rather than taking care to exclude those files that are unnecessary? If, like many companies, you do the former, you may find that you are also uploading the data file in which your ftp program stores the usernames and passwords that it uses when uploading. And, you guessed it, these files are often trivial to crack. Try searching the Web for ws_ftp.ini, for example, and you'll find many such data files. Then, to see just how serious the problem is, try searching for programs that can recover forgotten ws_ftp passwords from those. ini files.

In 1999 I was delivering a presentation at a security product sales conference on behalf of a company that wanted to highlight the importance of choosing strong passwords. We set up a Windows NT server in the foyer, and logged in with an administrator account that allowed the creation of new user accounts. As delegates arrived in the morning we invited each of them to create a new user account on the server and assign it a password which adhered to the rules that existed at the time within their organization regarding password complexity. Once the conference got underway I took the computer aside and started a copy of the L0phtCrack password cracker running on it. L0phtCrack started life as a tool produced by and for hackers who wanted to crack Windows and Unix passwords. Its authors subsequently 'went legit' and founded a security consultancy called @Stake, which was later acquired by antivirus specialists Symantec. The program uses both brute-force (try every possible combination) and a list of thousands of common passwords.

The current version of L0phtCrack, now rebranded as LC5, is marketed by Symantec as a password assessment tool that enables companies to ensure that the passwords chosen by users are sufficiently strong. It certainly lived up to its billing during our conference – by the time my presentation was underway at 2pm the program had cracked over 80% of the accounts that delegates had set up on the system. Some had taken a couple of hours, although the easier ones had been discovered in just seconds.

One delegate didn't hang around to listen to my presentation. He went straight back to the office to implement a new password policy for all employees. Having seen what L0phtCrack could do, he felt that immediate action was required, and that it couldn't even wait another hour.

In recent years, techniques have been developed to help prevent shoulder-surfing, the technique of discovering someone's password by simply watching over their shoulder as they enter it. Instead of requesting a user to enter their entire password, the system asks for just two or three characters from randomly chosen positions. Such techniques are popular in telephone and internet banking, to help defeat Trojan programs which log keystrokes and/or monitor mouse clicks. When used with purely numeric passwords, such a system can certainly reduce the opportunity for shoulder-surfing. However, a hacker who discovers three digits of a nine-digit password simply has to keep trying to log in repeatedly until the system asks for those particular three digits. To prevent this, the system should only change the selection of requested digits after a successful login, but not all systems do this in practice.

Another weakness with the partial password technique is that a crossword solving computer program or similar hand-held gadget can easily crack alphabetical passwords. If I notice someone entering p, a and a as the first, fourth and 8th characters of a password, typing p??a???a* into my crossword solver instantly brings up parabola as the most likely candidate. That's why numbers are always best for such situations, even though it reduces the total number of possible combinations.

Beyond the Password

Security experts refer to the three principles of authentication as:

- something you know

- something you have

- something you are

The password falls into the first of these categories – it is something you know. It's an incredibly cost-effective authentication mechanism because you merely have to tell someone something (i.e. a password). But the trouble with something you know is that it's all too easy to forget it and/or for someone else to get to know it too.

In cases where passwords are simply not secure enough, one alternative is to use the 'something you have' approach. The thing in question is usually some form of physical token containing a microchip of some sort, which must be read by some electronic device or other to provide authentication. For example, a smart card that must be passed through the slot in a reader or held up against a detector. You'll find out more about such devices when we cover phishing attacks in Chapter 17.

These devices are normally coupled with a traditional 'something you know' password to provide the best of both worlds. To prove your identity you must not only type in your traditional password, but also provide evidence that you have the device. And because the devices can't be copied, someone who discovers or guesses your password will only have half of the key rather than all of it.

Products that protect computers via the 'something you have' technique are widely available. To avoid the need to install new reader hardware on each of your PCs, some companies provide the "something you have" as an encrypted bank of data held on a chip that simply plugs into the computer's USB port when required.

Although these techniques are more expensive to roll out than traditional passwords, it does provide a much greater degree of security, and is therefore used in areas such as finance and defence. To provide a way into the system in the case of someone losing or damaging their hardware token, there's normally a provision for a super-user token which is normally kept securely locked away, but which can be used to override one or more standard tokens should the need arise.

To apply the 'something you have' technique to a system that you normally log into remotely rather than in person requires a slightly different approach. For example, connecting to a highly secure Web server or intranet can't be done by sliding your smartcard into a slot on whatever terminal (which could be anywhere in the world) that you happen to be using at the time. One provider of solutions to this problem is RSA, with its SecurID product. The SecurID authenticator is a small device that you carry on your key fob. On its small calculator-like display is a series of digits or letters that change every few seconds. When you need to log into a SecurID-protected system, you are asked for a password and also for the digits that are currently appearing on your authenticator device.

The algorithm that decides which digits are shown on the device at any one time is known only to the device and to the software which runs on the protected server, so if you enter those digits correctly the server knows that you are currently in physical possession of an authenticator device. Each authenticator also has a unique serial number, which is linked to your user account. So you have to use the correct authenticator to log into a particular account – someone else's device won't work.

Biometrics

The natural progression of the 'something you have' method of authentication ends up with systems that can uniquely identify a person without the need for them to carry an additional hardware token. Probably the best-known example of this 'something you are' technique is the fingerprint, though there are others too.

The eye is a particularly good candidate as it contains unique patterns that can help to positively identify someone (and, just as importantly, prove that someone is not who they are thought to be). The colours and patterns in the iris can be used for identification, as can the thousands of tiny blood vessels in the retina. Other methods include the sound of someone's voice or the way they sign their name on a pressure-sensitive pad, or even their particular smell.

Identifying someone through one or more of their characteristics like this is known as biometrics. As with hardware tokens such as SecurID, biometric technology is used extensively in high-security industries such as defence and banking, but is still making only slow inroads into other areas.

Fingerprint recognition is by far the most commonly used biometric. It's reliable and relatively cheap to roll out. It's also relatively non–intrusive, which can't be said of systems that scan retina or facial patterns, and require the user to press their face against a scanning device each time they log in.

Setting up a computer to use fingerprint recognition for authentication isn't difficult. You can easily buy fingerprint scanners as stand–alone devices with USB connectors, or built into an existing keyboard or mouse. Once the device is plugged in, you install the software and set up an administrator account. In administrator mode you can enrol someone as a user of the system by scanning their fingerprint and storing it on the system.

Subsequently, logging in is a matter of typing a username and then placing a finger on the reader. Many laptops now include fingerprint recognition as standard, to prevent access to the machine by anyone who is not authorized.

Biometrics means no more forgotten passwords. It's impossible to forget a fingerprint. In the event that access to a computer is needed in the absence of the finger's owner, the administrator password (which can usually be either a traditional password or a fingerprint) can normally be used.

Fingerprint recognition is finding its way into all sorts of devices. You can buy USB flash drives with a built-in fingerprint reader. This allows you to carry your important files around with you, but no one else can access the files if they manage to steal the USB stick because the data is automatically encrypted until the correct fingertip is placed on the scanner. One such example is Sony's Microvault, though many others are also available. If higher capacities are required, LaCie (**www.lacie.com**) produces external USB hard drives with inbuilt fingerprint reader, plus the necessary software drivers for Windows that allow you to create backups that can't be accessed except via fingerprint authentication.

LaCie also makes external drives that include built-in encryption which needs no fingerprint or password – to use the drive you have to plug in a small USB key device. Keep the key on your key fob and away from the drive when the drive isn't in use, and anyone who steals the drive will find that it is of no use whatsoever.

Full-face recognition is another option that is becoming popular and looks promising. Facecode (**www.facecode.co.uk**) sells a program that uses a computer's webcam for authentication. Once you've registered your face with the system and associated it with a particular user account on the machine, just look into the camera while the logon box is on the screen and the process is complete.

Duress

In ultra-high security environments, such as passwords which control the opening of a bank vault or the launching of a missile, hackers and other criminals are fully aware that the passwords or biometric material required to access the protected information are unlikely to be easily guessable or written down on a handy piece of paper. In such situations, coercing the legitimate user to carry out the operation, i.e. opening the vault or launching the missile, is the only option. The idea of someone being forced to type in a secret code with the barrel of a revolver pressed to their head may be the domain of James Bond films, but such things also happen in the real world too. Cases of muggers forcing nocturnal pedestrians to withdraw cash from ATM machines and hand it over are regularly reported.

A primary weapon in such cases is the duress password. This is a special password which, when typed or otherwise supplied, indicates to the recipient that it is being entered under duress and that assistance should be silently summoned.

In traditional passwords, consisting of letters or numbers typed on a keypad or keyboard, this simply requires the user to memorize two separate passwords. In biometrics, duress passwords are implemented similarly. For example, in fingerprint recognition, a user might signal duress by presenting his right thumb to the scanner rather than his left. The vault will still open, in order to avoid tipping off the criminals, but the police will also be on their way.

Further Considerations

A major factor in the adoption of biometric authentication is user acceptance. Everyone is used to typing a password or PIN, but having a part of one's body scanned is more intrusive, and many people feel uncomfortable doing so. Although the most widely used biometric technique, fingerprint readers still cause alarm in some people who associate fingerprint-taking with someone who's been arrested. Retina and iris scanners can also cause distress for those who dislike having to press their face or eyes against the closed mask that contains the scanner, perhaps for reasons of hygiene or claustrophobia.

But the greatest concern regarding the use of biometrics is of course their accuracy and security. How easy is it to defeat the system, and how often does it erroneously claim that the finger on the scanner is not the one that it really is?

In the early days, defeating biometric systems was relatively easy. Stories regularly appeared in the IT press from researchers who had fooled a fingerprint scanner with a plaster cast or rubber mould. One particularly gruesome story concerned residents of the Philippines, where senior citizens had to identify themselves by fingerprint when withdrawing their weekly pension payment. It was alleged that relatives of pensioners were not averse to cutting off the finger of a deceased relative before burial, so that they could continue to claim their money post-mortem.

Today's fingerprint readers are much more reliable, and certainly can't be fooled by lifeless models. However, one particular manufacturer did try to impress me at a security exhibition a few years ago with a revolutionary 'hand geometry' system. Rather than requiring a simple fingerprint for authentication, the user places his entire hand inside a small box, whereupon a camera takes dozens of measurements of the hand such as the lengths of each finger and the angles between them. I suggested that such a technique could be easily fooled by a rubber mould, at which point the sales person had no option but to admit that this was the case. He did, however, have the audacity to tell me that the great benefit of having a system that could be so easily fooled was that it was not subject to the Data Protection Act. I laughed and he sheepishly walked away to try to con some other potential buyers.

In the real world my experience with biometrics, and fingerprints in particular, is that the number of false negatives is very low. The system hardly ever fails to recognize a genuine finger. And if it does, you can of course override the system with a conventional username and password.

One-Time Passwords

The beauty of the traditional password, as opposed to hardware tokens or biometrics, is that it's cheap and easy. There's no additional hardware resources required and the facility comes as standard with every modern PC. Issue someone with a password, tell them not to forget it or write it down, and access control for that particular user is sorted. But the benefit of passwords is also their weakest link. Anyone who manages to discover someone else's password can use it with little chance of being detected and, crucially, neither the legitimate owner of the password nor the operators of the system will be aware that the password has been compromised.

One answer is to use one-time passwords. Instead of issuing a user with a single password, give them a printed list of, say, 50. Each time the user needs to log into the system he enters the next password on the list. If someone sees him type the password (so-called shoulder surfing), or the password is grabbed by a keystroke logger, then no damage is done because the password will not be accepted a second time. Once the list of 50 passwords is almost finished, the system automatically sends out a new list by post or by secure email.

One-time passwords provide much greater security than multiple-use passwords for relatively little extra effort or cost. However, there are still risks involved. In 2005 a group of hackers found a way to access the one-time password sheets issued to customers of a Scandinavian bank. The hackers set up a fake site and used phishing attacks to direct gullible customers to it. The fake site asked users for their banking username and password, and the next unused entry from their one-time password sheet. Not content with having captured all the information that they needed to create a fraudulent transaction, the hackers programmed their fake site so that, regardless of the one-time password that the user entered, the system claimed that the data was not valid and suggested that the user type in yet another entry from the sheet. The legitimate bank site had no option but to shut down while security staff worked out what to do.

Where Now?

The conventional password has been with us ever since computers needed to be able to identify people. The great benefit of password-based authentication is that it's cheap and easy to implement, but the greatest problem is that passwords can easily be guessed or stolen. Biometrics and one-time passwords clearly offer greater levels of security, but at an increased cost. Fingerprint readers may only cost $20 or so, but that's $20 more than a password-based system costs, and the figures soon mount up if you have tens or hundreds or thousands of employees.

However, if you look at the TCO (Total Cost of Ownership) of a password-based system it is not actually free at all. Technical support and help desk staff spend much of their time resetting forgotten passwords, and a fingerprint-based regime would largely eliminate this workload. The money saved on employing extra technical staff, if spent on a system that used some form of biometrics, would mean no additional cost yet a significant increase in security. Not to mention helpdesk staff who could get on with more useful tasks. But this is just wishful thinking as far as most organizations are concerned. Passwords are here to stay, and we have to accept that. Our job, therefore, is to make sure that we do everything we can to ensure that passwords do what they were designed to do as safely and reliably as possible.

▶ FUNDAMENTAL FIVE

Your action points for this chapter:

1. On all Windows computers, ensure that you use the Local Password Policy to set a minimum acceptable password length. ☐

2. Ensure that users change passwords regularly. The Local Security Policy can help to enforce this. ☐

3. Review your procedures for resetting the passwords of those users who claim to have forgotten theirs. Can you always be sure of the user's identity? ☐

4. Ensure that the default passwords supplied with new computing equipment have all been changed. ☐

5. Investigate the possible use of biometric security for protecting your most important computers. ☐

Your Information Security Policy

E very company needs a formal written document which spells out to staff precisely what they are allowed to use the company's systems for, what is prohibited, and what will happen to them if they break the rules. This document goes under various names but is most often known as an information security policy or an AUP (acceptable use policy).

Two printed copies of the policy should be given to every staff member as soon as possible after they join the organization (ideally on day one). The staff member should be asked to sign one copy, which should be safely filed by the company, and keep the other for their records. No one should be allowed to use the company's computer systems until they have signed the policy in acceptance of its terms.

A written policy, and a requirement that all staff sign it, may at first appear rather draconian, which is probably why many small and medium companies tend not to have one. But such a document really is a central component of any successful campaign to increase corporate IT security. Without a written policy, staff will be unaware of the rules. How can you discipline someone for inappropriate use of the Web unless everyone is in agreement as to what constitutes inappropriate use? Equally, staff need to be made aware that activities such as sharing passwords are dangerous and that they face disciplinary action if they do it. By putting their name to a written document, the rules are clear and unambiguous to all.

If you don't currently have a policy, you should draft one as a matter of urgency. If you have one but it's not been revised for some time, now might be a good time to retrieve it and ensure that it is up to date. For example, does it cover the use of relatively new technology such as USB flash drives or copying MP3 files from company computers to personal players?

It is not normally necessary for staff to sign a new copy of the policy each time a minor amendment is made. The policy should contain a clause that ensures that staff are aware that there may be a more recent version of the document on the internal Web site and that this will take priority. You may also wish to send out a bulk email to all staff each time the document is updated, which highlights the amendments.

Deciding on Content

The content of your policy document will be specific to your company, but obviously all policies have various themes in common. Many companies (and other organizations such as colleges and Government departments) make their polices available on their public Web sites (either deliberately or accidentally) so don't be afraid to look to these very useful resources to ensure that your policy covers everything that it needs to. Typing "information security policy" into your favourite search engine will bring up thousands of such documents. However, ensure that you respect the copyright regulations – feel free to take inspiration from polices on the Web, but don't copy entire sections verbatim.

If you want the easy option, the bible for anyone tasked with creating a policy is *Information Security Policies Made Easy* by Charles Cresson Wood. This 700-page book contains every possible clause that you could want, and all the text is included on a CD-ROM that accompanies the book. Fire up the CD in your computer, enter your company name, tick the boxes on the screen next to the required clauses, and the software will create a policy document for you. However, at $795 it's not a cheap option, and it's perfectly possible to do it yourself for a lot less. The package does, though, include hundreds of useful policies covering not just acceptable use, but also disaster recovery plans, non-disclosure agreements and much more besides.

Keep It Concise

There are various key internal publications that you need to create and maintain in your role as an IT security person. Some will go into great detail and spell out the minutiae of how you intend to deal with a particular problem if it arises, and the Disaster Recovery Plan is a good example. Other documents might be more brief, perhaps aimed at senior managers who need a mere overview of a particular situation (e.g. yes we have a backup procedure and we are confident that it works).

Your IT security policy must be brief – no more than two or three pages. If it's longer, staff simply won't bother reading it. Possibly the worst example I've ever seen runs to more than 90 pages. No one can remember such a massive set of rules, so the only way for staff to adhere to the regulations is to refer to the document continually throughout the day. Which they simply won't do.

Keep things simple. Just a few sentences for each topic. Explain the rule (thou shalt, or thou shalt not), and perhaps explain your reasoning, but don't go into great detail.

Topics for Inclusion

The wording and content of your AUP must be specific to your company and its line of business. Parts of it might look something like this:

Web surfing

Our internet connection is primarily intended for use on company business. You may use it to access Web sites of personal interest, but you must not intentionally visit sites that contain pornographic, racist or any other material that might be deemed offensive or which is unlawful.

You must not set up a Web server on your desktop PC, as this can be a serious security risk if not configured correctly.

Virus precautions

Antivirus software is installed on your computer. You must not attempt to disable it or prevent it from performing its daily update. If you fail to allow your antivirus software to update itself, there is a chance that your computer could become infected and subsequently attempt to infect machines belonging to our clients and partners.

Personal Email

You may use the company's network to send and receive personal email, but you must not transmit messages or attachments containing material that is offensive. If you receive offensive material in the form of spam, you must not reply to it or forward it – delete the message. You may not use our email system for commercial purposes.

You must not attempt to forge email such that it appears to come from someone other than yourself. You must not send email to colleagues or outsiders which contains offensive material or which could be regarded as material that attempts to bully, harass or offend.

You must not send unsolicited email to potential customers unless you have written authority (including by email) from them to do so.

Software Installation

You must not install any additional programs on your computer without permission. Contact the IT support desk if you wish to have a program installed. We work hard to ensure that we stay within the terms of our various software licence agreements, and we can only do this if all software installation requests are handled centrally.

The Firewall

We use a firewall to ensure that hackers cannot access our systems. We also use the firewall to prevent access from our network to a small number of services which are illegal or which cause excessive drain on our limited bandwidth. You are not permitted to attempt to circumvent these measures.

Encryption

If you wish to encrypt confidential information that is on your hard disk or on your area of the network file server, use the Windows Encrypting File System. Refer to the helpdesk Web site for details on how to enable this. No other encryption systems must be used.

The Law

Your use of our systems is subject to the Computer Misuse Act 1990, the Protection of Children Act 1978 and the Data Protection Act 1988. You must not use our systems to perform any operation that would contravene this legislation.

Logging and Surveillance

Our Web proxy servers record all activity, which means that a record is maintained of all Web sites that you visit. No other information is held, apart from the address of the site. This information is stored securely for a period of six months, after which it is deleted. You should not visit any Web site if you do not wish details of your visit to be recorded in our log files. The logs will only be accessed by a senior manager, and only if there is reasonable cause to do so, such as investigating suspected misuse of our systems or if we are requested to do so by the police.

If the company has reasonable grounds to suspect that you are misusing the company's computer systems, the company will, upon the authority of a senior manager, instigate covert surveillance techniques that might result in further information about your internet usage being recorded. However this will only be done in exceptional circumstances.

Passwords

You must not share your password with colleagues. You must change your Windows password every 30 days, and you will receive an automatic reminder to assist you in this matter. Do not write passwords down in a way that could allow them to be easily identified as passwords by colleagues or visitors. If you think that your account has been compromised, contact the help desk as soon as possible.

You must not log into the network with anyone else's password without written permission from a senior manager. You must not attempt to obtain or guess someone else's password.

Laptops

Privately-owned laptop computers must not be connected to the company's network without the permission of the IT support department. The department may wish to examine your laptop before granting such permission.

You must not use your laptop to transport confidential files out of the company's premises. Confidential files are those documented in the list that can be found on the intranet.

Use of Internet Forums

You must not post messages to public internet chat rooms and discussion forums in an official capacity or in a way that implies that you are posting on behalf of the company. You must not reveal your company email address in any public internet forum, as such places are often used by spammers to harvest email addresses.

Disposal of Equipment

Obsolete computers must be disposed of using official methods, details of which are available on the staff intranet. All information must be wiped from the hard disk first.

▶ FUNDAMENTAL FIVE

Your action points for this chapter:

1. Ensure that you have a policy which sets out to staff what they must, and must not, do when using the company's computer systems. ☐

2. Keep the document short and to the point. It is merely a set of rules, not a detailed list of procedures. ☐

3. Ensure that all staff sign a copy of the policy document. ☐

4. Keep the policy up to date, such as including references to new devices that come onto the market. ☐

5. Be seen to uphold the policy. If someone breaks the rules, they must be seen to be punished harshly but fairly according to documented procedures. Failure to treat all "offenders" equally is a criminal offence in many countries. ☐

Security Awareness Training

To work effectively, IT security must be regarded as an attitude rather than a product. This mantra is frequently recited by experts and consultants, and they are quite right to say it. Buying firewalls and antivirus software and intrusion detection, not to mention installing patches on all your servers and workstations, will only get you so far. Unless you can also persuade every staff member to embrace the concept, you are still at significant risk from an IT security breach of some kind because hackers know that the weakest link in a company's defences is almost always a person rather than a lump of technology. You can find more about how hackers exploit people in Chapter 34, which looks at social engineering.

So how do you get everyone to take security seriously, or at least to have a passing awareness of the risks? The answer is to roll out a program of security awareness training. It doesn't need to be in-depth. In fact, the shorter the better. After all, while IT security is one of your responsibilities, the typical mail room assistant, switchboard operator, marketing manager or caretaker probably never gives it a second thought. Yet it is essential that everyone – and I do mean everyone – in your organization receives some basic information.

Security awareness training is best done in person, if only because it's less boring for everyone concerned, and because it allows trainees to raise any particular concerns and to see for themselves that the company as a whole is committed to the process. If for whatever reason you are unable to conduct the training in person, then alternatives might include a private staff-only Web or intranet site, or a series of weekly emails sent to all staff over a period of a few months which cover a different topic every time. Autoresponder programs, which automatically send a series of messages over a period of time, can help here.

There's no need for the training to be particularly technical. An hour should be plenty. And there's no need for any hands-on experience or exercises – just a talk and perhaps a little PowerPoint. Whether the trainer is taken from in-house or you use an external training company is entirely up to you, but ensure that the presentation is lively and that the trainer is fully aware of the nature of your business. Although the security risks to a company that makes medical instruments are very similar to one which sells insurance, the mindset of the employees is very different.

As for class sizes, the sessions can be done *en masse* or in smaller groups. In the past I've often been asked to train small groups of around 10 employees and this has worked well. I have also trained the entire workforce of 600 employees of a merchant bank (four sessions in one day, with 150 staff in each) and this, too, caused very few problems. In general, the larger the audience, the less self-conscious they will be, and thus it will be easier to get a good discussion going.

Far more important than the size of the group being trained is their technical level. Talk to people about something they know, and they'll listen with interest. If the session is far too simple or way too complicated they'll switch off within the first couple of minutes, and the entire exercise will end up as a dangerous and expensive waste of time.

Don't assume that technical knowledge increases with seniority. However, you also can't assume that senior managers and directors will be prepared to attend a training session alongside very junior staff. If this looks like becoming a problem, arrange separate sessions. You will also need to train your technical staff (software developers, server administrators, etc.) separately because their technical knowledge will be high.

For each session, the three most important rules are:

1. Relevance.

2. Relevance.

3. Relevance.

Your typical employee doesn't care about IT security, at least not in the workplace. After all, the PC on his desk doesn't belong to him, and if it gets a virus or he loses a few documents there are people he can turn to in order to rectify the problem. It's the company's problem rather than his. So why can't he get on with the job he's paid to do and not worry about IT security?

The answer is simply that IT security affects us all, and that all of us could become the target of hackers, viruses, hackers and social engineers. Unless we each play our part, the company could face an electronic attack that could result in (in ascending order of seriousness):

■ Inconvenience to one or more staff

■ Lengthy computer downtime and lost business

■ Permanent loss of one or more important client

■ Theft of confidential information and its disclosure to competitors

■ Hefty fines or even jail sentences for senior staff

■ Closure of the business with the loss of all jobs

None of these events is fictional – they have all happened in the past to companies of my acquaintance. In one instance, a company that operated vending machines in hundreds of locations lost its key databases due to hackers. Without its list of vending machines, staff couldn't visit them in order to replenish the stock and retrieve the cash. Within a couple of months the company had ceased trading.

In another example, a company published daily newsletters by fax to clients in the financial services industry. A hacker broke into their distribution system and added, to the first page of the next day's newsletter, an image of a woman having sex with a horse. No one at the publishing company noticed the change, and the newsletter ended up on the fax machines of hundreds of clients the following morning. Within 48 hours, 50% of them had cancelled their subscriptions.

Session Format

The training session should be divided into two periods, possibly with a short "comfort break" between. In the first session, explain the purpose of the session and the benefits to be gained from attending. Wherever possible, portray them as benefits to the individuals rather than as benefits to the company. Thank everyone for attending, and explain how grateful the organization will be to anyone who acts on the advice gained during the training session in order to prevent an attack. For example, someone who has suspicions about an email attachment and therefore decides not to click on it until having consulted with the technical department.

Caution is a virtue when it comes it security, and no one should take risks regarding IT security because of commercial pressures. For example, if a report has to be with a client by 5pm but the sender is concerned that the file might be infected with a virus, it's much better to delay the transmission by 15 minutes while someone checks the file rather than sending it without regard for the potential consequences. Make it quite clear that any employee in this situation will not be penalized for putting security first.

In the second part of the presentation, cover the basics of IT security awareness, trying wherever possible to talk in language that's relevant to your company's area of business. Don't simply talk vaguely about viruses being able to wipe a hard disk and delete files, but give some examples of the data and departments that could be affected and the consequences if this were to happen. At all times, spell out that everyone has a part to play in ensuring that attackers can be kept out of the company's systems, and that it's not something that can be done by the technical staff alone.

Among the topics that you should cover are:

- Why hackers hack, and the techniques that they use. Explain that there's no such thing as a typical hacker – they do it for all sorts of reasons and come from all sorts of backgrounds. Some might even be insiders, so explain what you should do if you suspect a colleague;

- Why a hacker might want to target us. For example, because they want information that they know we have, or they just don't like us. Or maybe we're just a random target;

- The law regarding computer misuse. Yes, hacking and virus-spreading is illegal;

- Don't assume that an email message is really who it appears to be from;

- Never click on an email attachment unless you know what it is and who it's from. It may have been sent by a virus without the knowledge of the account holder;

- Beware of phishing scams. Never divulge bank details, both personal and corporate, via a Web site by clicking on a link in an email message. Always type the address directly into your browser or access it from your own Favourites menu;

- Never reply to spam, however offensive it is, and even if there's a "click here to remove yourself from our database" link. Just ignore or delete it;

- If your antivirus software warns you of a potential problem and you don't know what to do, contact an IT support person immediately.

Don't continue using the PC. If the computer is behaving in an unexpected way, disconnect it from the network by pulling out the network cable from the wall or from the computer;

- Never forward email warnings about viruses. They're probably hoaxes. Leave it to the IT support people;

- Remember to back up your important files (or, if your company has a central file store which is regularly backed up, make sure you always save your files to the central store rather than on your own PC);

- Encrypt confidential information, especially on portable devices such as laptops, mobile phones, PDAs and palmtop/handheld computers;

- Lock your Windows PC when away from your desk so no one else can use it or see your files;

- Don't misuse the Web, such as viewing or downloading pirated software or offensive/pornographic material. Doing so can result in prosecution for you and for the directors of the company;

- Never share or borrow someone else's password. If someone asks to borrow yours, always refuse – even if the request comes from someone in a more senior position;

- Keep your passwords safe, especially those where misuse can be instantly obvious such as those for updating the Web site;

- Never give out company information to someone on the phone or in person unless you can verify their identity and they have a good reason for needing the information. Avoid divulging information about the company's structure or facilities (e.g. what type of antivirus software do you use?) to telephone callers who pose as sales people – they may not be a genuine sales person at all.

Ensuring that staff don't share passwords with one another is essential for a number of reasons. The obvious one is that you need to prevent someone from using an account which has greater access privileges than those which they have been allocated, but there's another reason too: if staff share passwords you can no longer have faith in your security log files because an action which is recorded against one user's name might actually have been carried out by someone else. From a security management perspective, this is disastrous. If you prosecute someone for misusing your systems, for example, their defence lawyer will almost certainly have your evidence successfully dismissed because it is clearly unreliable. And if staff know that your logs are not to be trusted, they are more likely to abuse their position of trust because they know that, if caught, they can simply blame it on someone else.

Many years ago I was asked to do some consultancy work for one of the major European railways. The company had developed a new machine that was to be installed in thousands of small shops, allowing staff to sell train tickets over the counter. I was asked to examine the machine and the procedures for using it, to see if there were any obvious ways that staff in shops could fool the machine into generating free tickets for their friends. The only possible loophole that I discovered was that each user of the system had to log on before selling tickets, but there was only one username and password for each shop. The central server could therefore identify which outlet generated a particular ticket, but had no idea which staff member was involved. I pointed out the obvious flaw in my report.

Senior Management Commitment

Senior managers and directors of the company need to be involved in your security awareness training programme in two ways. First, at least one of them needs to be present during each training session, to demonstrate to employees that the company really does take the matter seriously and to answer any questions of policy and procedure that arise.

Secondly, senior managers are, in my experience, among the people who are most likely to click on an infected email attachment or run other unauthorized software. Sometimes they do it through ignorance, other times it's because they think they're above the rules which mere techies decree. In many cases, I've seen large multinational companies suffer horrendous virus infections across many thousands of PCs because a board-level director (in one case it was actually the IT director) didn't think that the rules about email attachments should apply to him.

Therefore, senior management needs to be included in your security awareness training. This is always difficult, both politically and from a time-management perspective. Don't even try to get all of them together at the same time – even if they do agree to attend, half will cancel on the day. A short session with each of them in turn, perhaps no longer than 15 minutes and arranged at their convenience, is better than no training at all. And of course it's not training but a strategic briefing – senior managers like to think that they don't need training.

Web Resources

Typing "security awareness training" into your favourite internet search engine will bring forth a plethora of products and training organizations that can help you, plus a lot of useful free literature from various Government organizations around the world. Most of the literature is very formal, suggesting that you start by undertaking a training needs analysis (a series of complex questionnaires sent to each employee) and then build your training programme accordingly. Such a process is slow and expensive and, in my experience, unnecessary. Most of it will be ignored by the trainees.

It's possible to buy security-related motivational posters and stationery which, when distributed around the office, help to drive home the message. Again, you'll find these on the Web and most suppliers will ship internationally. You could also consider creating a custom screen-saver for your company which displays a variety of messages along the "stay safe – think security" line whenever a PC is not being used.

Keep Records

Whether your security awareness programme is arranged by the training department, the IT people or the Director's 16 year old nephew who happens to "know a bit about security", keeping accurate and up-to-date records of the training sessions is vital. Ensure that you know who's been trained, and when. New staff should receive the training as soon as possible after they join the company, and everyone should be given a refresher course every year or two to take account of fading memories and new technology.

▶ FUNDAMENTAL FIVE

Your action points for this chapter:

1. Put together some basic information on IT security awareness for staff, perhaps on a Web page or in a series of weekly emails. ☐

2. Keep the material short and to the point. ☐

3. Ensure that all staff are included, from new employees to senior managers. ☐

4. Make the material relevant. ☐

5. Obtain the visible commitment to the project of senior managers, so that all staff realize that you take the subject seriously. ☐

8

Patch Management

S **oftware companies issue security patches regularly. Some do it on an as-required basis while others are more predictable. Adobe, for example, rarely issues security patches, and there's no predictable pattern as to their release schedule. Microsoft, on the other hand, issues its security patches on the second Tuesday of every month. By ensuring that its patches are announced on a known date, Microsoft allows its customers to ensure that they have the necessary manpower and technical facilities in place so that, if the patches are critical, they can be deployed before hackers manage to start exploiting them.**

In August 2005, Microsoft released a critical security patch for Windows 2000 that would prevent viruses from infecting unpatched machines. Just five days after Microsoft's warning, the Zotob virus had been written and deployed by the hacker community and badly affected a number of computers in companies such as CNN and the *New York Times*. Only by deploying patches as quickly as possible can you avoid such problems.

While most major software companies only ever issue two or three important security fixes per year, Microsoft issues around 100 updates for Windows, Internet Explorer and Office annually. Not all of these are officially classified as critical, but many are. Details can always be found at www.microsoft.com/security.

If your organization has only a handful of PCs and your IT support staff are on site, the process of patch management is relatively easy. Yet in larger companies the task is often much more difficult. Imagine a company with, say, 2000 staff PCs spread across seven different sites in four countries, each of which could at any time become the weakest link in the security chain by virtue of a single missing security patch which is exploited by a hacker in order to gain access to the company's entire global network.

It's not just standard desktop PCs that must be managed. What happens about laptops used by sales staff who spend most of their time out of the office, or by visiting engineers who don't actually work for your company but who need to connect to your network? What about your employees' home PCs? What about devices which are not used as desktop computers but which contain a Windows-based PC at their heart, such as advanced photocopiers, high-capacity printers, email kiosks, vending machines, the till in the on-site shop, dedicated video conferencing hardware, your telephone switchboard and your voicemail system? All are susceptible to attack and all must be kept up to date with security patches.

With recent versions of Windows, keeping the machine fully patched is fairly easy so long as it is connected to the internet. Configure the system to download and install updates automatically (this is the default with Windows XP Service Pack 2 but not on previous versions) and the job is done. Important Windows updates will be downloaded and installed automatically and, if a reboot is required, this will happen automatically too (unless someone is logged on as an administrator, in which case he or she will be prompted to ask if it's safe to restart).

Sometimes this isn't sufficient. If the machine isn't connected to the internet, it won't be updated. Also, some companies like to have control over which security patches are installed, but allowing Windows to download updates from Microsoft's own servers permits no such control.

A possible solution to this problem is SUS, or Server Update Services. This is a free product from Microsoft that you can download via the company's Web site. Install it on a computer that has a permanent internet connection, and it will automatically download copies of all Windows security patches to its own hard drive. You then choose which ones should be sent out to the computers on your network, and it does the rest. There are also some basic reporting features so you know which computers have received which updates.

Another useful feature of SUS is that, if your company's computers are configured to obtain their updates from your SUS server rather than via Microsoft's Web site, service packs which would otherwise have to be installed by someone with administrator privileges will be installed automatically without the need for someone with the necessary rights to visit the machine in person.

SUS is handy and free of charge, but it's not sufficient for many companies. Its reporting abilities are far from comprehensive, there's no facility to ban unpatched computers from being plugged into your network, and it doesn't handle patches other than those which fix holes in the Windows operating system or Internet Explorer (which is officially part of Windows rather than being an application). If you want something that is more full-featured than SUS, and are prepared to pay, then there are many excellent products on the market. A Web search for patch management will bring up links to dozens, which will enable you to draw up a shortlist of those that you should evaluate as being possibly suitable for your particular situation.

One well-known company in the patch management market is Shavlik (**www.shavlik.com**). Its HFNetChk makes it easy to automatically push patches out to any or all machines on your network, regardless of whether those machines are connected to the internet. Its excellent reporting facilities allow you to easily find out which machines have, or don't have, a particular patch file installed. Additional features such as bandwidth throttling allow you to ensure that the release of a patch is staggered across all of your company's computers rather than having them all hit your network at precisely the same time.

HFNetChk can analyse and patch not just Windows installations, but also Office, Exchange, SQL Server, Outlook and Java. Patching the Java Virtual Machine is one area in which the standard Windows Update facility that is built into the operating system is sadly lacking – updates tend to require administrator access in order to install, so if a user only ever logs into their PC with a non-admin account the Java updates will not be installed.

Another useful feature of Shavlik's product is a rollback facility, allowing you to easily remove patches if they are found to be causing problems. Although rare, there have been instances in the past where errors in patch files have led to major troubles such as servers that repeatedly crash. It is events such as these that have tended to tarnish the good name of the Automatic Update feature built into Windows. By agreeing to allow your computers to update themselves immediately when a patch is issued there is a real risk (albeit a small one) that a bug in a patch could render your entire network unusable. By using a third-party patch management product so as not to propagate the patches until you are sure that no major problems exist, you remove this risk.

MBSA

A highly useful tool in the arsenal of any IT security specialist is the Microsoft Baseline Security Analyser. MBSA scans one or more computers on your network and alerts you if any important Microsoft security patches are missing. It then provides links that enable those missing patches to be downloaded and installed. The program can also detect a number of configuration errors and other situations that can pose a potential security problem, such as accounts with easily guessable passwords or no password at all. MBSA was written by Shavlik and is based on HFNetChk so it has a good pedigree. It's also popular – Microsoft says that the program scans around three million computers each week. You can download it from **www.microsoft.com/mbsa**.

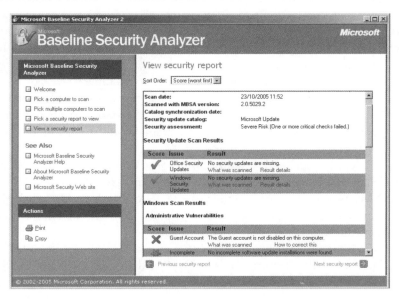

Another useful online source of information is the Web site of the National Infrastructure Security Coordination Centre at **www.niscc. gov.uk**, which issues warnings to all large businesses and Government organizations if hackers are known to be targeting specific business sectors. It's well worth keeping an occasional eye on this site.

Microsoft also makes available a free software download called the Security Assessment Tool. This is a questionnaire-based system that asks you about your current IT installations and suggests ways in which you could improve security. It's a free download from **www.securityguidance.com**.

▶ FUNDAMENTAL FIVE

Your action points for this chapter:

1. Ensure that all Windows-based computers are configured to download and install all new security patches automatically. ☐

2. Use Microsoft SUS and MBSA to roll out patches and to check that important patches have been installed. ☐

3. Implement procedures and/or technology to ensure that machines that don't contain all current security patches cannot connect to your network. ☐

4. Keep a regular eye on the Web sites of those who publish the application software that your company uses, to check for new security patches. ☐

5. If you are concerned about vulnerabilities in Internet Explorer, consider the use of an alternative browser. ☐

Windows Workstation Security

Those who sell computers pre-installed with Windows, antivirus software and a host of other applications tell their customers that the new machine is ready to use as soon as it has been unpacked from the box and plugged in. Equally, when you install a fresh copy of Windows onto a new hard drive the implication from the setup utility is that, once the operating system is installed, the computer is all ready to be used by an employee or a home-based user. This is not the case, and if you mistakenly believe it to be so then you are in for a few nasty surprises. Fresh out of the box, or when newly installed from CD, Windows is dangerously insecure, and there are a few things that you must do before you use it.

First, ensure that the hard disk has been formatted using the NTFS filing system rather than FAT or FAT32. If you're installing Windows from scratch you'll be offered the choice. NTFS is more secure and more resilient than FAT, so don't even consider anything else.

You must never allow an unpatched computer to connect to the internet, so a new installation of Windows should be patched by installing the latest service packs for Windows and Office from a CD that has been prepared on another computer. Alternatively, if you are using the Microsoft tools for creating company-wide installation CDs for Windows and/or Office, you can use a technique called slipstreaming to pre-patch the software before it gets installed.

Having ensured that Windows and all key applications have had the latest security patches installed, you should then install your company's standard antivirus software. Again, this must be updated to the latest version of the software and the virus signature files and should be done offline. Otherwise, if there is a virus-infected PC on your network that is continually seeking new unprotected machines to infect, the new computer will become infected as soon as it is connected to your network.

Assuming that the new computer will be operating within the confines of a corporate firewall, it can now be plugged into the network. If no such firewall exists, then install a personal firewall on the computer at this point. You may wish to use a dedicated product such as ZoneAlarm, or perhaps you will prefer to use one of the many antivirus programs that also include an optional firewall component such as Symantec's Internet Security Suite.

Once the new PC is plugged into the company network, ensure that all automatic-update features are enabled so that any new security patches will be installed automatically from now on.

User Accounts

Windows XP in both its Home and Professional incarnations normally sets up just one default user account, with full administrator privileges, and doesn't even require that the user enters a password before being allowed to use it. Many companies leave Windows in this default state and simply hand the computer to the user. This is an incredibly dangerous thing to do.

Before handing over the new computer to its user, you should always configure Windows to require a password, and set up a new account for the user. The precise way that you do this will depend upon various factors, such as whether your company network is domain-based or merely one or more workgroups. On a domain-based network, authentication is handled by a separate machine known as a domain controller, so the machine has to be added to the domain by someone with the knowledge and credentials that allow him to do so. On non-domain networks, authentication is handled by the PC itself, so an account must be created on that machine by someone who is in possession of its local administrator password.

Never, ever, allow your users to log into their PC using an administrator password. When you set up their login account, grant it only the minimum set of privileges that it requires (standard user or power user). Someone with an administrator account can install software and reconfigure the machine, which can cause major headaches for your technical support staff.

If a user logs into a PC using an administrator account then all of the programs he runs will run with greater privileges than would otherwise be the case. If the user inadvertently runs a virus-infected email attachment that tries to install a back door or some other item of malware, the installation will only succeed if the operating system allows it. So if the user (and therefore the malware) is running under the control of an account that does not have permission to install new software, the back door will not be installed.

Restricting user accounts can present occasional problems, such as if a user has a legitimate need to install a new application or printer and has to call upon the services of an IT support person. Yet this is a small price to pay, and is no reason to accept what might seem like the easier option of allowing all users to install new hardware and software unchecked.

By ensuring that users don't have access to administrator accounts, you also prevent accidental or deliberate removal of software. This can be just as important as preventing the installation of new programs. For example, someone (or a program that the user is running without their knowledge) running under an administrative account could remove or disable any antivirus software, personal firewall or other similar program.

Be Discreet

Ensure that the Windows user account names that you use in your company do not provide any clues to hackers. The default administrator account on every new Windows installation is 'Administrator' and this is the first one that every hacker tries, so you should always rename this account. Don't use 'admin' or 'manager', but something innocuous such as George or Yellow. Although Windows will allow you to rename the default administrator account, you can't remove it from the administrators group, so if you need to set up a standard user account you'll have to set up a new one from scratch.

When choosing passwords, pay particular attention to those of administrator accounts. These are the virtual keys to your kingdom, so make them long and complex, and ensure that they are known only to a few people. Each administrator should have his or her own administrator-level account rather than sharing one with someone else. This way, your log files will contain reliable details not just of any actions taken, but also who took them.

Each admin account user should also have a non–admin account, which they should use for all their routine non–admin duties. Administrator accounts should only be used when they are required, to avoid accidents caused by someone using an account that possesses more powers than they realized.

In Chapter 27 we shall discuss the Windows Encrypting File System, or EFS. One weakness with EFS concerns administrator accounts. The Windows default administrator account is designated as the Recovery Agent for EFS on a computer when Windows is first installed. This means that the Administrator account can read all of the files on that computer, even if they are encrypted, and even if the account is renamed from Administrator to something else. This is yet another reason why you must guard administrator accounts carefully.

Temporary Admin Permissions

If you are an administrator, i.e. you know the local admin password for a Windows computer, it can be frustrating if you need to sort out a problem that stems from the currently-logged-in user not having sufficient privileges. For example, the user might be trying to change a program's settings and is being denied access by the operating system.

The long–winded solution in such circumstances is:

1. The user logs off.

2. You log on with your administrator account.

3. You make the user a member of the administrators group.

4. You log off, and the user logs on again.

5. The user does what he needs to do.

6. The user logs off.

7. You log on as an administrator.

8. You remove the user from the administrators group.

9. You log off and the user logs on.

Thankfully there are a couple of easier ways. One is to use the Run As option. Right-click on the icon of the program you want to run, and choose Run As from the menu that appears. Enter the administrator username and password, and the program will run with the privileges of that account rather than those of the user who is currently logged in.

However, there is a problem with Run As. If you run a program in this way, any per-user settings that you change (rather than global ones) will be changed for the administrator rather than for the user. There are two ways around this. One is to use the long-winded solution listed above, instead of using Run As. The other is to download a useful program from the Web called MakeMeAdmin.

Once you have downloaded MakeMeAdmin, run it while logged in as the user. You'll be asked for the user's current password, and for the administrator username and password. Assuming you enter these correctly, you now have a command prompt (C : >) running under the user's account but which has administrative privileges. Once you have done what you need to do, type EXIT and everything is back to normal.

The Three-Finger Salute

Configure Windows so that users must press Ctrl-Alt-Delete and enter a valid username and password in order to log in. By default, Windows doesn't require either of these (assuming that the machine is not part of a domain), so anyone who turns on the computer can use it. This is clearly a bad idea in a company environment, even if it's acceptable in a domestic setting. To change this in Windows XP Pro, select Administrative Tools from the Control Panel, then choose Local Security Policy. In the left hand tree under security settings, click on 'local policies', highlight 'security options' and scroll in the right tree to 'interactive logon: do not require Ctrl+Alt+Del'. Set this option to Disabled.

Explore the options on the screen before you close the program – there may be others that will be of use in your company.

Local Security Policies

Modern versions of Windows (2000 onwards, but I shall concentrate on XP) include the facility to log almost everything that happens on the computer. To view the logs, right-click on My Computer and select Manage, then explore the Event Viewer section to browse the application, security and system logs (you need to be logged on as an administrator to do this). It's important to examine these logs occasionally as they can provide useful pointers regarding possible misuse of the system.

The computer's audit policy is where you specify which events get logged. To access this, select Administrative Tools from the Control Panel. Then choose Local Security Policy. Under Local Policies, click Audit Policy. The list of possible events to log is shown in the right-hand column. If you suspect unauthorized activity, take a copy of the log and keep it somewhere safe.

Having set the computer to require a Ctrl-Alt-Delete to log in and enabled logging, your next step is to enable a local password policy (again, assuming that the machine is not part of a domain). From the Control Panel select Administrative Tools and then choose Local Security Policy. Select Account Policies and then select Account Lockout Policy. From here you can set the maximum number of guesses that are allowed before the account is locked out, and the duration of the lockout. By default there is no lockout specified so a hacker with physical access to the machine, or via another computer on your network, can keep guessing passwords for as long as he likes. By setting a lockout policy of, say, 30 minutes after three unsuccessful attempts, this particular avenue into your systems is blocked.

If you allow users to be able to change their own passwords (it's an option that you can tick when setting up a user account via the Control Panel), you can enforce rules to ensure that they choose sensibly. Click on Password Policy and you can specify values such as the maximum age for a password before it must be changed, how many previous passwords are remembered (and thus can't be used again), and the minimum password length.

Another useful option when setting a password for a user is to force the user to change their password at the next logon. If an administrator changes a user's password, tick this box so that the administrator will no longer be aware of the user's new password and thus can't be blamed for subsequent misuse of the account.

Setting options such as password policies and lockouts is known as hardening Windows or locking down the system. A Web search on either of these terms will bring up much more information should you wish to explore this subject further. One useful Web site is **www.windowsecurity.com**.

Some Further Actions

Almost all PCs have a BIOS options page from where you can configure various settings that control how the computer operates. One very useful option lets you specify the boot device order. Ideally this should be set so that the computer boots from the hard disk first, and then from the CD drive if no bootable hard disk is found. This will ensure that no one can boot the machine from a CD-ROM once Windows is installed, but that Windows can be reinstalled if the drive fails and is replaced with a new, unformatted unit.

Failure to prevent users booting from other devices such as the CD drive, floppy disk or USB flash drive means that anyone who gains physical access to the computer can restart it and load any utility or operating system that they wish, bypassing the security precautions that you have established. Any information that is not encrypted can be accessed, even if you've used Windows to configure specific access permissions.

Once you have configured the BIOS boot options, enable password protection so that no one can change those options. All computers have such a facility in their BIOS pages and, although it's not foolproof (you can generally wipe the password by temporarily removing the small battery on the computer's motherboard), it adds another level of protection.

Default Accounts

A new Windows XP installation comes with a few default accounts as standard, in addition to the Administrator user. The best way to manage these, rather than select User Accounts from the Control Panel, is to right-click My Computer and choose Manage, then select Local Users And Groups. Delete any accounts that are not required.

Each Windows computer has a 'guest' account and it's important to configure the guest accounts correctly on each of your company's PCs. Unfortunately this can be fairly complicated, as the way in which Windows uses guest accounts varies greatly according to which version of Windows is in use and whether your network is domain-based.

On Windows 2000, assuming a non-domain network, if someone on computer A wants to connect to computer B over the network (to access files stored on it or to share a resource such as a printer), the user of computer A will normally be required to enter a valid username and password for computer B. Or alternatively, the user's username and password on A must also exist as a valid username and password on B.

If the guest account is enabled on machine B, then the above doesn't apply. Anyone on your LAN can connect to B, and Windows will automatically log them in as a guest user. You should, therefore, disable the guest account on all Windows 2000 machines to ensure that anyone who wants to connect to the machine has to provide a valid username and password.

With Windows XP Professional things are slightly different. All connections to machine B over the network are forced to use the guest account, even if the user of A supplies a valid non-guest username and password. Therefore, on a Windows XP Professional machine, you need to leave the guest account enabled if the machine will be accepting connections over the LAN from users who need to access shared files or other resources.

This behaviour in Windows XP, whereby all network connections are given guest access even if a different username and password are provided, is known as ForceGuest. Although it is enabled by default, and it makes good sense for security reasons, you can turn it off in the computer's local security policy if you wish.

With ForceGuest enabled, Windows XP Professional on a computer that is not joined to a domain uses Simple File Sharing to control permissions on files that are accessed over your network. Although this makes things easier, it reduces the amount of control that you have over who can access which files on that shared computer. It's recommended that you turn off Simple File Sharing. To do this go to My Computer and, from the Tools menu, click Folder Options and then select the View tab. Deselect the 'Use simple file sharing' box. Once you have done this, you can set the access permissions for any file or folder by right-clicking it and selecting Properties.

You can set up detailed access permissions for specific users and/or groups, rather than simply having catch-all permissions for a single guest account through which everyone has to connect.

File permissions are an important tool on a Windows machine. They allow you to restrict access to folders on a per-user or per-group basis. Windows XP automatically applies a degree of file protection – if users A and B both have accounts on a computer, user A will not be able to see the 'My Documents' area belonging to B. If you wish to protect other files or folders, simply right-click on the item and select Properties. You will generally see two relevant tabs at this point, namely Sharing and Security.

The Sharing tab is where you set the permissions for the network share rather than for the actual files and folders. The Security tab is for setting the file and folder permissions, which is done on a per-user or per-group basis and applies regardless of whether those files are being accessed by a local user or by someone over your LAN. Having separate permissions for the network share and the files/folders is confusing, and the easiest option is to set the share permissions so that everyone (i.e. the Everyone group) has either full control or read-only access, and then to use the Security tab to fine-tune those permissions to cater for groups or users.

Permission Problems

A depressingly high percentage of the problems that security professionals have to fix on a daily basis come down to an incorrect access privilege somewhere or other. Not all such problems are easy to solve, either, especially when you enter the realms of inherited permissions in which a file's permissions are not explicitly set but have permeated down from a folder higher up in the directory tree. While the easiest way to fix such problems is undoubtedly to grant people greater privileges than they actually need, either from the start or at the point that a problem comes to light, you must resist at all costs the temptation to do this. It will solve any problem in the short term, but will pose a serious security risk in the future.

Instruct users to lock their PC if they leave their desk. This prevents someone else (whether a staff member or a passing visitor) from accessing it, but is quicker than logging out and then having to log back in again. To lock Windows XP, just press Ctrl–Alt–Delete and then press K. Any programs that were running will continue to do so, and any documents that were open will remain so. The screen will be blanked, and contain only a message explaining that the computer has been locked and can only be unlocked by the original user or an administrator. To unlock and resume where you left off, just press Ctrl–Alt–Delete again and enter the account password.

A user who runs an ftp or Web server on their office computer without permission causes a significant security risk because hackers attack these services using tools that are widely available on the internet. Ensure that the ftp service is disabled, and that no Web server such as IIS or Apache has been installed. If the computer is within a corporate firewall, you should also block incoming ports so that attempts from outside the organization will fail to connect to any servers except those on a list of authorized machines.

There are various programs available on the internet for free download which will help you to find out whether a PC is running any unauthorized server software by telling you which, if any, of its TCP ports are listening (i.e. waiting for an incoming connection). You can also use the netstat command that is part of Windows – just go to a command prompt and type **netstat -an -p tcp** and the results will be displayed like this:

```
[C:\] netstat -an -p tcp
Active Connections

  Proto  Local Address          Foreign Address       State
  TCP    0.0.0.0:135            0.0.0.0:0             LISTENING
  TCP    0.0.0.0:445            0.0.0.0:0             LISTENING
  TCP    0.0.0.0:20202          0.0.0.0:0             LISTENING
  TCP    127.0.0.1:1027         0.0.0.0:0             LISTENING
  TCP    192.168.0.104:139      0.0.0.0:0             LISTENING
  TCP    192.168.0.104:1031     207.46.4.87:1863      ESTABLISHED
  TCP    192.168.0.104:1048     80.67.81.32:80        CLOSE_WAIT
  TCP    192.168.0.104:1050     80.67.81.30:80        CLOSE_WAIT
  TCP    192.168.0.104:1091     80.15.238.20:80       CLOSE_WAIT
```

For each port listed as LISTENING there is the potential for a connection to be accepted from an external computer via the internet and you need to find out why. In the example above, the listening ports are 135, 445, 20202, 1027 and 139. A Web search will help you track down the type of service associated with each port. Common port numbers include 21 (ftp server), 80 (Web server) and 25 (smtp mail server). A useful list of port numbers can be found on the Web at `http://www.iana.org/assignments/port-numbers`.

Adding -b to the end of the above command will cause the list to include the name of the program which established the listening port. For example:

```
[C:\] netstat -an -p tcp -b
Active Connections

Proto Local Address  Foreign Address State       PID
TCP  0.0.0.0:135    0.0.0.0:0       LISTENING   760
e:\windows\system32\WS2_32.dll
E:\WINDOWS\system32\RPCRT4.dll
e:\windows\system32\rpcss.dll
E:\WINDOWS\system32\svchost.exe
E:\WINDOWS\system32\ADVAPI32.dll
[svchost.exe]


TCP  0.0.0.0:445    0.0.0.0:0       LISTENING   4
[System]


TCP 0.0.0.0:2869    0.0.0.0:0       LISTENING   912
E:\WINDOWS\System32\httpapi.dll
e:\windows\system32\ssdpsrv.dll
E:\WINDOWS\system32\RPCRT4.dll
[svchost.exe]


TCP 127.0.0.1:1025  0.0.0.0:0       LISTENING   440
[alg.exe]


TCP 192.168.0.104:139 0.0.0.0:0     LISTENING   4
[System]
```

To find out why a program called alg.exe is listening for connections on port 1025, type the program's name into a search engine and you'll discover that it's part of Windows and is no cause for concern. Remember, too, that a listening port on a computer doesn't always mean that it will be able to respond to any incoming connections on that port – it all depends on how your firewall is set up. If your corporate firewall is blocking all incoming traffic on port 1025 then alg.exe will never receive anything at all.

If you want to examine port traffic in greater depth there's a free program available from Microsoft that will log all TCP/IP port access to and from the computer on which it's installed. This is a very useful diagnostic tool, especially if you're trying to investigate a possible security problem. A Web search for 'Microsoft Port Reporter Tool' will lead you to it.

Ensure that the Internet settings are configured correctly on the computer. From within Internet Explorer, select Internet Options from the Tools menu. On the General tab, in the Temporary Internet Files section, press the Settings button. Set the 'amount of disk space to use' to a fairly high value, depending on the amount of hard disk space available. Anything up to 1 GB is good. Not only will this speed up the user's Web browsing, but it will result in a lot of evidence being available for scrutiny if an employee is suspected of having viewed 'inappropriate material' on the Web.

Another option on the General tab lets you specify how many days the list of previously-viewed Web sites should be retained for. Again, the larger the value the more evidence you are gathering. This information is normally stored in \Documents and Settings\username\Local Settings\History.

Disk Quotas

All recent version of Windows support hard disk quotas. This allows you to specify the maximum amount of disk space that each user can occupy. Quotas can be per-user or per-group, and are easy to set up. Right-click on My Computer and choose Manage. Under Storage, click on Disk Management. Then right-click on the required drive, choose Properties, and select the Quota tab.

You can set both a quota level and a warning level. For example, you might set the quota at 500 MB and the warning at 400 MB, so that the user will receive warnings when his or her space is 80% full. You can also choose what happens once the quota is reached – continue to issue warnings, or deny the user the right to create any new files until he's deleted some existing ones. It's generally not a good idea to use the deny option because there's a real danger that a user will lose work if they have been editing or creating a document and then discover that they have nowhere to save it. Most programs will handle the situation sensibly, but not all do.

Disk quotas are a useful way to prevent one user or department hogging all the space on your file server. It's also a good way to prevent users from thinking that they can use their disk space at work to hoard MP3 music and downloaded movies. The other option is simply to keep adding new hard disks to your server as demand for storage increases. Although this is easy and cheap in the short term, it becomes less attractive once you factor in the additional costs of managing and backing up all those extra files.

File Extensions

Every file on a Windows-based PC normally has a three-character extension which identifies its type. Excel spreadsheets end with .XLS, for example, and Word documents have .DOC on the end. Text files use a .TXT extension, and so on. Although file extensions are not 100% reliable (you can rename a .DOC file to .XLS if you want to cause confusion), they are a useful indicator.

For reasons best known to itself, Windows XP does its best to hide file extensions from users. When you're viewing the contents of a directory in Explorer, for example, a file called Personnel Data.XLS will appear merely as Personnel Data. If the directory contains both a .DOC and a .XLS version of the same file, it will appear that there are duplicated names and working out which one to click on in order to open it can be tricky.

By hiding file extensions, Microsoft makes it easy for hackers to disguise the true intent of some files. For example, if someone emails you an attachment called BROCHURE, it's difficult to tell whether it's brochure.doc or brochure.exe. If it's the latter, clicking on it could cause untold damage to your computers because .EXE files are programs rather than simple documents.

There are many file types which can contain executable content and which will run a program (possibly an undesirable one) if you click on the filename. The most common is .EXE but there are others. Viruses frequently use a .SCR file to send themselves to unsuspecting users, as most people are not familiar with this file type which is normally used by programs which install a new Windows screen saver.

Because Windows allows filenames that include dots, consider the case of someone emailing a file called BROCHURE.DOC to you. Is this a harmless Word document? Actually, no. It's an executable file called BROCHURE.DOC.EXE but Windows has removed the extension (the .EXE part). To avoid becoming a victim of ambiguity, configure all of your Windows workstations to display file extensions as nature intended. In the case of Windows XP, open My Computer and then, from the Tools menu, select Folder Options. On the View tab, clear the 'hide extensions for known file types' checkbox.

The Registry

The database known as the registry is the most important file on a Windows computer. Most programs use the registry to store their configuration data, as does Windows itself. Windows ships with a registry editor program called RegEdit that allows a user with sufficient privileges to edit any entry in the registry, or to export the registry to a text file for perusal elsewhere.

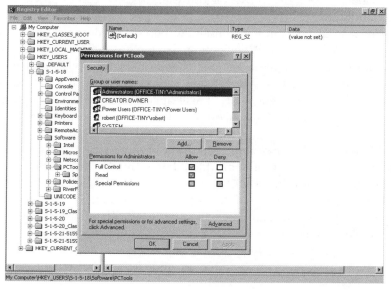

RegEdit allows you to set access permissions for individual areas of the registry. Few people bother to do this, but it's a very useful technique to help protect a computer. Simply fire up RegEdit, right-click on a particular branch (I've selected PC Tools here) and choose Permissions. By setting the permissions on registry entries you can prevent staff from changing a program's settings, even if that program doesn't have an inbuilt facility that allows you to do this.

Windows is notoriously bad at performing basic housekeeping on the registry, which can result in this critical database becoming fragmented, over-large, and filled with obsolete information that can safely be deleted or archived. Attempting to do this yourself is difficult, because the typical registry contains thousands of entries with meaningless names. Thankfully, there are some excellent programs that can do the job for you. My favourite is Registry Mechanic (**www.pctools.com**), which costs around £20 for a single copy up to £689 for a company-wide site licence.

Mortal Coils

Eventually a PC reaches the end of its life and upgrading the processor or RAM or hard disk becomes uneconomical. It's time to throw away the machine and replace it. In many countries, disposing of electronic equipment is not simply a matter of dumping it in the nearest skip, so beware of doing so. You may well be legally required to call upon the services of a specialist contractor who can remove the toxic and/or valuable materials.

Alternatively you can give or sell the machine to staff, a local school, a charity, or anyone else. Or even sell it on eBay. Sadly such deeds are often more trouble than they're worth. If money changes hands then it has to be accounted for. If there's a copy of Windows on the hard disk then, technically, you may find that the licence originally supplied with the computer forbids you from reselling it or even giving it away. Applications, too, are normally non-transferable.

Whatever you decide to do with your old computers, it's essential that you wipe all confidential information from the hard disk before the machine leaves your premises. Similar rules apply if you dispose of old hard disks, perhaps because they have been removed from machines that are being upgraded.

Simply deleting every data file and then emptying the Windows recycle bin is not sufficient – undeleting files from a hard disk is trivial to anyone who has the correct software. Formatting the hard disk is not always sufficient either – if you inadvertently choose the 'quick' format option then the operation can be reversed in just a couple of seconds.

There are plenty of programs around that make a thorough job of wiping a hard disk. A Web search for hard disk wiping software or secure erasure programs will find lots of them for you. If you fail to use such a program every time you dispose of a hard disk, whether as part of a usable computer or not, you risk hackers (or merely the curious) attempting to read the contents. Such activity is very common. In 2004, security company Pointsec bought 100 second-hand hard disks on eBay. Each had been wiped, according to the vendors, yet Pointsec was able to recover data from 70 of them. One particular drive, purchased for less than $10, contained information from one of Europe's largest financial services groups including pension plans, customer databases, financial information, payroll records, personnel details, login codes, and administrator passwords for their intranet. There were more than 70 Excel documents of customers' email addresses, dates of birth, their home addresses, telephone numbers and other highly confidential information.

Pointsec carried out the exercise for purely publicity reasons, and the news of its discoveries made the TV and newspapers worldwide. In this particular case it was agreed not to name the company whose data-wiping efforts were so lax. The next time it happens, the culprits might not be so lucky.

FUNDAMENTAL FIVE

Your action points for this chapter:

1. Ensure that all your Windows workstations and laptops are fully loaded with all the current operating system security patches. ☐

2. At least once a month, check the Web sites of the vendors of your company's major applications to ensure that you are not missing out on important application patches. ☐

3. Never plug a new PC into your network until it is properly patched and has had antivirus software installed. ☐

4. Never allow users to operate their computer with an administrator-level account. *Bona fide* administrators should also be issued with a user-level account and should use this except when they need administrator access. ☐

5. Use the Local Security Policy and Local Password Policy under Windows XP to ensure that users choose strong passwords and change them regularly. ☐

10

Basic Server Security

W hile the temporary loss of a key PC or laptop might inconvenience a handful of people, the loss of a key server for even a short period could prove catastrophic. Consider the effect on a business such as eBay or Amazon if the server which handled all their customers' credit card payments went down for just a couple of hours. Or if a hacker managed to corrupt the file server on which all 3000 employees of a multinational organization store their documents. Servers are often a single point of failure in many companies, especially those with neither the forethought nor the finance to install spare capacity.

Possibly the most famous single points of failure currently operating in IT are the top-level root DNS name servers that contain the definitive record of the IP addresses associated with internet domain names. When you type **www.defeatingthehacker.com** into your Web browser, a

DNS name server has to provide a look-up facility to convert defeatingth-ehacker.com into an IP address of 70.96.188.34. Only when your Web browser knows the IP address of the Web server can it connect to that server and retrieve html files from it.

Although there are thousands of DNS servers around the world, they all ultimately update themselves from a master copy, and the consequences of this top-level server failing or becoming corrupted are severe. It could result in every .com or .co.uk domain being unreachable by anyone who doesn't know the IP address of the computer that they are attempting to contact.

Correct configuration and protection of servers is a complex and continual task, and a variety of excellent books and Web sites exist which cover the precise details of how to do it. In the limited space available in this book it's impossible to cover all of the in-depth configuration options for the various permutations of server roles (Web, file store, mail, ftp, etc.) and operating system platforms (Windows 2000, XP, 2003, Linux, Solaris, etc.) that are in common use within server environments. Therefore this chapter will cover only some general must-do advice that is applicable to all server situations, with the strong suggestion that you supplement it with some additional research.

Microsoft Small Business Server

Many small companies don't have a central file server on which staff keep their documents. They prefer instead to rely on simpler technology where each PC is networked but there is no central file store or mail server. In smaller organizations this can often make good sense, especially if you don't have the necessary skills available to keep the server running and properly managed. However, a server-based network has a couple of major advantages. Most importantly, a central file store to which users can save their document files, rather than asking them to use their local hard disks, means that you can apply a proper encryption and backup regime to all of your company's data at a stroke.

Configuring a PC to store all of the user's document files on a server rather than the local hard disk is easy – just change the My Documents setting to point to the user's directory on the server and all applications will then obey the new setting.

Of all the server software aimed at small and medium companies, the best-known is Microsoft's Small Business Server or SBS. Unlike Linux, it costs money, but it's only a few hundred pounds, and most people find that Windows-based workstations talk best to a Windows-based server. It would be unwise, to say the least, to be tempted by a Linux-based server simply to save money unless you had access to someone with the necessary skills to set up and maintain it.

SBS provides all the server-based facilities that a small business needs, right out of the box, including a central file store and shared internet access for all. There's also an intranet, based on Microsoft SharePoint, that allows you to create Web sites for internal consumption such as newsletters, document libraries and events. There's an email server that's based on Exchange Server, remote access facilities that allow staff to access their files via the Web from a traditional PC or a mobile device, and there are also remote administration facilities. It also includes Outlook Web Access that allows staff to access their email over the Web using a standard browser, but with the look and feel of a real Microsoft Outlook session. SBS also includes a Web server, should you wish to host your public Web site on your own machine, although you'll probably find it easier and safer to delegate this role to an external hosting company.

Server operating systems are not fit-and-forget products. They require ongoing maintenance to ensure that they are running safely and securely. SBS is no exception, so a careful reading of the information at www.microsoft.com/sbs is highly recommended.

Physical Security

There is no more important starting point when it comes to server security than to ensure that the machine is physically protected. No one except authorized administrators should be allowed physical access to the server – all other users should connect remotely via your LAN or the internet. With physical access to the machine, an unauthorized user can attack the computer's content by various means, such as installing a Trojan or a password grabber, or a password cracker such as L0phtCrack. By booting the machine from a floppy disk, CD or USB flash drive he will have total control.

If you believe Microsoft's warnings that a forgotten Windows administrator password will render your server unusable, requiring you to format the drive and start again, check out www.winternals.com for another angle. The company sells a variety of very useful products, including one that will change a lost or forgotten admin password. Thankfully, it requires physical access to the machine in question and can't be run over the network.

A USB flash drive can also allow a trespasser to copy confidential files quickly and easily for instant take-away, or to use a program that can copy the server's list of encrypted passwords for cracking off-site at his leisure.

Physical security should be applied to all of your essential IT assets, and not simply by locking servers in a dedicated cupboard or room. When I talk to hackers (the bad guys) and penetration testers (good guys who pretend to be bad – see Chapter 14), they often tell me that they find physical security systems easier to bypass than non-physical ones such as passwords and firewalls. Sometimes this means simply walking straight past the target company's reception area, dressed as an engineer and carrying a couple of computer components. If this fails, plan B involves gaining entry to a meeting room, cupboard or service area which is situated in the public area of the building before one reaches the reception area. If this fails too, then plan C involves gaining access by making an appointment to visit the company (perhaps for a job interview or as a potential supplier), being escorted through the reception area and then slipping unnoticed into another part of the building under the pretence of needing to use the toilet.

Password-protecting all PCs, and locking their keyboards if an employee is away from their desk, will help to ensure that unauthorized visitors to your building can't easily access your systems to copy files or install software such as keystroke loggers or Trojans. But hackers and penetration testers also have another technique for accessing your information, which takes just a few seconds to carry out and which can take place in an empty meeting room, cupboard, or any other part of your building. All they need is to find an unoccupied network socket into which they plug either a laptop or, for longer-term access, a Wireless Access Point. Once the WAP is plugged in, the hacker can then access your network from any nearby location until such time as you happen to notice the WAP.

Do you know where all your Ethernet sockets are? Are there any in unattended locations such as meeting rooms and cable ducts? Are any of those locations outside of your secure area, accessible by people who have not yet passed by your reception desk? Do you implement any form of control to restrict or monitor what gets connected to those sockets? If not, carry out some basic risk assessment to determine whether it would be worth you doing so.

Your physical security precautions should extend not just to unmonitored network sockets, but to any area of your premises which could allow hackers to gain access to confidential information directly or indirectly. When hackers are unable to crack passwords or bypass firewalls they often fall back on tried and trusted techniques such as bin-raiding (also known as dumpster diving), which involves nothing more than browsing the contents of companies' rubbish bins in search of printouts or other media that might contain private information or even passwords. Although low-tech, bin-raiding still gets practised by hackers today – especially those hacking for financial gain rather than fun. Never throw away confidential items such as salary spreadsheets, program listings or customer data without shredding it. If a hard disk develops errors and you're tempted to chuck it into the nearest skip, remember that a hacker can recover most of its contents. Throw it heavily onto the ground in the car park a couple of times before laying it finally to rest.

If you haven't invested in a shredder yet, and a procedure which specifies how and when it should be used, consider doing so. Make sure that it's used properly, however. I was once visiting the offices of a public relations company who were assisting me with a magazine article that I was writing about one of their clients. In the waste bin next to me was a spreadsheet containing personal details of every employee, including their salary. Although the document had been through the shredder and cut into strips, each strip was a perfectly readable row of the spreadsheet because the sheets had been put into the machine the wrong way round.

Another episode which shows the importance of physical security occurred a few years ago. At the time I was working in London, editing an IT newsletter for a company based in Australia. Each month we had to send a package from London to Sydney, which was collected from our offices by a major international courier company. If deadlines were tight, no collection was available and I had to deliver the package to the courier's customer reception centre at Heathrow Airport. For reasons that I never quite understood, the customer reception centre had actually been built within a secure area, protected from thieves and terrorists by large guards and even larger dogs. But if I was dropping off a package I was simply waved through, into a part of the airport in which I could easily view, touch and interfere with anyone's cargo.

Keen to point out that this wasn't particularly secure, I mentioned it in a column that I used to contribute to a monthly IT security magazine and thought nothing more of it. A few months later, when I next had cause to visit the airport and this particular courier company, a brand new customer reception centre had been constructed outside of the secure area. I complimented the reception staff on their brand new facility. "Yes, apparently someone wrote in a magazine that the old one wasn't secure" he said. "Really", I said, but decided not to elaborate.

Power Protection

All your servers should be connected to an uninterruptible power supply (UPS). The UPS contains a battery that is continually recharged from the mains, capable of providing sustained mains voltage (230v or 110v depending on location) for around an hour in the event of a power failure.

All but the cheapest UPSs have the facility to signal to the servers that the mains power has failed, via a USB or serial cable. You do, of course, need to be running a server operating system which is capable of receiving and acting upon this signal (most modern versions of Windows and Unix can do this). When the UPS's battery is reaching the point at which it can no longer sustain the server during a power outage, it will signal to the server so that the computer can automatically shut itself down cleanly and without any risk of data corruption.

Most computer hardware (both servers and workstations) lets you specify what happens when power is restored after a mains failure. This option is normally accessed via the BIOS settings screen. Commonly, this option is set by default to do nothing, in which case the server will not return after a power failure unless someone manually presses its power-on button. If you wish the server to restart of its own accord, ensure that this BIOS option has been set to allow the computer to turn itself on when power is restored.

If the power failure was caused by a surge, it is highly likely that one or more circuit breakers or fuses will have been tripped. So once again the server will not be available upon restoration of the power supply until some manual action has been carried out. If this is a problem, ensure that you have procedures in place for someone to deal with it.

If you have lots of servers, or you anticipate long and frequent losses of external power, battery-based UPSes won't suffice. The alternative is a petrol or diesel generator that is equipped with the necessary sensors and battery-based starter so that it can begin to supply power to critical services when required.

Whatever your contingency plans for coping with the loss of mains power, testing them regularly is important. Tests should be carried out in real-world situations, i.e. with all servers running, which obviously requires a great deal of faith. If you have a generator, remember to keep its fuel tank topped up at all times. A friend of mine tells the story of a company which installed a generator, which they tested every week because it was so critical to the company's operations. When a real power failure did occur, the generator died after just a few minutes because no one had thought to replace all of the diesel that the tests had consumed.

Change your Banners

Most servers display a brief welcome message after a user has successfully logged on. The precise wording of the message can normally be configured through a registry entry or other option. Such banners are a great way to remind users that, for example, their access to the server is logged and that they must abide by the terms of your Acceptable Use Policy or other document. However, never let your banners divulge information that might be useful to a hacker. Banners such as the following are common but are best avoided:

> **Welcome to the XyCo FTP Server**
> **Today is Friday 9th Nov 2006**
> **Please Log In**
> **Forgotten your password? Call Mike Allen on 2668.**

Including a contact name and number for the person who deals with lost or forgotten passwords is clearly a security risk, as is identifying the name of the company whose server this is. Even a line as innocuous as 'Please Log In' is inadvisable, because anti-hacking legislation often states that it only covers unauthorized access, and hackers have been known to claim in their defence that they were accepting an explicit invitation to use the system.

If your company operates mail (SMTP), Web or FTP servers that are accessible over the internet, be aware that all servers contain default pre-assigned banners which provide a clue as to the server software which is running. Hackers use this information when looking for machines to attack. Each time Microsoft issues a patch to fix a critical loophole in its IIS Web Server, for example, hackers around the world quickly fire up their automated programs to scour the internet in search of sites which are still running unpatched software.

It's widely known that most outgoing mail servers are named mail or smtp and that they listen on port 25. So if I attempt to guess the name of the BBC's mail server and to connect to it via the command `telnet mail.bbc.co.uk 25` I am greeted by the message:

```
220 gateg.kw.bbc.co.uk ESMTP Sendmail 8.11.2/8.11.2;
```

This banner tells me which SMTP server software the corporation uses (ESMTP is Microsoft Exchange) and precisely which version of Sendmail. The situation is similar with FTP file-transfer servers. If I connect to the public FTP server run by networking company Novell I am greeted by:

```
Connected to thelev.provo.novell.com.
220-ftp.novell.com NcFTPd Server (licensed copy) ready.
```

Once again, I now know which FTP server software the company uses.

Retrieving details about Web server software is slightly more complicated, but the tools to do it are freely available for immediate download from the Web. One such tool is httprint, available at `http://net square.com/httprint/`, which will automatically retrieve a variety of information about any Web server at which you happen to direct it.

You can help to make hackers' lives more difficult by changing the default banners on your Web, mail and ftp servers. Precise details vary according to the type of server software you're using, and if your server is hosted by a separate company then you'll probably have to ask them to do it for you as you may not have sufficient privileges to change this yourself.

RAID

IT security isn't just about protecting your systems from attack by hackers. Remember the holy trinity of confidentiality, integrity and availability. With servers especially, availability is just as important as confidentiality and integrity, which is something that many security managers forget.

Ensure that your server hardware has a degree of fault-tolerance. Dual power supplies help, as the system can then continue operating if one of them develops a fault. Without a UPS, though, the server will still grind to a halt if there's a power failure, because both UPSs will be connected into the same circuit. In theory you can get around this by plugging them into different ring circuits (perhaps on different floors of your building) via the use of long extension cords, but this is best avoided unless you know exactly what you are doing. If the two power sockets are on different phases then you risk serious damage to all of your equipment. Also, anyone who needs to work on the power in the vicinity and turns off the circuit nearest that server will assume, wrongly in this case, that the supply has been shut off.

Hard disks are prone to failure, and a failed drive in a server can spell disaster. The solution is a technology called RAID (Redundant Array of Independent Disks). It is available in a variety of permutations, each of which offers different levels of fault tolerance, but the most commonly used setup is known as RAID 5. This requires at least three drives, and a special hard disk controller card.

With a RAID 5 system, the three (or more) physical disk drives appear as one logical unit. So a trio of 200 GB drives will actually appear as a single drive offering 600 GB of storage. However, one drive's worth of data (200 GB in this case, but actually spread across all the drives) is used to store checksum information. The end result is that, if a single drive fails, you simply replace it with a new one and the RAID controller still has enough information available from the remaining drives in order to reconstruct the contents of the broken drive onto the new one. Most RAID systems are even hot-swappable, which means that you can replace a broken drive without switching off the server, so users will never know that a drive has been replaced.

Clearly, if more than one drive fails then you have a problem. Also, calculating the contents of the failed drive and writing it to the new one takes many hours and is generally performed as a low-priority process in order that the server doesn't slow down while this is happening. If another drive fails during this time, the system won't be capable of recovering itself and you might well have to perform a full restore from a backup.

▶ FUNDAMENTAL FIVE

Your action points for this chapter:

1. Remember that availability is just as important as confidentiality when it comes to servers. ☐

2. Physical security is vital for servers, to ensure that hackers cannot boot the system from a CD or floppy and override all your security settings. ☐

3. Consider the purchase of an uninterruptible power supply so that the server will shut down gracefully if the power fails. ☐

4. Consider the use of RAID systems so that a failing hard disk will not cause data loss or downtime. ☐

5. Change your server logon banners so that hackers cannot easily identify which server software you use. ☐

11

Understanding Firewalls

A computer which is connected to the internet becomes part of a single global network. Whether that computer is a powerful multi-user Web server or a small desktop or laptop PC, and whether it's connected to the internet via a leased line, broadband, cable or dial-up modem is irrelevant. Unless you take steps to prevent it, every computer on the internet is accessible to every other one.

In some cases, this is exactly what you want to happen. If you run a Web server that offers information to the public, such as google.com, then you want everyone who has an internet connection to be able to access your site. But clearly this isn't always the case. Your desktop PC may be linked to the internet so that you can browse the Web and send email, for example, but you don't want the world's 800 million registered internet users to be able to connect to your PC and view your files as if it were a public Web server.

Computers connected to the internet normally communicate via a protocol (a language) called TCP/IP. Communications take place over channels known as ports, and there are around 65,000 available ports. Common services such as Web traffic, email and ftp file transfers have their own standard port numbers. Web (http) traffic uses port 80, SMTP email uses port 25 and ftp transfers use port 21. Programmers who design systems which communicate over the internet are free to use any numbered port above 1024.

A firewall is an electronic filter that allows you to block communications over the internet according to their source, destination, direction or port number. For example, you might have a firewall between your company's LAN and the wider internet which is configured to block all incoming traffic on port 80. This port, you will recall, is the one used by Web servers, so by blocking incoming port 80 you will ensure that anyone who has installed a Web server application on their desktop PC won't actually receive any visitors. While this is a useful security precaution, you won't want to prevent your company's public Web site from receiving any visits so you would enter that server's IP address into the firewall as a specific exception to the rule. This will ensure that port–80 traffic destined for your authorized server will get through, while attempts to connect to any other Web server on your company LAN will be blocked.

Another common use of firewalls is to allow specific employees, contractors or suppliers to access your systems remotely. For example, the easiest way to maintain your Web site remotely is to implement an ftp server that allows new files to be uploaded. Yet ftp is notoriously insecure because the protocol doesn't use any encryption. You can add an extra layer of security by setting up some rules in your firewall so that the ftp server can only be contacted by those who are connecting from a certain list of specified IP addresses. These will be the addresses of the computers used by your trusted people.

A firewall which filters data according to its destination port number offers a great deal of protection from hackers, but can sometimes miss a trick. A technique known as tunnelling allows internet traffic to be sent over non–standard ports. This is often done for legitimate purposes but can also be exploited by hackers, and it can confuse simple firewalls. For example, some programs which allow telephone calls over the internet use tunnelling techniques to communicate via port 80, which is normally used only by Web sites. This avoids problems with corporate firewalls, which would prohibit the use of such software (and therefore severely limit sales) if it used a non-standard port which was blocked by default.

Many firewall products now employ a technique called SPI or Stateful Packet Inspection. They examine the full content of each data packet, rather than simply inferring the packet's content according to its destination port. If you're shopping around for a firewall, look for one that includes SPI.

Firewalls come in many forms. Some are independent devices designed to protect all computers on the LAN to which the firewall is attached. Some (known as personal firewalls) are programs which run on a desktop PC or laptop, designed to protect that computer only. A personal firewall program has been included as part of Windows XP since the product was launched, but it was not enabled by default and was relatively easy to defeat. When Microsoft upgraded Windows XP to Service Pack 2, the firewall was improved and is now turned on by default.

A firewall is essential if your company's computers are linked to the internet. A single dedicated firewall protecting the gateway between your LAN and the internet removes the need for each desktop and laptop on your LAN to have a personal firewall, and this is by far the best solution. While personal firewalls clearly offer better protection than no firewall at all, they are not without risks. Experts generally agree that running a firewall program alongside various other applications on a computer is unwise, because a Trojan or virus (or merely a bug) could cause the firewall to crash or stop working. Conversely, a dedicated firewall running on a computer that does nothing else presents much less of a risk because it can get on with its job unhindered by other programs.

To understand just how important a firewall is, we need to consider the steps that a hacker typically takes when he is attempting to attack a particular computer. Armed with the IP address of the computer, he normally starts by performing a port scan. This means attempting to initiate a communication on each of the remote computer's 65,000 ports in turn. If a port responds, there's a chance that the hacker can exploit this to gain entry. For example, if there's a response on port 21 then there's probably an ftp server running, so the hacker might look for wrongly-configured file permissions that allow him to upload or download files that he shouldn't be allowed to see. If there's a response form port 80 then there's a Web server running, which might be exploitable if the latest collection of server patches hasn't been installed.

Port-scanning software is easy to acquire. Probably the best known example is nmap, which is freely downloadable from the internet and a favourite tool of both hackers and security consultants.

Trojan horse programs communicate via the internet, just like legitimate applications. The Back Orifice program, once it is run by an unsuspecting user who clicks on an email attachment without considering the consequences, installs itself on victim's PC and listens for incoming connections on port 54321. It will obey a variety of instructions that arrive on this port, such as allowing a hacker to view or delete any file on the affected computer. If you browse through your firewall's log files you will find hundreds of incoming connections on port 54321 which your firewall has blocked – these represent hackers scouring the internet for computers which are listening on port 54321 and which therefore are running a copy of Back Orifice which the hacker can easily wake up.

Most programs that listen for incoming TCP/IP connections allow you to specify which port they use. Although port 21 is the commonly accepted default for ftp servers, your ftp server software almost certainly allows you to change this to any value you like. This adds a small additional layer of security to your ftp server, because anyone who wants to connect to it will need to know the port number as well as the IP address. However, a port scanner program is quite capable of discovering the nature of each service which is running on every open port, so using such a technique in the belief that it makes your server significantly more secure is misguided.

Logs

One of the keys to effective security is to enable every logging facility that is ever offered to you, and firewall logs are no exception. This will ensure that you have a record of every attempt that is made to connect to your network, or to whatever computers are behind (i.e. protected by) the firewall. Your logs, which should be safely stored and archived, will generally contain details such as the source IP address (i.e. where the attempt came from), the destination IP address and port (i.e. which part of your network the hacker was targeting), times and dates, and assorted other technical information. Unfortunately, firewall log files don't make for easy reading and tend to fill up quickly with millions of lines of impenetrable information such as:

FWIN,2005/10/20,09:37:16 +1:00 GMT,81.168.90.113:3102,81.168.54.237:1433,TCP
FWIN,2005/10/20,09:38:32 +1:00 GMT,81.168.65.171:1217,81.168.54.237:1433,TCP
FWIN,2005/10/20,09:38:52 +1:00 GMT,81.168.248.87:2514,81.168.54.237:445,TCP
FWIN,2005/10/20,09:39:06 +1:00 GMT,81.168.155.180:4058,81.168.54.237:135,TCP
FWIN,2005/10/20,09:40:08 +1:00 GMT,217.173.102.121:2126,81.168.54.237:1433,TCP
FWIN,2005/10/20,09:40:36 +1:00 GMT,81.168.92.237:4132,81.168.54.237:135,TCP
FWIN,2005/10/20,09:41:16 +1:00 GMT,81.168.155.180:4057,81.168.54.237:445,TCP
FWIN,2005/10/20,09:44:58 +1:00 GMT,81.168.12.255:4937,81.168.54.237:445,TCP

Thankfully there are many programs around that can analyse firewall logs and turn them into meaningful reports. Most firewalls use industry-standard formats for their log files so the majority of report generators work with the majority of firewalls. Here's a graph produced by Stonylake Firewall Reporter, to neatly illustrate that a picture really is worth a thousand words. This particular example shows which incoming ports were most frequently blocked.

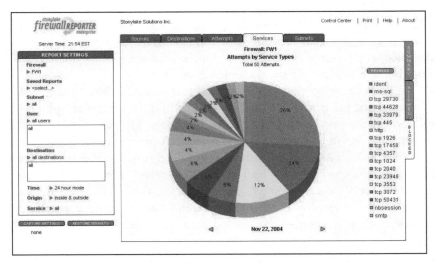

If your log file shows that a suspected attack is coming from a particular IP address, a trip to www.ripe.net will allow you to look up the details of the company to whom that address is assigned. Another useful site that can help you find out about the company or individual behind an IP address is www.completewhois.com. Remember, though, that many users of the internet are issued with dynamic IP addresses and thus the ripe.net search will lead you only as far as the culprit's internet service provider. Linking a particular user to a particular IP address at a given time will require the co-operation of the ISP and/or the police.

Although firewalls are described as being designed to block unwanted traffic into (and out of) computers, describing their action as blocking is slightly misleading. Blocking implies that the hacker, or at least the person who generates the blocked attempt at communicating, receives some notification that their communication has been blocked. In reality, firewalls go to great lengths to ensure that those who initiate a prohibited connection receive absolutely no response whatsoever, which will hopefully lead them to assume that there is actually no computer connected to the particular address. This is known as stealth mode, and helps to defeat a port-scanner.

The DMZ

A firewall blocks access to your computers from internet-based hackers. It will prevent your staff from installing Web or email or ftp servers on their computers, and it will prevent your internal network servers (which are designed to provide services only to people who are within your firewall) from being accessible via the wider internet.

This scheme works well if you don't run any public-facing servers of your own, i.e. if all your email and Web and ftp servers are physically located on the premises of third-party providers. However, if your Web server, say, is on your company's premises, your firewall brings with it a dilemma. If your Web server is inside the firewall and is part of your LAN, someone who hacks the Web server can potentially gain access to every other computer on your network. That's every PC and laptop on every employee's desk, and possibly the machines at employees' homes if they happen to be dialled into your company's network at the time.

The solution is to set up something called a demilitarized zone or DMZ (the term is military in origin). In computing, a DMZ is a separate semi-protected network of one or more computers which is controlled by the firewall. Anyone who accesses one of the computers in the DMZ, whether with or without permission, is not connecting to your internal network, and therefore cannot break out of the DMZ. The alternative to a DMZ would be to put your Web server on your LAN and for the firewall to allow public Web traffic to reach your LAN. This is clearly a bad idea, and if you're currently doing this then it makes sense to stop it as soon as possible. Instead, place the Web server in a DMZ.

Bypassing the Firewall

A penetration tester is someone who, with your permission, tries to hack into your company's computers and produces a report that tells you about the weaknesses that he managed to find. We'll discuss this in more detail in Chapter 14. When I ask penetration testers how often they manage to bypass a company's firewall, they talk of a 70% success rate. Yet if you peruse the glossy brochures, Web sites, magazine reviews and case studies published by those who sell firewalls, the implication is always that the product offers 100% protection and is completely unhackable. So who's telling the truth? Actually, everyone is.

A firewall which is correctly configured and physically protected is totally secure, but human error and ignorance lead to many companies discovering that their firewall isn't quite as wonderful as the vendor promised when it was installed. Most importantly, a firewall protects your computers from hackers who attempt to connect to you over the internet. Yet although most companies spend the majority of their IT security budget on keeping internet-based hackers out, the truth is that most computer misuse takes place on your premises inside the perimeter of your firewall. An employee who takes home a copy of your customer database prior to his resignation will never encounter your firewall. Nor will a hacker who bribes one of your employees with £10,000 to hand over a copy of that database. And nor will a hacker who telephones a gullible employee, pretends to be a senior partner in the organization, and insists that the database is emailed to his account right away because he's in the middle of an important presentation and his laptop has crashed. All of these techniques will allow people to bypass your firewall, and they are used thousands of times every day around the world by hackers and penetration testers.

A firewall that is configured to block outgoing traffic can also be defeated fairly easily. By all means configure your firewall to prevent your staff from looking at hardcore pornography or downloading illegal music tracks. But if a dishonest staff member can't access these sites via his internet connection on your LAN, what's to stop him plugging £20 worth of modem into his computer, sticking the other end into the telephone socket and accessing the banned material via another internet service provider? Absolutely nothing at all. Such behaviour is all the more dangerous because, while the employee is dialled into this additional ISP and is also connected to your LAN, there is a real possibility that a hacker can enter his PC via the dial-up connection, unprotected by your firewall, and attack all of the computers on your network.

It is therefore essential that all staff are aware that using a modem to access the internet from a company PC without explicit permission is dangerous and strictly prohibited. When you buy computers, make sure that they don't include modems as standard unless you really need them.

A tool such as SiSoft Sandra (**www.sisoftware.co.uk**) provides an easy way to check that there's no other banned hardware attached to the computer. Such programs are a useful addition to a security person's toolkit as they provide a detailed inventory of a PC's hardware and software so you can check whether components have been added or removed without permission.

Occasionally, a firewall can actually cause problems rather than solve them. In June 2005, the commercial television network ITV inadvertently broadcast details of a pornographic Web site on its lunchtime news programme in the UK. The address of the site was intended to be a fictional example of the genre and the journalist who compiled the report checked that it didn't exist by typing its URL into his Web browser. An error message appeared which led the journalist to assume that no site by that name was in operation. In truth, the site did indeed exist but had been blocked by the ITV firewall.

Of course, instances of firewalls causing problems are very rare and it is essential that you employ one to assist in protecting your company's computers. However, remember that a firewall is not a fit-and-forget product. As well as requiring regular examinations of log files, it will need frequent configuration changes as your security rules evolve, such as allowing access to your servers by new members of staff. An annual audit should also be performed, which should involve senior IT staff considering the firewall permissions list and deciding whether all those who have access to a particular resource really still need it.

Lies, Damned Lies and Hacking Competitions

Security companies use various methods to market their products, and a popular choice among producers of firewalls is the hacking competition. The company sets up one of its firewalls and then challenges the hacker community to attempt to break into the server that it is protecting. After a few weeks, once the deadline has passed, the vendor proudly announces in its advertising that its firewall stood up to many millions of attempted attacks.

Don't be fooled by such competitions. They don't prove that this particular firewall is unhackable. They merely reinforce my earlier warnings that a firewall will only protect you if it is correctly configured. Furthermore, the rules of most hacking contests clearly state that social engineering attacks are against the rules, as are a host of other techniques such as attempting to gain physical access to the server or initiating a Denial of Service Attack against it. You can't make such rules in the real world so it's unfair for them to be included in contests either.

▶ FUNDAMENTAL FIVE

Your action points for this chapter:

1. Hackers often break through firewalls because they are not correctly configured. Ensure that yours is set up properly. ☐

2. Enable all logging facilities, and archive the logs to a safe store on a regular basis. ☐

3. Be aware of the difference between a central firewall at your network's point of connection to the internet versus personal firewall software running on each workstation. ☐

4. Examine your firewall logs regularly for signs of unauthorized activity. ☐

5. Remember that a firewall prevents outsiders getting into your systems. It does nothing to prevent attacks that originate inside the firewall. ☐

12

Protecting Your Web Site

Y our Web site is the public face of your organization to all of those who visit it. Whether your site gets 100 hits a day or 100 million, it's important to spend some regular time ensuring that it's secure. The same is true whether the server on which your site's pages reside is based on your premises or at a co-location company, or if you simply rent some space on the server of a third-party hosting provider. Ultimate responsibility for the server's content still rests with you, and it is your company that will bear the consequences if hackers attack the site.

Web servers and Web sites are the number one target of hackers. Set up an ftp or email server and your firewall will maybe catch a handful of attempts each day to break into it. A newly configured Web server, however, will see hundreds of attempts during the same time. Protecting your Web site must therefore be near the top of your security to-do list.

Back It Up

There's a multitude of inconveniences which hackers enjoy bestowing on owners of Web sites, one of which is unauthorized alteration of content. This is known as defacement. Thousands of Web sites are defaced every month, by hackers who manage to exploit bugs in Web server software or make a lucky guess at a password. Most defacements never make the headlines but some very high-profile sites have been targeted over the years. In the US, members of the CIA (Central Intelligence Agency) once arrived in the office to discover that the front page of their Web site proudly welcomed visitors to the Central Stupidity Agency. Bill Clinton's site was also targeted, at the time of the Monica Lewinsky affair, by hackers who amended all the hyperlinks on the site and redirected them to the playboy.com home page.

To protect against Web site defacement attacks, ensure that your Web server is fully patched (or that your hosting provider can provide the necessary proof that this is done regularly, if you don't operate your own server). You must also back up your Web site regularly so that it can easily be recreated from a known-good copy if required. Remember to back up not just the static html pages but also any back-end database-driven content such as MySQL tables.

Keep tight control over the passwords that are used to maintain your site. No one except administrators should have root access to the server. Those who contribute to the content of the site should each have their own password, to aid accountability, and each account should allow the user access to their own area of the site and no other.

If you run your own Web server, use your firewall to assist in protecting it. Access via FTP to upload new files should be limited by IP address and available only from known locations (either a specific computer on a specific person's desk, or at least to prohibit access by computers other than those on company premises). As with all passwords, remember to change or disable them if a user leaves the company or changes roles.

If you use a content management system to facilitate Web-based updating via html forms, ensure that the admin system is properly protected. I've encountered systems in the past where anyone who surfs to, say, `www.mywebsite.com/admin` is presented with the admin menu without being asked for a password.

Highly visible defacements, such as changing the name of the organization to something grossly offensive or replacing all the pictures on the front page of the site with porn, have one saving grace. It's immediately apparent that the site has been hacked and so the task of changing all the passwords and restoring the content from a backup can begin immediately. But what if a hacker broke into your site and simply changed a couple of words here and there, in files that were buried deep inside the structure of the site? For example, if one or two of the prices in your online catalogue were increased just enough that you were now slightly more expensive than your competitor. How quickly would you notice these minor changes? Or would you actually ever notice at all? One way to avoid such problems is to use a checksum program that can detect changes to files.

Communications data (who accessed which Web site when, who emailed whom) is incredibly important in the fight against all sorts of crime. The fight against global terrorism relies heavily on this type of intelligence. If someone is arrested on suspicion of being a terrorist, what better way to find the names of his accomplices than by checking the telephone companies' databases to see who he called, and who has called him, during the past few weeks. This is why so many national governments are trying hard to force internet service providers to retain email and Web access logs rather than destroying them. All Web servers have the facility to log activity and yours is no exception. Ensure that logging is turned on and that all options are enabled. The more information you can retain about who accesses your Web site, and from where, the better prepared you will be if you ever need to investigate possible misuse.

Archive the log files regularly to tape, DVD or another server if they are taking up too much space on the Web server. Consider buying a program that can produce useful reports from Web server logs, to help you locate patterns of unusual activity. Even the smallest amount of data can help prevent and detect crime, even if its precise usefulness can't be judged from the start. CCTV camera footage, for example, is still of great use even if the pictures are very blurred and the offender's face can't be identified, because the pictures allow investigators to see what the offender touched and, therefore, which objects should be dusted for fingerprints.

Basic HTTP Authentication

It's easy to add username and password authentication to one or more sections of your Web site. There's no programming involved. You simply create two special text files and upload them into the folder or directory that you want to protect. One file contains the necessary commands to enable the authentication facility and the other contains the list of valid usernames and passwords. Once you have done this, anyone who attempts to view a page that resides in the protected folder will automatically receive a pop-up dialogue box in his Web browser, requesting a username and password. This works in all browsers and is supported by most of the well-known Web servers including Apache and IIS. The feature is known as Basic HTTP Authentication.

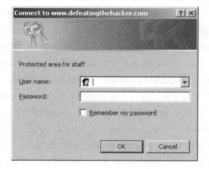

To use basic http authentication, start by creating the .htaccess file which enables the feature. Here's what the file should look like:

```
AuthUserFile /home/oursite/public_html/staff/.htpasswd
AuthName "Protected Area for Staff"
AuthType basic
<Limit GET>
require valid-user
</Limit>
```

Upload the file into the directory that you wish to protect. A few points to note:

■ The name of this file must be .htaccess (note the dot in front). You may find that your PC won't let you create a file of this name. In which case, give it a more sensible name such as htaccess.txt and use your ftp program to rename it once you have uploaded it to the Web server.

■ The first line of the file, which starts with AuthUserFile, must contain the path to the .htpasswd file (which we'll discuss shortly). You will probably need to change the /home/oursite/public _html/staff part to something which is relevant to your server. In this particular example, we are protecting a directory called staff.

■ The AuthName line lets you specify some text which the Web browser will display within the dialogue box.

Having created your .htaccess file, you can now create the file which contains the usernames and passwords. Call it .htpasswd (see the note above about renaming it once it has been uploaded to the server) and place it in the same directory as the protected pages and the .htaccess file. Here's an example .htpasswd file:

```
holly:CERvekVZDDINw
olivia:LKmimHQzZX5wE
```

Again, a couple of points to note:

■ Each entry consists of a username (holly and olivia in this case) and a password separated by a colon.

■ Each username:password pair must go on a separate line in the file

The passwords must be entered in a special encrypted format, hence the rather strange looking text in the above example. The easiest way to find out the encrypted form of a password is to search the Web for an online htpasswd generator, and you'll find various sites that will do the conversion for you instantly. In the above example, I entered a username of holly and a password of Gremlin into the generator and it produced the holly:CERvekVZDDINw line ready to copy and paste into my .htpasswd file. Because the generator has no idea which site you intend to use your .htpasswd file on, it's quite safe to use online password generators.

Brute Force

Although htaccess/htpasswd authentication is incredibly useful, one potential fly in the ointment is a brute force attack in which a hacker uses an automated program to try thousands of passwords every minute. Programs to attack Web servers in this way are available for download on the Internet – one such is known as Brutus.

Hardening htaccess authentication requires some additional programming, and is definitely recommended. One method is to log the IP address of each person who tries to connect to the site, and to block any visitor who has made, say, 10 unsuccessful login attempts from the same IP address within the past 24 hours. If your site is written in a scripting language such as PHP and uses a database technology such as MySQL, this is not difficult to do.

Another option, which uses PHP but doesn't require a database, is to use PHP's 'sleep' command to introduce a short delay between a user entering a username/password and the site allowing or denying access. A delay of five seconds won't cause any major inconvenience to legitimate users but will make brute-force cracking of the site unfeasible.

Domain Names

Your internet domain name (yourcompany.com or yourcompany.co.uk, for example) is one of your organization's most important electronic assets. If someone else manages to gain ownership of it they can redirect every employee's email and every page of your Web site. Ensure that you renew your domain name in good time in order to prevent the name being flagged as unwanted and thus available to whoever buys it first.

Domain names are rented rather than bought outright, typically for periods of between 1 and 10 years. The company through which you registered your names will normally contact you when they are due for renewal, but errors sometimes happen, so it's important to keep your own note of the renewal dates and to act in plenty of time. Failure to pay the renewal invoices on time will, at the very least, mean that your name (and thus your Web sites and email) is inactive for a few days. If the renewal continues unpaid, the domain name will be returned to the pool of available names and can then be claimed by the first taker.

Before renewing a domain name, check the invoice carefully. Unless you specify otherwise, your company's details are added to a public database whenever you register a domain name. This lists your company's name and address, the name of the person who handled the registration, and the domain name's expiry date. This makes it easy for unscrupulous registration companies to send out invoices for names that were not registered by them, in the hope that you'll unwittingly pay the invoice, and thus change the company that holds your registration. More often than not, you will end up with no better service at a greatly increased price from a company whose business practices are at best questionable.

If you don't have your own domain name, by the way, it makes a great deal of sense to get one rather than relying on that of a third party. If your company is Clever Engineering Ltd, your email address needs to be something like sales@cleverengineering.com rather than cleverengineering@btinternet.com or cleverengineering@hotmail.com. Not only does having your own domain name for email portray a company which is properly aware of technology, it also means that you can change email providers without having to reprint all your stationery, repaint your vehicle liveries and so on. Just log onto your domain name control page, change the name of the email service to which cleverengineering.com gets directed, and the job is done. Your customers can continue to mail you at cleverengineering.com as before.

Make sure that you register all of the necessary domain names for your company and its brands. If your organization is called Ultra Foods and your best-known products are Mega Beans and Ultra Sausages, make sure you register ultrafoods.com, ultra-foods.com, megabeans.com, ultra-sausages.com, mega-beans.com, ultra-sausages.com and all of the regional versions for the territories in which you operate (e.g. megabeans.co.uk and ultrasausages.com.au, for example). Take care to avoid ambiguity when choosing your domain name, however. The Italian branch of a company called Powergen proudly resided at powergenitalia.com for many months until they realized their mistake.

If you're launching a new product, register the necessary domain names before you publicize the launch, otherwise someone will get there before you in the hope that you'll pay lots of money in return for them handing over the domain registration certificate. Most of the national domain registrars have official dispute procedures which can force squatters to hand over domains that have clearly been registered for the purpose of extortion, but it's not always easy to prove that you have the automatic right to 'your' name. A famous case involved the British Airports Authority, which owns and operates most of Britain's airports including Heathrow. Before BAA registered baa.com, someone got there first and created a site for those interested in sheep. After much legal wrangling BAA got its domain, but it was a costly battle and the company should have known better.

On July 22nd 2005, Microsoft announced that the successor to Windows XP would be named Windows Vista. Wisely, the company registered windowsvista.com on 31st March and windowsvista.co.uk on April 1st. Other country domains were also registered around the same time. Yet windowsvistatips.com and windowsvistasecurity.com, and dozens of other variations on the theme, were registered by companies and individuals other than Microsoft on 22nd July, which goes to show that those who indulge in speculative domain registrations are very quick off the mark.

Finding out who owns an existing domain name is easy. One method is to go to any of the numerous Web sites that offer domain registration services and attempt to register the name in question. You'll be informed that it already exists, and there will normally be a link that takes you to information about who owns it. Try looking up your company's domain names to see what information is publicly available – you may be surprised at just how much is on display. Spammers and marketing organizations are known to use this information, so you may wish to amend it to remove items that you no longer wish to remain in the public domain. This can usually be arranged via the company that registered the domain for you.

Web Programming Security

Many Web sites today are database-driven rather than comprising separate html files. The text of the entire site is held in a database on the server, and a suite of programs written in languages such as PHP or Perl extract the content as required, add the necessary formatting commands to select fonts and colours, and generate html code on the fly. The Web page that is seen by the person sitting at their Web browser doesn't actually exist as an html file on the server – it is assembled from its various components at the time that the surfer requests it.

Database-driven sites have two main advantages over static collections of html files. The most useful is the separation of presentation (all those style sheets) from content (the actual text that appears on the pages). This makes it very easy for the programs that run the site to apply different presentation schemes to the site without needing more than one copy of the text. At the click of a mouse, the user of the site can see the standard page, or a printer-friendly version, a dyslexia-friendly version without the fussy backgrounds, a narrow version for viewing on palmtops, or anything else that your programmers wish to add.

The other benefit of database-driven sites is that they can be updated without the need for anyone to use an html editor or an ftp upload tool. Typically, amending an item on such a site involves surfing to a particular editing page, supplying a username and password, and specifying the page that is to be edited. The text from that page is then retrieved from the database and presented on-screen in a Web-based form for editing, and the process is completed by clicking on a Submit button. This can be done from anywhere where a computer and a Web browser are available.

With the move to database-driven Web sites, the security implications are enormous. You must ensure that the usernames and passwords that permit changes to the database are kept private, of course, but this is just the start. I recently bought a product via a UK Web site called FotoSense. Once I had placed the order, I looked up the purchase on the site by logging in, going to the My Account section, and clicking on the item's name in the Previous Purchases section. The details of my order were displayed, and I happened to notice that the page's URL was:

www.fotosense.co.uk/account_orders.asp?orderID=13442.

By changing the value of the order number (13442 in this case), I could view the details of every order on the system, including the date, item, and amount paid. By stepping back from 13442, one order at a time, I could build up a total picture of how many items the company sells via its Web site each day, and the amount of money taken. Such information would be of mere curiosity to me but hugely valuable to the company's competitors, so I telephoned the company behind the Ebox Pro software that powers the site. Their official comment was "That's not really an issue", and that their software is secure "because it doesn't leak personal information such as credit card numbers".

Plastic card fraud and identity theft are hot topics, and a company that allows such details to be accessed by hackers will of course be rightly criticized. But if you sell online you must appreciate that security is about more than one thing, otherwise your online business is doomed to failure. Security loopholes in third-party ecommerce products are not uncommon. If you rely on such software for any aspect of your online presence, it pays (literally) to check the vendor's Web site regularly in case there are fixes and patches that you need to download and install. And it pays to think like a hacker sometimes, because that's the only way that you'll be able to detect potential problems such as this one.

PHP/MySQL Site Security

The programs that operate database-driven sites are vulnerable to hackers, who can (and do) exploit bugs in those programs to gain unauthorized access to the site. It is impossible to provide a detailed guide to creating secure database-driven Web sites in a book such as this, especially as there are so many different combinations of server software (Apache, Windows IIS, etc.), database engines (Oracle, MySQL, Microsoft SQL Server, etc.) and programming languages (PHP, Perl, ASP, Python and many more). The most popular development environment is the PHP language and the MySQL database system, so the remainder of this chapter will provide some advice on creating secure PHP/MySQL sites.

Try to keep confidential information out of your PHP files. Normally, a PHP program runs when someone surfs to its URL (e.g. www.yoursite.com/catalogue.php), at which point the PHP program generates some HTML code that the visitor's browser can display. Visitors should never get to see the PHP code itself, but hackers occasionally manage to do so. If, as most programmers do, you store within your PHP files the necessary passwords to access your MySQL database, then your entire content database is instantly vulnerable. To avoid this, put the database access passwords in a file with a .inc.php extension (such as dbaccess.inc.php), place this file in a directory which is above the Web server's document root (and thus not accessible to surfers of your site), and refer to the file in your PHP code with a require_once command. By doing things this way, your PHP code can read the included file easily but hackers will find it much more difficult.

Ensure that register_globals is turned off in your installation of PHP. This is the default setting in PHP version 4.2 and above, but won't be the case if you are using an older version on your server or if it has been deliberately turned off to make programming easier. With register_globals turned on, hackers (or indeed anyone) can fairly easily access the content of any variable in your PHP code. Similarly, get into the habit of starting all your PHP programs with an `error_reporting (E_ALL)` command, to ensure that you receive the maximum number of warnings about possible errors and security weaknesses in your code.

Many companies use ready-made PHP programs to run their Web site. These programs, known as Content Management Systems, can be downloaded free of charge from sites such as `www.opensourcecms.com` and the best-known players include Mambo, Drupal and Nuke. Those who require a discussion forum on their Web site can also obtain free software, with the best-known example being phpBB. If you use a ready-made CMS or forum product, whether open source (free) or commercial, ensure that you keep the program fully patched and up to date. If a security patch is issued for the particular software that you use, hackers can scan the entire internet in minutes to search for installations that have not yet installed the patch and are thus open to exploitation.

As with all software, remember to check that all of the files associated with installation are removed once the product has been set up and configured, otherwise the hacker can re-run the setup program and wipe your content database. If you are required to change the access permissions on certain data files during installation so that configuration data such as database access passwords can be written to them, remember to change the permissions back to their normal read-only status once the setup is complete.

If you are programming a Web site that requires users to log in with a username and password to see protected content, take care to ensure that the authentication routines can't be easily bypassed. When a user correctly supplies valid credentials, use a cookie or a session variable to flag that this has happened, and check the flag every time that the user tries to access a protected page. Don't simply assume that, because a user was correctly logged in when they viewed the first page of your protected site, they are still logged in when they try to surf to a different page in the same site. They may have typed the URL directly into their browser, or reached the page via a search engine, rather than arriving via your login screen.

Never use client-side code, such as Javascript or hidden form fields, for security-related functions such as password validation or database query selection. Unlike PHP, where the code is not normally visible to users, client-side code can be seen by anyone who clicks View Source in their Web browser.

Back up your PHP script files frequently, and don't store the backups on the Web server. Remember to back up your SQL database files too. Use software such as PHPMyAdmin or mysqldump, which backs up databases in portable ASCII format. Never simply back up the binary files because they will not be accessible if you move to a different database server, Web server or operating system.

For an excellent source of further advice on how to protect Web-based applications, the Open Web Application Security Project at www.owasp.com is well worth a look. It's updated regularly and is free to access.

Common Web Hack Techniques

The techniques that hackers use to break into Web sites have been given names such as 'SQL injections', 'cross-site scripting', 'cookie poisoning' and 'form variable tampering'. A brief explanation of some of these follows, if only to remind you that protecting your Web site from attack in an effective manner requires more effort than simply changing an ftp password and backing up your files every few months.

SQL injection attacks occur frequently where programmers don't properly validate input. The method is difficult to understand if you don't have a passing familiarity with PHP and SQL, so please accept my apologies if the following few paragraphs mean nothing to you.

Let's take the commonly-encountered example of a protected Web site where an on-screen form contains two boxes into which you are invited to enter a username and a password. We'll use the $u variable in our PHP code to store the username that is entered, and $p to store the password. Once the form has been filled in, the contents of those two variables get passed into an SQL database query such as:

SELECT COUNT (*) FROM USERS WHERE USERNAME = '$u' AND PASSWORD = '$p'

This query returns the total number of records in the table of users in which the username and password match the values that were entered into the form. Many Web sites use this technique for authentication. If the returned count is greater than zero, we can assume that the username and password that were entered into the form represent those of a valid user, and so access to the protected site is granted.

Let's have a quick look under the hood and observe the code in action, to appreciate how an SQL injection attack works. If a user enters a username of **HANNAH** and a password of **KATIE** into the form the resulting SQL query, once the entered data has been used to replace the $u and $p variables, will be:

```
SELECT COUNT (*) FROM USERS
WHERE USERNAME = 'HANNAH' AND PASSWORD = 'KATIE'
```

No problem there. But consider what happens if a hacker enters a username of **HANNAH** and a password of:

DUNNO' OR '3' = '3

The resulting SQL code will end up as:

```
SELECT COUNT (*) FROM USERS
WHERE USERNAME = 'HANNAH' AND PASSWORD = 'DUNNO' OR '3' = '3'
```

We now have a query that will count the number of records in which the username/password pair is **HANNAH/DUNNO** or in which **3** equals **3**. Clearly, **3** will equal **3** for every record of the users table, and so the count of the number of valid records will be greater than zero. The hacker is now considered a valid user and will be granted access to the secure Web site.

Avoiding this vulnerability requires that all dangerous characters (in this case the single quote mark) are stripped from input before it is fed into any SQL query. Many programmers fail to do this adequately, and security fixes for well-known Web applications to fix such weaknesses are released regularly. Failure to apply these patches to your systems can result in your protected site being open to anyone without the need to supply a valid password.

Thankfully, appreciating the risks involved in cookie-poisoning is much less technical. A cookie is a text file that is written to a user's hard disk by a Web site that the user is visiting, which can be used to store a small amount of information. The site can subsequently retrieve that information. For example, if you visit a shopping site and you browse the collection of toasters, the site might set a cookie on your PC with a name of 'browsed' and a value of 'toasters'. Next time you visit the site, the site checks your computer to see if there's a 'browsed' cookie on your PC and, if so, the site automatically takes you back to the toasters section.

Cookies are protected by a strict security mechanism. A site can only access its own cookies so there's no way that a competing shopping site could discover that you've recently been looking for a toaster, or change the contents from toasters to kettles. But although Web sites can't access other sites' cookies remotely, anyone with physical access to the user's PC and the necessary software can do so. I could change the toaster cookie on my PC to kettles and, next time I browsed the shopping site, it would assume that I was last browsing the kettles section.

Some sites use cookies to handle authentication. For example, if I log into a protected site and I supply a valid username and password, the site might set a cookie called 'logged_in' on my computer, with a value of 'yes'. Each time I access a protected page, the site checks that the cookie exists to save me having to keep entering my username and password on every page.

If I was to use a cookie editing program on my PC, I could create a cookie called 'logged_in' with a value of 'yes'. Having done this, I could then access any of the site's protected pages without ever being asked to identify myself. This is cookie poisoning and is another favourite Web-hacker technique. To prevent being caught out, you must ensure that your Web sites don't rely on simple cookies for authentication.

Finally in this examination of common Web hacking techniques, we will take a brief look at form variable tampering. Let's take the example of a secure Web site from which a user can buy a Beatles boxed set of CDs for

£100. The user clicks on this particular item and an order form appears, into which he can type his name, address and credit card details. The user clicks on the View Source option in the File menu on his browser to look at the html code for the form. In addition to the form fields for name, address and credit card details, there are also two 'hidden' form fields which contain the item's catalogue number and price. When the user submits the form, his personal details plus the contents of those hidden fields are sent to the credit card payment processing system, his card is debited, and the transaction takes place.

But the user doesn't simply fill in the form and press the Submit button. Instead, he copies the html code that comprises the form and uploads it to his own Web server, changing the value in the hidden price field from 100 to 50. He then submits the form and the data is passed to the card processing company, which promptly charges him £50 for the product because that's what was in the price field.

Form injection attacks, as these are called, used to be common. The practice is gradually becoming less widespread as online vendors wake up to the fact that they need to write Web sites that can detect tampering. When you pay for something via Paypal, for example, the Paypal system sends back the price to the vendor's Web site so that the site can check that the price that has been charged to the customer's card is the same price as appears in the product catalogue. If it is not, then the sale can be cancelled and any other appropriate action taken.

Some hackers even have the audacity to change prices to negative values which, in the case of sites that are incredibly poorly programmed, result in the customer's card being credited rather than charged.

You can find a lot more information about creating secure Web-based applications in a book published by Microsoft called *Improving Web Application Security: Threats and Countermeasures*. It runs to almost 1000 pages, and you can download it for free as a PDF file – go to Microsoft's Web site and type threats_countermeasures.pdf into the search box there. As you might expect, the book concentrates on Microsoft's own technologies rather than open-source software such as PHP, but it's worth a read regardless of your development platform.

▶ **FUNDAMENTAL FIVE**

Your action points for this chapter:

1. Web sites are the number one target for hackers, so protecting your public presence on the internet should be near the top of your priority list. ☐

2. Ensure that the contents of your Web site are backed up regularly, including SQL database tables, PHP/ASP script files, and html documents. ☐

3. If you need to restrict access to areas of your Web site, use Basic HTTP Authentication. ☐

4. Renew your domain names in good time or you risk losing the right to use them. ☐

5. If you write your own Web applications, refer to the OWASP Web site for useful security guidelines. ☐

DANGER

13

Wireless Networking

W iring an office for network access is expensive and disruptive and, however you do it, you'll still probably find that you don't have enough sockets or that they're in the wrong place. Wireless networking was touted as the solution to these problems. Plug a Wireless Access Point (WAP) into an Ethernet socket and anyone who sits within range of the WAP using a device that has wireless networking capability can connect instantly to the Web or the office network. Most modern laptops now have wireless connectivity built in, as do many palmtops and smartphones. For those computers that don't, wireless cards for desktops and laptops can be obtained for around £20.

For easy home-based wireless connectivity, around £80 will buy you a combined wireless access point, router and ADSL modem. Plug it into your telephone socket on a line which has been enabled for broadband service and you've got a wireless network that allows all your computers to talk to each other and to the internet.

Wireless networking is known colloquially as WiFi. It's also known as 802.11, after the name of the committee at the IEEE (Institute of Electrical and Electronics Engineers) that designed the standard. WiFi comes in various flavours, with such interesting names as 802.11a, 802.11b and 802.11g, each of which offers similar facilities but at different maximum speeds.

WiFi offers a much-needed solution to a real problem, and companies were quick to deploy it. Within traditional organizations it means, for example, that staff with suitably-equipped laptops can check email and access networked files from anywhere in the building without needing to locate a spare desk. In academia, students at a college or university can simply fire up their laptop and access the network from any classroom or other nearby location – clearly much cheaper than having to run bunches of network cables to each room on the campus. But WiFi has rapidly become the centre of attention for the hacking fraternity. Sometimes they simply seek a free internet connection, while other times they use the WiFi link to break into a company's private files.

When you take a new WAP out of its box and plug it into your network, the default settings normally offer very little in the way of security. Sometimes none at all. Although this means that anyone in your organization whose laptop has wireless facilities can now use your network, so can anyone else within range. And that range is generally considerable (typically 300 feet indoors, and around 1200 feet outdoors).

For the hacker, locating an unprotected WiFi connection is easy. Any laptop or palmtop with wireless capability will automatically display the name of all access points within range and, at the click of a mouse, attempt to connect to any of them. The process can be greatly aided by programs that search for WAPs and display information to help the hacker decide which is the best (fastest connection, strongest signal and so on). NetStumbler is the best-known of these, and it can be downloaded from the internet for free.

With WiFi use being so prevalent, the chances of a hacker (or a legitimate business traveller in need of a quick email fix) finding a free connection in any large city is surprisingly high. Hijacking someone else's bandwidth in this way is generally illegal in most countries, however. In July 2005, for example, a British man was fined £500 for 'dishonestly obtaining a communications service' under the Communications Act 2003 when he was convicted of using a neighbour's wireless connection without permission.

From the start, the 802.11 wireless network protocol included an encryption system to prevent hackers from intercepting data over the airwaves. The encryption was known as WEP, or Wired Equivalent Privacy. Researchers quickly discovered that WEP was fairly easy to crack, so a new encryption system called WPA (Wireless Protected Access) was devised as part of the latest 802.11g standard. This is much harder to crack, but is possible via a dictionary attack if the owner of the WAP has used a simple password.

If you are considering installing WiFi in your company, or have already done so, you need to address the security issues. The tips below generally apply to WiFi connections in offices as well as domestic installations. If you use wireless at home, your altruistic tendencies might tempt you to open up the service to neighbours. However, bear in mind that, without the correct security, your neighbours will have access to all your private files and not just the Web. Also, if your home broadband account allows only a finite amount of usage per month before additional per-gigabyte charges begin, you may find that your altruism is expensive.

Protecting your WiFi Connection

Disable SSID broadcasting. Unless you do this, the SSID (Service Set Identifier) of your wireless network is broadcast over the air without encryption every few seconds and any passing user can browse the list of available networks. The SSID includes the name that you have assigned to your wireless LAN (WLAN), which makes it easy to identify. SSID broadcasting is great if you want to allow roaming users to connect, but it's much safer to manually configure each authorized user's computer or other device with the necessary SSID that they need rather than advertising it to the world in general.

A hacker with the necessary software can still discover the SSIDs of local WLANs if he has the necessary software available, by intercepting other data that travels across the airwaves, but disabling explicit broadcasts is recommended. You should also configure your SSID so as not to divulge any clues as to the identity of the WLAN's owner. For example, if your company is called Ultra Foods, don't set up an SSID of UltraFoods but instead use something like WLAN1.

Next, make sure that you've changed all the default passwords on your WAP. There will probably be more than one way into the WAP's administration menu (from which you can change the SSID, add users, change its IP address and so on). Make sure that you are aware of all routes, and that all passwords are changed. Use strong passwords – I always recommend two unconnected words separated by a digit, such as mango7leopard.

Log onto the Web site of your WAP's manufacturer and download the latest software (known as firmware) for the device. Check the Web site at least once a month and, if the manufacturer offers an email newsletter that provides timely security alerts, sign up for it.

Ensure that you use WPA rather than WEP encryption. Set it to the highest strength available on your WAP (usually 128 bit) and use a strong encryption key (password). You should change this key every month.

Every computer that has networking facilities, whether wireless or wired, has a MAC (Media Access Control) address. This is a 12-character number such as 12-7A-22-19-4D-5A. MAC filtering, which most recent WAPs support, allows you to set up the WAP so that it will only allow connections from computers with specific MAC addresses that you manually add to a list. Although MAC address filtering is highly recommended as yet another tool in your arsenal of wireless LAN security techniques, many computers allow the user to configure their own MAC address and set it to any value that they choose (so-called MAC address spoofing) so the technique isn't 100% secure. It is still very much worth deploying, however.

If your WAP or base station has a logging facility, enable all options and check the log files regularly to see who's been using your WLAN. Investigate any possible abuses.

Find your WLANs

How many wireless networks are there in your company? How many WAPs and base stations are there? Because the hardware is so cheap and useful, you may find that there are actually more than you realize, and that staff have simply connected such devices to your wired network without your knowledge or permission. And if you don't know about them, chances are that they are not correctly configured for effective security.

To locate the wireless networks in your company, start by downloading a copy of NetStumbler from `http://www.stumbler.net`. Wander around your building(s) with a laptop that's running the software and see whether it detects any open networks.

A slightly less cumbersome method, at least for initial detection pending further investigation, is to invest in a small device which fits on your key fob and which simply lights an LED if it detects a wireless connection. These typically sell for under £20. Look under the Products section on `www.myirock.com` for an example, although there are many other similar models available – your local hardware supplier probably stocks them.

BlueTooth and Infrared

There are other wireless technologies used for transferring data between computers, most notably Bluetooth and Infrared. Infrared is used primarily to transmit (or Beam) small amounts of data such as contact details between personal organizers or mobile phones. Because it has a range of only a few feet it is considered to be sufficiently hacker-proof.

Bluetooth is a general-purpose wireless technology, designed to replace cables for tasks such as transferring pictures from digital cameras, connecting a cordless keyboard or mouse to a computer, and linking an earpiece to a mobile phone. However there is also a LAN Access facility built into the Bluetooth specification. If a desktop PC with an internet connection has a Bluetooth adaptor installed, any device with Bluetooth capability (such as a palmtop computer) can use it to make a wireless connection to the internet. Bluetooth as found in most portable devices has a range of only 10 metres or so, but it's possible to buy Bluetooth adaptors for desktop PCs that have a range of 100 metres.

It is recommended that you don't allow staff to install Bluetooth hardware on their desktop PCs without good reason and, if such hardware is installed, you should configure the drivers with care so that unnecessary features such as LAN Access are not enabled. Furthermore, if your mobile phones or PDAs have Bluetooth capability, turning off the feature when it's not required will increase both battery life and security.

▶ FUNDAMENTAL FIVE

Your action points for this chapter:

1. Buy a portable wireless detector so you can easily and quickly find out if staff or departments have set up wireless access points without your knowledge. ☐

2. Disable SSID broadcasting to make it harder for unauthorized people to stumble across your signal. ☐

3. Ensure that you check the Web site for your access points and other wireless equipment regularly for security patches and firmware upgrades. ☐

4. Enable MAC address filtering to control that computers can connect to your wireless network. ☐

5. If your access point supports it, use WPA encryption rather than WEP. ☐

14

Penetration Testing

There's only one way to discover the true state of your company's IT security, and that's to try breaking it. It's possible to do this yourself using automated software products which try to mimic the behaviour of a typical hacker, and such products will be discussed later in this chapter. But the best way to discover the full truth about the state of your security is to undergo a penetration test.

On the face of it, penetration testing is a fairly simple process. You employ a firm of security consultants to hack into your network using whatever means they wish. This is done on the understanding that the testers don't damage anything, don't divulge what they discover to any third parties, and they produce a report for you that identifies the holes in your security and explains how to plug them.

Almost all large organizations in both the private and public sector undergo penetration tests on a regular basis (typically once every year or two). The event offers an unparalleled opportunity for the organization to find out the true state of its IT security. But the whole exercise is not without its problems, most notably regarding cost and trust.

Employing a penetration testing company (sometimes known as a Tiger Team) is not cheap. For even the smallest company, expect to pay a few thousand pounds. But it's always money well spent because it results either in reassurance and peace of mind, or huge relief that the main loopholes in your security have been discovered by good guys, and that you can fix them before it's too late.

Finding a reputable, trustworthy penetration testing company is difficult. Some companies specialize in the practice, or at least are specialist security consultants. Others are more general management consultancies or even accountants, who have realized that there's money in IT security and have recruited some techies. Of those who actually carry out the testing, many are ex-hackers who learned their skills on the job, while some are much more academic and have honed their talents by reading textbooks and practicing on their own test networks in computer labs. All of which leads to a dilemma. Do you choose ex-hackers, who will do a good job but might not be trustworthy? Or do you choose accountants, who are probably trustworthy but possibly not as skilled?

I suggest that you choose the specialist security consultancies rather than the opportunist accountants. Don't worry about them using ex-hackers, so long as they are well-managed. Most importantly, get personal recommendations from colleagues and counterparts. Next time you're invited to a sales seminar by a security company, take the opportunity to go along, even if you're not particularly interested in the products being marketed. Such events are a great way to meet fellow delegates who have similar problems to yours, and an informal chat with such people over lunch or coffee will yield more useful information than reading a thousand white papers and brochures on the Web.

Before you Begin

Once you have chosen your pen test provider, there are some legal and procedural niceties that should be completed before the fun starts. Ensure that the company has your written permission to attempt to break into your systems, otherwise they are committing a criminal offence. Next, choose a time for the test to take place. Choose sensibly. For example, don't get your Web server tested just as your latest advertising campaign is driving potential new customers to your site, in case the test results in the site being unreachable.

Ensure that the testing company has professional indemnity insurance to cover them if anything unexpected should happen. Avoid companies that refuse to take responsibility for any mishaps and whose standard terms say that 'we cannot be held responsible for any damage to your systems or data that our tests may cause'. Employing testers under these terms puts you in a worse position than merely allowing yourself to be attacked by real hackers.

Pen tests work best when very few people know that they are happening. Senior management should be informed, because it helps to demonstrate that you are on top of the security problem. Other employees should not be informed unless there's a need to do so. Technical staff, i.e. those people who manage the equipment that is being targeted by the pen testers, are best kept out of the loop but at least one senior person in the department should be aware of what's going on in order that he or she can intervene if necessary. For example, if the administrators notice that a server is being attacked and want to shut down the machine or call the police, they can be informed that there is no need to do so because the attackers are on your side.

The subject of damage limitation must also be discussed and agreed upon. How far should the testers go to prove a hunch correct? Is it acceptable for them to initiate a Denial of Service attack that crashes your Web or email server and inconveniences your customers? Are there any mission–critical systems that should be left untested, or any systems that are known to be fragile and which should be treated with extra care?

Decide how thoroughly you intend to brief the testers as to the structure of your systems. Do you want them to adopt the persona of a curious external hacker who knows very little about your company, or a dishonest employee who knows the names and IP addresses of all your workstations, routers, switches and servers? The former is generally the preferred option, although this tends to increase costs slightly because the testers have to spend time discovering the topology of your systems before they can begin to attack them in more depth. It does, though, more accurately simulate the activity of real hackers. If you intend to go down this route, be sure not to let too much information slip during your initial consultations with the testers.

Confidentiality should be top of your agenda when talking to pen test companies. Ensure that you have their written assurance that information they discover during the course of their activities will remain strictly confidential, and that such information is stored securely when on their premises. If they pepper their sales pitch with horror stories about how easily they managed to break into customers' systems in the past, and those stories include strong clues as to the identity of the clients, beware. Your failings might be added to the sales pitch next time around.

Confidentiality falls into two categories when a pen test is performed. Not only are potential weaknesses in your system identified, but the testers might also encounter confidential data during their activities (e.g. if they manage to break the encryption on your customer accounts database). Make sure you agree how each will be dealt with.

Finally, talk about the deliverables. What form will the report take, and how long after the test will you receive it? What areas will be covered? Will the testers attempt to break into just your key servers, or will they include switches and routers and firewalls? Will they do a complete port scan? Will they try to defeat your intrusion detection system?

Tools and Techniques

Hackers use a wide variety of programs and techniques to break into a computer. They often start by performing a port scan to discover areas of the target system that deserve further attention, and then choose additional software tools according to the port that they find unguarded. Much of the software that hackers use is freely downloadable from the internet, but some hackers also write their own code on as as-needed basis when particular obstacles to the success of the hack come to light.

A good penetration testing team works in a similar way. They use a mixture of publicly available programs, proprietary programs written in-house and not available to anyone else, and small *ad-hoc* programs written as the test proceeds. Ask your pen testers what they use. If their entire software toolkit comprises programs that any hacker can download for free from the internet, look elsewhere. If you get fobbed off with excuses, such as 'the list of software is confidential', the same advice applies. Remember that you have a lot more to lose than they do if the whole exercise goes badly wrong.

Discuss where the testers will operate from. Clearly it's best that they don't operate from within your premises, and certainly not from any location that is within your firewall and thus not representative of a hacker's location. Generally, testers work from their own offices, accessing your systems via the internet. They might also make some visits to your premises in an attempt to locate wireless networks and to perform some social engineering. In most cases, clients are not invited to watch the penetration testers at work but, if you particularly wish to do so, perhaps because of your concerns over confidentiality, then ask. If your request is denied, don't be afraid to ask why.

Optional Extras

Some companies employ penetration testers because they are concerned solely with the risks from distant hackers attacking their systems via the internet from locations all over the world. Therefore, the testing encompasses only key items of equipment such as mail servers, Web servers, network file stores and so on. However, if you wish to get a complete picture as to the overall security of all your electronic assets, the testers' remit needs to be extended.

Consider including some social engineering as part of the test. Here, the testers attempt to contact staff by various means such as telephone and email and trick them into divulging confidential information. In March 2005, the IRS (Inland Revenue) in the US was the target of such a test, carried out by inspectors from the Treasury Department who posed as computer technicians. They telephoned 100 users to ask them to temporarily change their passwords to specific words 'in order to help resolve a problem with the network'. Of those 100 employees, 35 instantly agreed. A worryingly high number, but much better than the 71 who failed a similar test four years previously.

Such activity can be enlightening and very revealing, but take care not to subject victims to public ridicule – if you include the results in a staff newsletter then ensure that they are suitably anonymised. However, consider bestowing public praise or even a small gift upon those who manage to see through the testers' disguise.

If you have any wireless network facilities, or you think that you might have, add this to the penetration testers' agenda. This will of course require that they visit your premises, but they should be able to carry out their experiments from a nearby location such as the car park rather than requiring entry to your offices.

Consider whether you wish the testers to attempt to gain physical access to equipment rather than merely accessing it electronically. Are you concerned that hackers or other unwanted visitors could gain access to your offices or servers without your knowledge, either to steal equipment or copy information? If so, most pen testing companies will be more than willing to undertake testing in these areas. Again, public praise (such as a company-wide email or a mention in the staff newsletter) for those who deny the testers access will generally be appreciated by recipients.

When the Report Arrives

Most companies who hire penetration testers are confident that the report will not bring to their attention any major vulnerabilities that require immediate attention. Yet most end up sorely disappointed when the report does just that. Therefore, ensure that you will have sufficient manpower available to implement the report's recommendations within days, if not hours, of its receipt. Before this, you will also need to ensure that there is time available to be able to digest the report, and to discuss it with key colleagues such as senior managers and relevant technical staff. Budget-holders should also be notified that they might be called upon at short notice to authorize some urgent expenditure on hardware and software that might be required to shore up the most dangerous holes.

Before undertaking any action, make sure that you fully understand the report from the testers. Make sure, too, that you agree with its findings, and seek clarification from the testers if you are unsure. Although not common, testers do occasionally embellish their reports and exaggerate the impact of some discovered weaknesses, in order to justify their existence or to generate additional subsequent consultancy.

The DIY Options

If you don't want the risk or expense of employing professional penetration testers, one option is to buy a program that automatically scans your network looking for vulnerabilities. If you've ever tried the Microsoft Baseline Security Analyser (MBSA), which is a free tool from Microsoft that alerts you to missing security patches on a PC or server, then you will be familiar with the concept. You install the software on a PC, enter the details of the network that you wish to scan, and the program automatically attempts to locate vulnerabilities such as open ports, missing security patches, accounts with blank or easily guessable passwords, incorrectly configured network shares, and so on.

Examples of automated vulnerability scanners include Sunbelt's Network Security Inspector (`www.sunbelt-software.com`) and GFI's LANguard Network Security Scanner (`www.gfi.com`). The Sunbelt program costs around $1900 and its database contains over 3000 known vulnerabilities that the software is able to search for. LANguard is cheaper at around $1000 for a licence for scanning a network of unlimited size, and is also available in a cut-down free version so that you can get a feel for how it works.

Using an automated vulnerability scanner has one advantage over full pen testing, namely that you can keep running the software and fixing problems until everything appears to be secure. Once you've paid for the software you can run it as often as you like, whereas re-testing with professional testers will cost extra. But the downside is that the software is not intelligent. It can only scan for vulnerabilities that are in its database, and although the database is updated frequently the program can't think as a hacker does. So while an automated scanner is a very useful addition to your toolkit, you shouldn't assume that a clean bill of health from such a product means that you would also receive such a rating from a real penetration test.

One pen testing organization describes such tools as giving a false sense of security and suggests that they should never be used. I disagree with this outright condemnation, but it is important to be aware of their shortcomings. However, they are certainly better than nothing at all, and they offer excellent value for money.

If you run an Exchange server, one incredibly useful tool is Best Practice Analyser, a download from Microsoft that alerts you to any discrepancies between the way your server is configured and the recommended way of doing things. You can get it from `www.microsoft.com/exchange/downloads` and it's totally free. There are various programs specifically designed to test the security of Web sites by initiating common attacks such as SQL injection and cross-site scripting. Check out www.acunetix.com for one example.

There is also another way of performing a DIY pen test on your key systems. Most hackers operate by using programs that are freely available on the internet, such as the nmap port scanner. By obtaining these tools and installing them on a spare PC, you can attempt to hack into your own systems. However, while such a technique is perfectly legal and is certainly cheap, the risks are substantial unless you know how to use the tools and interpret their results.

The Tsunami Site Case

The law as it affects penetration testing in the UK suffered a major blow to its reputation in October 2005 following the conviction of a computer security consultant and lecturer called Daniel Cuthbert. On 31st December 2004, Cuthbert made an online donation to the relief fund for victims of the Asian tsunami that had occurred 5 days earlier. Having failed to receive a confirmatory 'thank you' message from the system, he was worried that he might have just unwittingly submitted his credit card details to a spoof Web site run by hackers. In an attempt to find out more about the site, he typed ../../.. into the address bar of his Web browser. This is a common technique used by hackers, which exploits a bug in some Web servers and allows them to see parts of the site that are not normally available to the public. Having tried this twice, and received no response, he assumed that the site was genuine and took no further action.

Unbeknown to Cuthbert, his actions had triggered the Intrusion Detection System at the company that operated the site, and the company called the police. Cuthbert consequently found himself in court, accused under the Computer Misuse Act of intending to gain unauthorized access to a computer system. The Judge, with 'some considerable regret', had no option but to find Daniel Cuthbert guilty. He was fined. He had also already been dismissed from his job.

The majority of the IT security community felt that prosecuting Daniel Cuthbert was unfair, and that it would damage the relationship between the police and the security experts on whom they often need to depend. It does, though, highlight the extreme care that you need to take when performing a penetration test if you are to be confident that you are not acting illegally.

▶ FUNDAMENTAL FIVE

Your action points for this chapter:

1. If you employ an external company to probe your systems, choose carefully. Ask for reference sites. ☐

2. Before the test commences, ensure that you will have the time and money to put things right when the report arrives. ☐

3. Ensure that the testing company has your written authority to proceed with the test. ☐

4. Decide in advance how far you wish the testers to go. Should they include social engineering? ☐

5. How much disruption should the testers be allowed to cause? Should they be allowed to initiate a Denial of Service attack? ☐

15

Security Through Obscurity

Defeating hackers requires many different techniques. You can use encryption to protect confidential files, or usernames and passwords to guard a private Web site. To prevent unauthorized copying of document files you can use digital rights management, and to block access to your servers you can install a firewall. But whatever security product, system or service you use, there's always one thing that never changes: the security precautions that you have taken are overt and visible, and the hacker will be aware of them.

Providing potential hackers with clear evidence of your security systems makes good sense and is a useful deterrent. But there's also another option, known as Security Through Obscurity (STO), which takes a completely different approach. In STO, the mere existence of the protected system is the secret and so there is no need to provide any additional security.

A good example of STO is that of leaving a spare door key under the mat or inside a flower pot. There's no need to protect the key any further, because no one except the owner (and anyone who has been told of its existence by the owner) will know that it's there. Another example that appears regularly in fiction is the secret doorway disguised as a bookcase. Pull on a particular 'book' in a certain way and the shelves magically revolve to reveal a hidden passage. The door is never locked. It doesn't need to be, because no one knows it exists.

Security Through Obscurity is often used to protect information systems. For example, a company's Web site that provides information for the public might also contain some private pages for employees only. Yet instead of adding password protection to the staff-only pages, they are simply hidden behind an obscure URL. I even know of Web sites that use similar techniques to hide not just private information, but also the editing facilities – anyone who knows the secret URL can change the content of the site.

Security Through Obscurity is a much-used technique because it's quick and easy. Implementing this form of security means not having to implement any security at all, and simply hoping that the hackers won't discover your secret. The fundamental problem with this approach is twofold: first, there's a chance that the hackers will discover your secret. Secondly, and much more important, you won't realize that your secret is out until it's too late. Until the content of your Web site changes, or someone breaks into your house, or someone finds your secret passage.

There are plenty of tools available to help hackers defeat STO security, the best-known of which is the humble search engine. By entering the correct incantation into Google, for example, the hacker can find URLs that include a folder called admin. He then surfs to that directory in the hope of being presented with an admin menu and not being asked for a password.

One further example of STO is the Caesar Cipher, a primitive form of encryption dating from 2000 years ago in which each letter of the plaintext is substituted with a letter that is three positions later in the alphabet. A becomes D, B becomes E and so on, and thus computer becomes frpsxwhu. At first glance, the code appears uncrackable, but a little investigation and experimentation will uncover the secret and then open up all the information that has ever been protected using this method.

Compare this with a conventional modern-day encryption algorithm which depends on highly complex mathematical formulas which would take many years for even the most powerful computer to solve. Everyone knows the secret but they simply don't have the resources to solve it. Back in the real world, this is like leaving your spare key under the mat of a house a couple of miles away. Anyone who finds it will know what it is, but trying to discover which house it fits is simply not practical.

Multiple Protection Methods

STO is not recommended as the sole method of protecting an electronic resource, but it is often a useful component of an overall strategy. Every network server comes with a default account that has ultimate power. Under Windows this account has a username of Administrator, while under Unix and Linux it's known as root. It makes good sense to change this name to something else, but don't assume that this is all you need to do in order to defeat the hackers.

Equally, a degree of STO can help prevent ftp servers from being attacked. The convention for ftp is that the server listens on port 21. Hackers therefore search for ftp servers by attempting to connect to port 21 on a range of machines. By configuring your ftp server to listen on, say, port 2121, you fly under the radar of such hackers. Again, remember that any hacker who carries out a full port-scan will still find your hidden server so the technique is not infallible. Plus, anyone who wishes to connect to your ftp server will need to change the default settings on their ftp client software so that it connects on port 2121, which can require additional support effort.

Security books and journals are full of dire warnings about Security Through Obscurity, and why you should never consider using it. Certainly you should never deploy it as the sole way to protect anything. But as part of an overall strategy, it certainly adds something. For example, a security consultant of my acquaintance set up a pair of SQL database servers and connected them to the internet. One was configured to listen on the default port 1434, the other on non-standard port 1435. The server on port 1434 received hundreds of probes from port-scanning hackers every day. The server on the non-standard port remained untouched for a full year.

To indicate why STO isn't a good way to protect computers, here's an edited extract from the log file of a real Web site that I set up for a client. The report shows those pages which couldn't be delivered to the user who requested them, along with the reason as to why that request could not be satisfied (the first column shows the number of times that the particular entry appears in the log). You will see that two people tried surfing to a non–existent page called author.exe, presumably in the hope that it would allow them to change the content of the site. And 21 people tried surfing to cmd.exe in the hope that it would open a Windows command prompt in their browser from which they could control my Web server.

```
2    Not Found = /_vti_bin/_vti_aut/author.exe
74   Not Found = /_vti_bin/_vti_aut/fp30reg.dll
93   Not Found = /_vti_bin/owssvr.dll
13   Not Found = /_vti_inf.html
46   Not Found = /help/Help.html
374  Not Found = /pages/
21   Not Found = /scripts/..%255c%255c../winnt/system32/cmd.exe
1    Not Found = /scripts/..%c1%9c../winnt/system32/cmd.exe
9    Not Found = /scripts/nsiislog.dll
1    Not Found = /scripts/root.exe
1    Not Found = /services/reading/admissions.html
2    Not Found = /sortal/@X@course.course_id@X@.htm
1    Method Not Allowed = /testhost.htm
2    Method Not Allowed = /www.arplhmd.cjb.net_@@RNDSTR@@
1    Method Not Allowed = /xtf.htm
22   Method Not Allowed = 1.3.3.7:1337
1    Not Implemented = /scripts/..%C1%9C../winnt/system32/cmd.exe
1    Not Implemented = /scripts/..%e0%80%af../winnt/system32/cmd.exe
2    Not Implemented = /scripts/root.exe
1    Not Implemented = /scripts/scripts/..%252f../winnt/system32/cmd.exe
```

In computing, everything has its place. Hackers tend to know what those places are. On Windows, for example, the cmd.exe program which gives you a C:> command prompt lives in the/winnt/system32 directory. Therefore, when you install software on a Web server it makes good sense to choose a directory other than the default one which is offered to you. In addition, make sure that you always remove any unnecessary files from the installation directory once they are no longer required. A common hacker technique is to look for installation files that were not deleted after the installation was completed. If the hacker can re-run the installation file, he can reinstall the software with his own choice of administrator password. Plus, of course, he can wipe all the data and other settings from your current installation.

Software Crackers

When Microsoft launched version 4 of Windows NT a few years ago, the company gave away free four-month evaluation copies by the thousand at trade shows and even on magazine covers. It was then discovered that anyone who downloaded the latest service pack and applied it to their evaluation copy would end up with a full version that never expired. You may not have heard of this episode, as Microsoft's PR team did its best to explain to journalists (myself included) that printing details of their cock-up would be a Very Bad Idea. Their strategy succeeded in the short term, but the long-term damage to the company's reputation among journalists was serious.

As this example illustrates, one of the hacker's favourite pastimes is to defeat the protection systems that are built into software. In most cases, the crackers have no wish to use the software – they simply need to prove to themselves that they are smarter than the people who designed the security feature. For this reason, using STO in your company's own software is a bad move.

When Lotus launched the latest version of its Organiser program for Windows back in December 1995, many admired the built-in password protection feature which ensured that users could keep their personal information private. One evening, with nothing better to do, I decided to find out just how secure it was. After just half an hour I'd worked out that the program didn't use any encryption. It simply stored the password in an encoded form at the beginning of the data file. If I replaced the encoded password with zeroes, the program no longer requested a password before opening the file. This simple discovery immediately rendered useless the protection that the company's many customers had presumably applied to hundreds of thousands of highly confidential personal files. Had Lotus implemented proper encryption, rather than merely pretending to have done so, the situation would never have arisen.

You should never use STO in isolation, and never put yourself in the position where significant damage or embarrassment could be caused if the secret were to be discovered. A key under the mat is a good idea, but that's no excuse not to lock the door too.

FUNDAMENTAL FIVE

Your action points for this chapter:

1. Be aware of the dangers inherent in using Security Through Obscurity as the sole protection mechanism for a system. Primarily, you won't know that it has been breached. ☐

2. Running an ftp server on a port other than 21 is a useful additional security step. ☐

3. Running a Web server on a port other than 80 does little to increase security because anyone who needs to access the site will have to be informed of the port number. ☐

4. Examine your Web server logs for signs of hackers attempting to access private files in known locations. ☐

5. When installing software on your Web server, don't use the default file or directory locations. ☐

16

Windows Vista

Microsoft has a habit of making bold claims whenever it announces new versions of its software. Windows 3.0, Windows 95, Windows NT, Windows 2000 and Windows XP were all billed as 'the best Windows ever'. Hardly surprising, of course, given that no company ever intentionally launches a new product that isn't quite as good as the old one.

It's certainly true that the security facilities included in Windows have improved greatly since version 1 was launched 20 years ago. But even today there are serious drawbacks, perhaps the greatest of which is the ubiquitous administrator account. Without administrator privileges, common tasks such as installing new software, adjusting the computer's clock, creating a new internet connection or setting up a new printer are forbidden. Therefore many users, especially at home or those working for small companies, use the computer in administrator mode all the time.

This is especially true with laptops, where the network configuration needs to be changed each time the machine is transported between a home environment, office, and client sites. Each will require settings to be tweaked before it can be connected to the internet, and Windows XP doesn't allow these to be altered by anyone except an administrator. Consequently, companies often have no option but to allow users administrator access to their laptops so that they can connect them to the internet from wherever they happen to be.

Microsoft, and every security expert I've ever met, continue to point out that you should never use a computer in administrator mode unless you need to. For all other times, the advice is to set up a user account that doesn't have administrator privileges. The reason is simple. If you accidentally download a virus or you become the victim of some other malicious software, the damage that the malware is able to wreak will be limited because of the access privileges granted to a non-administrator account. A virus that tries to format the hard disk or change the telephone number of your dial-up internet connection simply won't be allowed to proceed. But most people regard this protection as an inconvenience rather than a benefit.

At the heart of Windows Vista, the successor to Windows XP, is a new way of working. Most programs automatically run with reduced privileges, even if you log into the computer with an administrator account. If the program tries to perform a forbidden operation, the user must provide confirmation in order for the operation to proceed. According to how the computer has been configured, confirmation involves answering yes or no to a dialogue box prompt, or entering the username and password of an account that has local administrator privileges. This prevents viruses and other malware from spreading and from damaging systems but doesn't block users from performing legitimate tasks. This new feature is known as user account protection, and is just one of the ways that Microsoft is attempting to ensure that administrator privileges aren't misused in Vista, either by users or by errant software.

Another new Vista security feature helps to avoid problems caused by registry permissions. The registry is where Windows, and almost every application, stores its configuration settings and other key information.

Whenever you change a setting in Windows, such as the network IP address or the default numbering format for Excel, this gets stored in the registry. Although the registry is effectively a single file, it's possible to apply different access permissions to various parts of it. Only administrators can change the machine's IP address, for example, but standard users can change the Excel numbering format (unless an administrator has changed the default security for this particular part of the registry).

Under Windows XP and all previous versions, if you don't have permission to change a registry setting then there's little that you can do about it – Windows simply won't let you do it. With Windows Vista, all attempts to change registry settings will succeed but, if you don't have permission to change the setting for all users, it will be changed only for your particular user account. This is to be known as registry virtualization.

Microsoft hopes that user account protection and registry virtualization will finally persuade both home and company users of Windows to configure the operating system according to best-practice guidelines, and not allow the system to run in administrator mode all the time. Assuming that this proves to be the case, it should help reduce the speed at which malware can damage files and spread between computers.

Firewall and Internet Explorer

The original release of Windows XP included a rudimentary firewall but its features were limited and it was not enabled by default. Service Pack 2 improved the firewall and ensured that it was enabled, but it still lacked many of the features found in other products. Most notably, it only filters incoming traffic. This helps to stop hackers but won't, for example, prevent users from accessing banned Web sites such as file sharing systems, or block a virus or Trojan from sending confidential information to an external site without permission. The Windows Vista firewall finally includes both inbound and outbound filtering, providing much greater facilities to ensure the safety and security of the PC and its files.

Internet Explorer version 7 is available as standard with Windows Vista or as an optional download for XP. It has been extensively upgraded to improve security. The program runs with very limited system privileges, even if the user is logged in as an administrator. Installing new software or browser plug-ins, or changing important settings such as the home page or the default search engine, requires explicit confirmation so malicious Web sites will find it much harder to dupe unsuspecting visitors. In addition, the on-screen indication that the site is protected by SSL encryption is now much more visible and obvious, rather than the previous tiny symbol of a closed padlock. Writing to any part of the hard disk except the Temporary Internet Files folder (where cookies and cached pages are stored) will no longer be possible for the Web browser or for any add-in that it runs.

IE7 includes a new phishing filter, which continually refers back to a master database of Web sites that are known to be operated by people intent on stealing personal information. This database is updated many times each day, which will hopefully limit the amount of time that a phishing site can remain active without its effects being blocked.

Network Access Protection

Perhaps the most important security improvement in Windows Vista, from a corporate viewpoint, is Network Access Protection. This allows network administrators to prevent a computer from being connected to the company network unless it meets minimum security requirements such as having up-to-date security patches and antivirus software installed. The network administrator can specify what happens if a sub-standard computer is plugged in – it can either be denied access to the network entirely, or can be given access to a restricted environment from which the missing software can be downloaded and installed.

Although this facility has been available from a handful of third-party providers in the past, its inclusion as a standard component of Windows is to be welcomed. Network Access Protection will be of immense benefit to companies who run large networks that are open to anyone who can find an unused network socket into which they can plug their laptop, PDA or any other device. Perhaps the only downside is that the feature only works if the network server is also running Windows Vista – existing Windows XP or 2000 servers will need to be upgraded. *Plus ça change.*

Smart Cards

More and more companies are beginning to investigate the use of hardware devices rather than passwords for user authentication. To help drive this, Vista makes it easier for programmers to create new ways for logging in. This should lead to a rise in the number of smart card readers, fingerprint scanners and other devices available. In addition, the Encrypting File System now allows users to export their encryption keys to a smart card, thus allowing the device to act as the key to encrypted information on a Windows Vista computer.

Another enhancement to the encrypting file system is the concept of full-drive encryption, known as Secure Startup. This encrypts all of the hard disk, including the boot sector and swap file, rather than just a selection of data directories. This has a number of advantages, especially when used on a modern computer that has a Trusted Platform Module (TPM) chip installed. The TPM chip will prevent the computer from starting unless it is booted from the copy of Windows that is installed on the hard disk. Any attempt to boot the computer in any other way, such as from a bootable Windows or Linux CD, will fail and the machine (and all its data) will remain inaccessible.

Currently, anyone with physical access to a server can boot it from another copy of Windows XP or 2000 and reset the administrator password to one of their choosing. TPM will prevent this technique from working. It will also help to reduce the value of stolen laptops, as all of the files on the machine will be unreadable.

Looking Ahead

Windows has come a long way since making its first appearance more than 20 years ago. But any program that is used by more than 90% of the world's computers is clearly going to attract the attention of 90% of the world's hackers too. While some hackers and virus-writers do target Unix and other non-Windows systems, the majority of them prefer to aim their efforts at Microsoft and its products. Windows Vista certainly appears to offer some genuine improvements that will help to protect computers and the information they hold.

FUNDAMENTAL FIVE

Your action points for this chapter:

1. Remember that no operating system is 100% secure nor offers a total panacea. You must still work to stay in control and to defeat the hackers. ☐

2. If you are not yet ready to consider upgrading to Windows Vista but the concept of Secure Startup appeals, consider ensuring that all new computers that you buy include the TPM chip. ☐

3. If you do not intend to upgrade to Windows Vista for the time being, upgrading existing Windows XP installations to version 7 of Internet Explorer will offer additional security safeguards. ☐

4. If Network Access Protection appeals, remember that this will require a server upgrade so start planning for this. ☐

5. Experts generally advise against using version 1 of any new operating system. Don't rush to be an early adopter. Let others find the bugs. ☐

Email

When I first started out as an IT journalist working full-time on a magazine in 1983, I spent the majority of my working day on the phone talking to companies and publicity people in search of a good story. Nowadays, despite doing a job that's very similar, I use the telephone maybe once or twice a week. Everything happens by email. Why phone someone and risk interrupting them when you can send them an email and then move on to the next entry on the to-do list?

The trouble is, email is unreliable. There's no guarantee that a message you send will arrive, or that it won't be intercepted *en route*. There's no easy way to tell whether a message that hits your inbox is free from viruses or even that it really was sent by the person whom it appears to come from. If we were starting from here, there's no way that any sane business consultant would allow us to put so much trust and reliance into a facility, which frankly is broken beyond repair. But that's the way it is, and we have to find some way to live with it. And to trust it.

Let's start with the concept of faked or spoofed mail. That is, the ability for someone to send a message which appears to come from someone else. You've undoubtedly received spoofed messages in the past, as it's a technique used by spammers. They often use a program that contains a dictionary of hundreds of thousands of words, and their system automatically picks 2 or 3 at random to create a different sender every time. Many anti-spam systems work by regarding multiple messages from the same sender as spam, so this technique helps the spammers to ensure that their messages don't get blocked.

The ease with which email can be forged was demonstrated after a British man was arrested in connection with emails sent in the aftermath of the Asian tsunami in December 2004. Relatives seeking information about their loved ones had posted messages on a Web forum. The man had emailed them, pretending to be from the Foreign Office Bureau in Thailand, informing them that their relatives' bodies had been found. It was all a cruel hoax.

Sending fake mail is easy. All you need is a telnet program (there's one included free with Windows), an internet connection and an SMTP mail server to connect to. To send a spoof mail you use the telnet program to connect to the mail server, specify the recipient and the sender and the text of the message, and then the server does the rest. When it comes to specifying the sender, you can type absolutely anything you want. Legitimate email programs such as Outlook will, of course, specify your own name as the sender, but there's nothing in the rules that says that they have to. The SMTP server has no way of checking or verifying.

Here's a telnet session log where I connect to my ISP's mail server (the lines in bold are the bits that I typed) and sent a mail to myself (robert.schifreen@gmail.com) which appears to originate from the_team at the BBC.

```
C:>telnet smtp.my_isp.co.uk 25
220 mra05.ex.your_isp.net.uk ESMTP
helo schifreen.co.uk
250 mra05.ex.your_isp.net.uk
mail from: the_team@bbc.co.uk
250 Ok
rcpt to: robert.schifreen@gmail.com
```

```
250 Ok
data
354 End data with <CR><LF>.<CR><LF>
Subject: Important message

Hi, this is an important email for you from the BBC.

Regards,

The Team
.
250 Ok: queued as 4BFA9D47E1
quit
221 Bye
C:>
```

A few seconds later, the message arrived in my Gmail inbox:

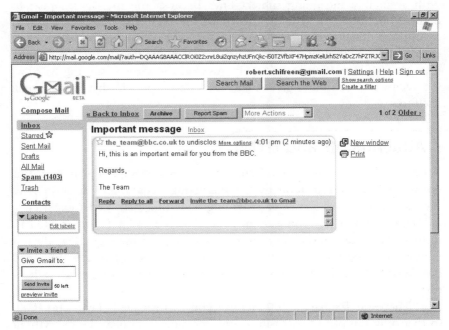

At first glance, and indeed at a second glance, the message looks genuine
enough. The sender is shown as `the_team@bbc.co.uk`. It's only if you
examine the headers of the message, which are not normally displayed, that
you get to see the technical information about the origins of the message

which can provide clues as to whether or not it is genuine. This is beyond the capabilities (and interest) of the typical recipient who, in this case, judges the book by its content and never looks at the cover.

Every email program, even Web-based systems such as Google's Gmail, allow you to view the headers of a message. Should you wish to find out more about deciphering email headers, there are many Web sites that tell you how. `http://spam.surferbeware.com/spam-deciphering-headers.htm` is a good place to start.

Mail spoofing is not merely the domain of spammers. Viruses use the technique, coupled with a bit of psychology and technical trickery, to assist in their efforts to spread to as many computers as possible. It is common for a virus to access the address book on a victim's computer, or to trawl all of the documents on their hard disk in search of valid email addresses. The virus then sends a copy of itself to these people, with a suitably intriguing subject line. Because the messages appear to come from someone who is known to the recipient, most people will open them. They will then discover, too late, that the holiday snaps from their friend or the proposal from their colleague is actually nothing of the sort. By the time they realize their mistake, the virus is starting to trawl the recipient's computer in search of yet more people that it can email itself to.

Attachments and HTML

When email was a service or a facility, messages consisted of plain text. But email has been seized upon by the marketing departments at companies such as Microsoft as a way of providing us with a rich media experience so plain text is out. You can now send messages in RTF or HTML format, and thus choose fonts and colours for the message. The default editor for composing new messages in Outlook is not merely Notepad but Word. HTML also allows messages to contain images as well as text.

Microsoft Exchange 2003 allows you to turn off HTML and RTF so that only the plain text of incoming messages is displayed – everything else such as graphics and links are stripped out. You can do the same thing with Exchange XP, but it requires a registry hack rather than being a menu option. Personally, I never use Outlook without this no–HTML option enabled. It's much safer and makes most messages a lot easier to read.

By using Word as the default email editor and by allowing messages to include HTML commands, you open your computer to possible infection by viruses that would otherwise pass you by. Plain text editors can't execute Word macro viruses, and spyware which hides behind graphics that are loaded from a remote server via an html hyperlink won't run either. Although it's fun to be able to embellish emails with fancy colours, fonts and graphics, it's also essential that you limit the number of ways in which your company's computers can potentially be compromised (the attack surface, to use the military jargon which is now finding its way into IT parlance). Therefore, you should always configure Outlook so that Word is not the default editor and that messages are composed and displayed in plain text format.

Email attachments represent one of the biggest risks in IT security. They allow unwanted files to come in, and, as we shall see later, they also allow staff to smuggle information out. Ask anyone who looks after corporate PCs for a living, and they'll tell you that the biggest day-to-day problem is viruses and that the majority of these arrive via email attachments.

As has already been mentioned, viruses frequently spread by emailing themselves to unsuspecting victims as email attachments. The recipient clicks on the attachment, the program runs, and the virus springs into action. Attachments pose other problems too. They can contain not just documents (including Word .doc files that can hide macro viruses) but also executable program files, batch files, screen savers (basically another form of executable file), and more. If you don't already do so, you should consider configuring your mail server to prevent users from sending executable files in attachments, but admittedly this does make your entire email system less useful. A compromise is to allow .ZIP files to be passed around, and to inform users that they will have to zip their executable files if they want to send such items to colleagues. This will still block viruses that arrive as .EXE files.

The golden rule with email attachments is never to click on one to open it unless you are confident that it is genuine. Although many tech-savvy users know this, most computer users don't. And because few viruses have the manners to announce to the user that their machine is now infected, it can be weeks before the problem is detected. By which time, for some companies, it might be too late.

Phishing and Pharming

Criminals are constantly working to find new ways of using email to defraud consumers and companies alike. In recent years, phishing has become a lucrative and worryingly easy way for them to do so. It has all the advantages of spam, in that it uses email as a ludicrously cheap distribution medium. But it is also far more lucrative for the perpetrators. According to Gartner, US banks and credit card companies wrote off $1.2 billion in 2004 as a result of customer losses due to phishing attacks. Clearly a not-insignificant figure, and one that the financial industry is desperate to prevent from increasing even further.

Phishing is a very simple crime to carry out and it works so well because there's still a low level of security awareness among most internet users, especially (but certainly not exclusively) older people. It involves sending out emails that purport to come from the recipient's online bank, advising that there is a problem of some sort with the account and that the user needs to log into the bank's system to resolve it. There is, helpfully, a link in the email message that takes the user directly to the login page on the bank's Web site.

The trick, of course, is that the Web site is actually a fake. It relies on the fact that html pages on Web sites are never private (you can look at the source code of any page by selecting Source from the View menu in your Web browser). So the criminals copy the html code to make up a login page on their own server that looks just like the real one, except that the usernames, passwords and PIN codes which are entered are retained by the hackers and, within minutes, the hapless victim discovers that the contents of their bank account have been transferred elsewhere.

If your email reader can't display html, then it can't display links to fake bank sites – at least not in a form that the unsuspecting recipient can click onto. This is just one reason why it pays to disable the ability of your email program to display incoming messages in HTML format.

Phishing is so-called because it involves fishing for passwords and other personal information. The non-standard spelling follows a long-standing tradition in hacking circles which started 40 years ago with the alliterative 'phone phreaking'. This is the technique of misusing the telephone network to obtain free calls, typically by playing tones of specific frequencies down the line in order to mimic the signals that payphones used to send to the exchange to inform the system that the user had inserted a coin. The most famous phreaker was a man called John Draper, who acquired the nickname of Captain Crunch when he discovered that the childrens' whistle given away free in boxes of Cap'n Crunch breakfast cereal in the US in the 1970's operated at just the right frequency to do this.

Because email is so cheap to send, phishers don't bother with the normal niceties that concern the marketing departments of financial institutions. Phishers don't bother going to the trouble of ensuring that mail purporting to come from bank X doesn't get sent to someone whose account is actually with bank Y. Recipients who don't have an account will simply ignore the mail, or possibly complain by replying to the message. Needless to say, complaints go unanswered.

Although the victims of phishing highlighted by the media are generally domestic users of online banking systems, or gullible pensioners who now wish they'd stuck with keeping their cash under the bed, corporate accounts can, and do, get raided by this method too. If your company uses online banking or other services such as share dealing, you must ensure that all staff with access to the login information are aware of how to spot possible bogus requests. This includes:

1. Banks never ask for passwords or other security information by email. If you receive such an email, even if it appears important (e.g. your account will be shut down if you do not reply), assume that it is bogus unless you can prove otherwise.

2. Banks never ask for passwords, etc. on the phone. If anyone calls and asks for such information, and claims to be from the bank, ask for the caller's name and call them back by looking up the number for the bank on its official Web site or in the telephone directory.

3. Never click on links within phishing emails, even if you are merely suspicious and have no intention of entering real information into the username and password boxes. The bogus sites might also hide a virus.

4. If you're concerned about the authenticity of a Web site into which you are entering confidential information, look for a closed padlock symbol on the status line at the bottom of your Web browser which indicates that you are connected to a secure encrypted server. Double-click on the padlock and you should see details about the company to which it was issued. This should be the name of the organisation whose site you are currently browsing, or a recognized subsidiary. Check the name carefully for devious mis-spellings.

5. Phishers and hackers sometimes try to gain victims' confidence by appearing to know part of a confidential number and merely requiring confirmation of the remainder. For example, some hackers send out emails which purport to be from credit card companies and which ask you to confirm, for security purposes, the first digits of your card that ends in 9225. Many people assume that no one would know the last four digits except the card issuer, and fail to notice that most town-centre rubbish bins contain thousands of discarded credit card receipts from electronic terminals in shops which, for security reasons, show only the final four digits of the customer's card number.

6. All financial services companies have dedicated staff to handle complaints about phishing scams, and contact numbers are usually listed on the companies' Web sites. If you think that your company has been a victim, contact the bank or card company concerned immediately.

At the end of 2005, the banking industry revealed a new weapon against phishers. Customers of Lloyds TSB are now issued with a small authentication device which they carry on their key fob. When the unit's button is pressed it displays a series of digits. Logging into the online banking account requires the customer to enter their username and password as normal, as well as the numbers that are displayed on the authentication device. Assuming that the authentication succeeds, this means that the customer has physical possession of the device and, therefore, that the person logging in is the actual customer rather than a hacker or phisher.

Although the financial industry has always refused to divulge how much it is losing through phishing attacks, the rollout of hardware identification tokens clearly indicates that the amounts involved are substantial. These devices cost several tens of pounds each, in small quantities, and have never been used in large-scale consumer applications before. Clearly the problem of phishing, in terms of both lost revenue and customer apprehension, is a significant problem.

Although devices such as this should greatly reduce online fraud, there are still risks involved. When the customer presses the button to activate the device, the six-digit number which is generated is valid for 30 seconds – just enough time for the user to type them into the e-banking Web site. But possibly, just enough time for the customer to type them into a fake site, and for that fake site to instantly make use of them via an automatic program that uses them to log into the genuine site.

On The Pharm

Despite the similar-sounding name, pharming has very little connection with phishing. It doesn't involve sending out email, and it's not a widely practised technique as it requires a fair amount of hacking expertise. It does, though, produce similar results for the hackers, in that it can help them to guide unsuspecting visitors into fake e-banking Web sites.

Pharming involves manually altering a DNS server. DNS is the Domain Name Service, which is a directory that converts IP addresses into friendly names. Without DNS, you'd have to type 207.46.130.108 into your Web browser instead of `www.microsoft.com`. Pharming involves hacking into the database of a DNS server and changing the IP address entry of a site, so that people who type the site's name into their Web browser will find themselves at a fake site which appears to be totally genuine.

Scams

Before phishing, the most common internet email scam was the 419 trick, and such attacks are still continuing in great numbers. The original 419 emails contained messages such as "Greetings, you do not know me but a mutual acquaintance passed me your details. I am the son of the late Prime Minister of Nigeria, and I'll give you 30% of the proceeds if you'd be so kind as to let me use your bank account to transfer $20 million out of a dormant bank account belonging to my late father".

Although most of the original 419 emails originated in Nigeria, and were thus named after the section number of the Nigerian Penal Code which outlaws the practice, nowadays the numerous variations on an original theme are just as likely to come from almost anywhere.

There are two ways that the 419 criminals make their money. Sometimes they request that you pay them a few thousand dollars so that they have the necessary funds to bribe those who have permission to release the millions. Other times, they ask for your bank account details and some of your company's letterhead as proof of your ID and to ensure that your share can be wired to you at the earliest opportunity. These details are then used to forge a letter to your bank authorising not a credit but a withdrawal.

All the time, the scammers continue the pretence that the 30% of $20 million is on its way, so that they can continually ask the victim for more cash advances, letterhead, and other confidential information. The Metropolitan police in London have said that, at any one time, there are a couple of dozen greedy businessmen hanging around in hotel lounges eagerly anticipating the arrival of a man with a suitcase full of money. Who is, of course, not coming.

If you wish to report advance fee fraud emails, the Met have an email address at `fraud.alert@met.police.uk` and they also publish further information at `www.met.police.uk/fraudalert/419.htm`. If you'd rather gain satisfaction from seeing 419 scammers hoisted by their own petards, `www.419eater.com` is a fascinating account of the efforts by a group of people to play the scammers at their own game and con them into identifying themselves.

But for all the technology that goes into creating and sending email, one of the most common security incidents happens not because of any inherent weakness in the internet, nor through hacker activity, but by simple user error. It happens when someone sends a message to a large list of people by copying and pasting the list of recipients into the message's 'to:' field rather than remembering to use the 'bcc:' field. This results in each recipient seeing not only the message, but the list of recipients too. Which is often confidential and/or valuable, such as the database of subscribers to an electronic newsletter or the registered users of a particular product. User education is the best way to prevent this happening, so make sure you include it in your security awareness training programme.

Personal vs. Private

Most companies allow staff to send and receive private email through the company's systems, so long as it is not taken to excess and that the company's email systems are not used to transmit illegal material. If your company allows such practice then there are a few rules that you should spell out to all employees.

First, staff might reasonably assume that private email sent or received using the company system is totally private. This is rarely the case in practice, because all companies need to monitor their networks for reasons of performance and security, so there is a small chance that personal email might be read by administrative staff. This should be made clear to all employees.

Be aware that, even if you notify staff that personal communications might be intercepted, such action is still regarded as intrusive and should be done only when necessary and certainly not as a matter of routine. In some countries, notably Germany, it is illegal for a company to monitor private communications and so many companies have had no option but to ban staff from using corporate systems for personal purposes. However, the

German law is generally an exception rather than the norm, and companies in all countries must be aware that banning personal use of the email system does not legitimize routine monitoring of what remains, i.e. all business–related messages.

▶ FUNDAMENTAL FIVE

Your action points for this chapter:

1. Consider implementing a training programme to ensure that all employees are aware of the dangers of unsolicited email messages and attachments. ☐

2. You must never reply to spam. Ensure that everyone knows this. ☐

3. Never open an email attachment unless you are confident that it is safe. ☐

4. Consider investigating the use of encryption to ensure the confidentiality of private email communications. ☐

5. Ensure that staff are aware of the rules when using the company's email system for sending and receiving personal communications. ☐

18

The Curse of Spam

A ccording to Symantec, which provides a filtering service for its corporate subscribers, the company is detecting and removing more than 2 billion spam messages every week. It's said that spam represents 60% of all internet email. Microsoft, which owns the Hotmail service, claims that its filters remove more than 3 billion spam messages from its members' mailboxes every day. Anyone who tells you that spam isn't a problem is either lucky or lying.

Unsolicited email costs us all dearly in real financial terms, not to mention the fact that it's often grossly offensive. Take a company with 1500 employees. If each of them spends just one minute per day deleting the spam from their mailbox, that's three man-years of wasted time every year. Companies who sell anti-spam software love to point out statistics such as this, to persuade you that their product will pay for itself in no time. This is entirely untrue, of course, because if the spammers all disappeared tomorrow our mythical company wouldn't be able to consequently make three members of staff redundant. However, there's no doubt that spam is a major inconvenience even if not a tangible cost.

In addition to being irritating and offensive, spam can also cause a denial of service. In April 2005, the head of Greater Manchester Police in northern England was subjected to a spam attack. At its peak, Mike Todd was receiving 2000 emails an hour. Some were personally offensive and threatening, others were faked so they appeared to originate from George W. Bush. The major inconvenience was that legitimate, important messages might have been lost among the detritus. Presumably, someone had to be employed to sift the huge quantity of messages rather than merely deleting everything and waiting for the attack to die down.

Could your email system could cope with such an attack? If not, now is the time to consider what you might do to reduce the impact that such an attack might have upon your critical systems and your ability to continue working.

Detecting Spam

There are various products, services and techniques that can help reduce the amount of spam that arrives in your employees' mailboxes. You're probably already employing at least one of these techniques, but there's no harm in deploying two or more. The primary methods for spam reduction are:

- Sign up to an external service that retrieves all of your company's email, removes the spam, then forwards the remaining non-spam messages to a separate address. It is this address that you connect to in order to read your mail. One major player in this market is Messagelabs (`www.messagelabs.com`). Another is Brightmail, now owned by Symantec.

- Install some spam detection software on your corporate mail server to remove or mark spam before it arrives in your employees' mailboxes. One such product is Spam Assassin, which is available free of charge. The Web pages at `http://spamassassin.apache.org/tests.html` contain a list of all the tests that Spam Assassin performs, and the weighting that it gives each result, in order to determine whether a message should be regarded as spam. Usefully, details of the deciding factors are added to the header of each message so that, if you choose to examine your spam once it has arrived in your filtered mail folder, you can find out precisely why it was classified as such.

- Run software on your users' desktops that removes spam. Cloudmark (**www.cloudmark.com**) makes one of the best-known programs of this type, which works in an innovative way. If a user regards a certain item in his mailbox as being spam, he clicks a button to notify the Cloudmark servers. Once a few people have done this, and thus it is clear that this message is indeed spam, the Cloudmark database of known-spam messages is updated to include this message and it will automatically be removed from the mailboxes of all other Cloudmark subscribers.

- If you use Microsoft Exchange Server 2003 or above, and Microsoft Outlook 2003 or above on your PCs, this product has extensive anti-spam features built in. If you haven't already investigated them, it's well worth doing so.

- Whatever email client you use on staff desktops, most have the ability to create rules that will isolate or delete messages that contain certain words. You can create a very basic spam detector by searching for words such as sex, Viagra, Cialis, and any other terms that crop up regularly in your unwanted mail.

Spammers go to great lengths to avoid their offerings being deleted or marked as spam. The most common technique is to ensure that every message appears unique and thus difficult to identify as a mass-mailing. Early versions of spam-sending software used to do this by sprinkling a handful of random words (from a built-in dictionary included with the software) into each message. Later techniques included adding basic thesaurus functionality to the software, so while one recipient might be offered huge erections another might be offered a large building. Which just goes to show that thesaurus-based spamming doesn't always work.

Spammers also buy lists of email addresses from dishonest insiders. In the summer of 2005 an employee of AOL was jailed for 15 months after he admitted selling a database of 92 million AOL users' email addresses to spammers for $28,000. It is estimated that his actions resulted in seven billion spam emails being sent to AOL subscribers.

Because spammers are so sophisticated, keeping on top of the problem is not always easy. Being able to detect spam requires you to keep an up-to-date database of known spam messages, in a similar way that antivirus companies must continually revise their list of virus signatures.

Prevention's Better than Cure

By far the best way to avoid spam is to keep your company's email addresses off the databases that spammers use. This is easier said than done, however. I've seen cases where someone has created a brand new email account on a public server such as Hotmail and has started receiving spam within an hour. Of course Hotmail and other similar services such as Gmail offer spam filtering, but it was still fascinating to see that the spam folder started to accumulate content so quickly.

There are a few useful tips that you should follow if you want to help keep your company's email addresses away from the spammers:

- When allocating new email addresses to staff, it helps to include non-standard characters such as digits. An address such as `john.smith63@yourcompay.com` is less likely to be generated by a random address generator than plain old john.smith.

- Ensure that all staff are informed that they should never reply to a spam message. Not even to complain about its content or to request removal from the spammer's database. In almost all cases, clicking on the 'remove me from your database' link merely identifies that the spammer has found an active email address which gets read, and the amount of spam sent to that address will multiply very quickly as it gets passed among the spamming fraternity.

- Configure your company's email server so that, if anyone has an Out Of Office message turned on, the server will only send it to addresses within the organization and not to external addresses. This has the downside of not informing external people that the recipient is out of the office, of course, but aids security (it's not a good idea for everyone to know who's not at their desk) and will avoid the situation where your company's mail server responds to every spam message which arrives in the mailboxes of people who are on holiday.

■ Ensure that staff do not use their company email addresses to submit entries to spammer-heavy parts of the internet such as Internet Relay Chat (IRC), Web-based discussion forums or Usenet newsgroups. Encourage them to create non-company email addresses for such things, using free systems such as Hotmail, Gmail or Yahoo. If you need an email address for a one-off purpose, such as registering to download a piece of shareware, `www.mailinator.com` is worth knowing about. Simply make up any email address (e.g. `robert@mailinator.com`) and specify this when the shareware's site asks for it. To retrieve your mail, e.g. if the site is going to email a password to you before you can download your shareware, just go to mailinator.com, type 'robert' into the box, and there's your mail. No registration required, nor passwords. Which does, of course, mean that you can read other people's mail by typing in common names. A great way to pass an afternoon if you're feeling bored, and perfectly legal. Well, probably.

■ Spammers generate lists of email addresses by harvesting them from Web sites. If your company's Web site contains any email addresses, such as contact addresses for customer services or named staff, you can bet that the spammers will find them using their automated tools. A handy way around this is to use a Javascript program on your Web pages to display an email address. The end result is that the person viewing your site still sees the address, but the source code of the page contains not a valid recognizable email address (i.e. a string of characters with an @ symbol in the middle) but a chunk of Javascript code. For example, if you place the following code in a Web page it will display a clickable mail link which will send me an email if you click it:

```
<SCRIPT language=javascript>
<!--
var username = "robert.schifreen";
var hostname = "gmail.com";
```

```
var linktext = username + "@" + hostname;
document.write("<a href=" + "mail" + "to:" + username +
"@" + hostname + ">" + linktext + "</a>")
//-->
</SCRIPT>
```

Developments

Although technology has yet to come up with a guaranteed method to block all spam, new ideas are constantly being developed. One such idea, already in widespread use, is for the owners of domains names to be able to specify which IP addresses are permitted to send email that appears to originate from their domain. When an email is received, the receiving system can then look up the details in a central database and, if the IP address of the sender is not listed as being authorized to send mail from that domain, the message is assumed to be spam, and it can be flagged or deleted.

There are two competing technologies in this arena. One is from Microsoft and is known as Sender ID (see **www.microsoft.com/ senderid**). The other is called SPF, or Sender Policy Framework (**spf.pobox.com**).

The Future of Spam

Despite the best efforts of the companies that produce anti-spam software, not to mention the improvements that continue to be added by Microsoft to Windows and to Exchange Server, the concept of unsolicited electronic communications isn't going to become a thing of the past. It's a cost-effective marketing and sales tool, even if only because the very low costs associated with the technique mean that response rates can be incredibly low and yet still result in a profit for the spammer.

If techniques such as Sender ID mean that hijacking someone else's computer become technically impossible, spammers will still find other ways to spread their message. Legitimate bulk-email companies already exist, and a surprisingly high number of respectable big-name companies use their services to send messages to customers by email and by cellphone text message. Many countries already have opt-in legislation that prevents such companies from sending information to anyone who has not explicitly consented to receiving marketing information in this way, but the loopholes and deceptive practices are already widely understood and will continue to be exploited. For example, when did you last see a credit card application form where the main sales text was the same size as the 'tick this box if you don't want to receive opportunities from carefully-selected business partners' section?

New technology will also add to the arsenal of opportunities available to electronic marketers. VoIP, or Voice over IP, allows us to make free telephone calls using the internet. The technology to distribute audio spam in this way is simple. Although some companies already use automatic telephone diallers linked to audio playback systems to place cold sales calls to potential customers ('you have won a free holiday – press 9 if you want to speak to an operator'), use of such systems will only increase if the cost of making each call reaches zero.

Most marketing managers expect a response rate of around 1 or 2% to a traditional printed mail shot. Use the internet and you can still make a profit on a rate of 0.01% because the fixed costs are so low and there's an almost infinite supply of email addresses to continually bombard. Databases of such addresses are incredibly cheap to buy – just a few hundred dollars for tens of millions of addresses. And if the address doesn't exist, you haven't wasted the cost of some paper, envelope and a postage stamp.

Summary

Even conservative estimates put the amount of spam on the internet at around 50% of all email, which amounts to tens of billions of messages every week. Thankfully there are a number of steps that you can take to reduce the amount of spam that your staff encounter such as signing up to an external filtering service, or installing software on your own servers or workstations.

There are also steps that you must take to ensure that spammers don't manage to obtain details of your company's email addresses. Obfuscate the email addresses that appear on your Web site, and don't post real addresses on public discussion forums.

But most importantly, you must never reply to spam. Sometimes the temptation to reply is great, and the spammers know this. They use clever psychological techniques, such as the 'you have been subscribed to the Big Gay Cocks email list – click here to unsubscribe' message that I received recently. The more offensive and worrying the message, the more likely that recipients will click the link to request removal, and thus the longer the vicious circle will be perpetuated.

FUNDAMENTAL FIVE

Your action points for this chapter:

1. Ensure that you have anti-spam systems in place to help reduce the amount of unwanted email being received by your employees. ☐

2. Educate employees in the best way to deal with spam, i.e. never to open the messages nor to reply to them. ☐

3. Never reveal your real email address in a public discussion forum or newsgroup – set up a temporary address on a system such as Hotmail. ☐

4. Use obfuscation techniques such as Javascript to prevent spammers from harvesting addresses from your Web site. ☐

5. Everyone hates spam, and everyone hates spammers. Make sure that your marketing people are never tempted to use email as a marketing tool. ☐

19

Viruses

Computer viruses are a major nuisance and cause huge amounts of damage. They delete files from users' computers or email confidential data to the world at large, and they install programs which allow hackers, spammers and perpetrators of Distributed Denial of Service attacks to enter the machine at will. And crucially, having done its damage, the virus then attempts to copy itself to other computers via email or via the victim's own network. It is this copying or cloning which defines the program as a true virus. A program which merely deletes files or installs a back door but which doesn't subsequently try to copy itself to other computers is known as a Trojan Horse. Not, of course, that those whose computers are infected by trojans or viruses tend to care about the precise etymology of their affliction as they watch their files being deleted.

While the vast majority of viruses affect only Windows PCs, users of other hardware and software platforms such as Linux, Macintosh, PDAs and even mobile phones are not immune. There are real viruses in circulation that affect each of these platforms, and the risk to Linux and Mac machines increases greatly if you run a Windows emulator such as WINE. As a general rule, all computers should be running antivirus software. Better safe than sorry, as they say.

What Viruses Can Do

Although a program merely has to attempt to spread copies of itself to other computers to qualify as an official virus, the vast majority of viruses do other things in addition to this. In most cases these additional actions are malicious, done purely because the sick mind of the cyber-vandal who wrote the program or adapted it from an existing one thought it might be fun. The concept of a 'good virus' has occasionally been mooted by IT experts, such as a program which spreads among computers searching for problems on those machines and automatically fixing them without needing to concern the users. Widespread distrust by the world of corporate IT soon put an end to such suggestions and no such schemes currently exist, to the best of my knowledge.

Among the malicious actions which viruses commonly carry out on infected computers are the following. As to which would be most damaging to your company, only you can decide:

▰ Installing a spamming back-door or robot (also known as a bot). This is a facility that allows spammers to connect to the infected computer at will, in order to send spam via the user's email account. One of the major obstacles affecting all spammers is that they require a constant supply of email accounts from which to send their messages, because commercial email service providers will close down any account that they discover is being used to send spam. By installing sophisticated back door software on PCs through viruses, the spammers always have a continuous supply of email servers and accounts to exploit.

▰ Distributed Denial of Service Attack zombie bots. A Denial of Service Attack (see Chapter 30) is a hacking technique that involves crashing a computer by flooding it with more requests than it can handle.

To be most effective, such an attack must originate from more than one source in order that the flooding can be as heavy as possible and difficult to trace. The best way to do this is to program lots (like, tens of thousands) of individual computers around the world to attack the target simultaneously on a given date. To do this, the attackers create a virus that turns an infected PC into a sleeping (zombie) participant in a forthcoming attack. Once the virus is installed, the zombie is able to respond to commands from the perpetrators of the attack and start sending out requests to the victim. When the creators of the virus have managed to infect sufficient computers, they send out a signal via the internet and all of the zombie robots (bots, in hacker-speak) spring into life. The target system doesn't stand a chance.

■ Send or delete files. The virus scans the victim's hard disk in search of particular files, and either deletes them or emails them to the creators of the virus. Or in some cases, uploads them to a hacker Web site for the world to see.

■ Install a remote-access back door. The virus installs a program that allows hackers to connect to the infected computer at will, to use its facilities and copy its files. One famous remote-access program created by hackers a few years ago was named Back Orifice, as a pun on Microsoft's business software suite called Back Office. Among the less harmful facilities offered to remote users was the ability to open and close the CD drive drawer remotely. Hardly of major concern, though it did confuse a lot of people at the time.

■ Install a keystroke logger. This is a program that logs every key that a user presses, and stores it in a file on the hard disk for subsequent retrieval. Keystroke loggers are extremely useful in the corporate world when the need arises to discreetly investigate a staff member who is suspected of misusing their computer. Such programs are also used by hackers and virus-writers to steal passwords, and viruses are often the vehicle that is used to install them. Once the file of recorded keystrokes is retrieved, it can be used to gain unauthorized access to confidential computer systems and online banking facilities.

■ Install a screen grabber. Operators of secure systems, especially online banking facilities, have attempted to counter the deployment of keystroke loggers by switching to other forms of input for authentication. For example, instead of having to type in a password, the user has to select each letter in turn from a series of menus and boxes that must be clicked with the mouse. This defeated the keystroke loggers, but it wasn't long before the criminals programmed their way out of the situation by switching to screen-grabbers that record a continuous movie of the screen's contents rather than simply logging keystrokes.

All of these actions are carried out by real viruses that exist now. It's highly possible that at least one action from the list above is happening on a computer in your company right now, if you can't guarantee that all machines are running antivirus software and that the software has been updated on every machine within the last couple of days. The only way to know for sure is to run antivirus software. If you have your suspicions that a machine is infected but your antivirus software says otherwise, there's no harm in running another antivirus product too. However, most operating systems (including Windows) don't like having two such programs installed, so uninstall one and reboot the machine before installing the other.

How Viruses Spread

If an infected computer is connected to a LAN or WAN, the virus may attempt to use the network to seek out other computers. This depends upon the network configuration and access privileges. Remember that a virus is just like any other program and so can only do what it is permitted to do by the operating system. The virus will be running under the same user ID as the person who is currently logged in so, if that person has administrative privileges, the virus will have more avenues open to it than if it was running under a restricted user's account.

While many viruses try to spread, or cause damage, via a network connection, the most common way that viruses travel between computers is through email. This is in contrast to the early days, a decade ago, when they spread by copying themselves to the boot sector of whatever floppy disk was in the A: drive. When that disk was used to boot another computer, or when an infected disk was accidentally left in a drive while the computer was being rebooted, the virus would execute. The demise of floppy drives has rendered such methods obsolete and none of the major viruses in circulation today employs this technique.

Spreading by email is easy. The virus simply scans the hard disk of the computer on which it resides, looking for email addresses in documents and other files. Because so many people in medium and large companies use Microsoft Outlook for their email and their contact book, a common technique is to scan the Outlook address book and send the virus to everyone in it. The recipients will get an attachment that appears to come from someone they know and will therefore trust it. Especially if the attachment is accompanied by a message from the recipient's contact that says something like 'Here's that picture you wanted' or 'try this – you'll love it'. So the recipient clicks on the attachment, the virus program runs, and the process starts again on yet another machine.

While installing antivirus software is of course a very important way to prevent a computer from falling prey to a virus, an equally important line of defence is never to click on an attachment unless you are confident that it is from a trusted source. Ensure that all your staff know this. Antivirus software is not 100% effective, especially against new viruses that the scanner is as yet unable to recognize. Therefore, you must regard the education of users as highly as installing antivirus software on their computers.

Microsoft is, thankfully, slowly taking steps to help prevent viruses spreading via Outlook and Windows. Recent versions of Outlook will alert the user if a program appears to be making multiple attempts to look up information in the address book, or if a program is trying to add itself to the registry to instruct Windows to automatically load and run the program each time the computer is turned on. All of this is a great help in the ongoing fight, but don't get complacent. Without proper antivirus software running on all workstations and Windows-based servers, and some basic ongoing education for all your users, your company will fall prey to a virus attack at some point. It's a fact of life in the information age.

How to Avoid Infection

According to the purveyors of antivirus software, viruses aren't a problem. Assuming that you install their software, of course. Because once you have done so, they say, you can relax in the knowledge that all of your company's computers are protected. Sadly, of course, it doesn't work like that. Even if you install antivirus software on all the PCs in your company, and configure the software to update itself regularly, you will still suffer from viruses. Among the reasons for this which I have personally encountered among my clients are:

- A visitor such as a sales rep or external consultant brings an infected laptop onto company premises, connects it to the corporate network, and it immediately starts attempting to locate other machines to infect.

- Staff or engineers, in contravention of the company's rules, install a new PC and don't get around to installing the antivirus software straight away. During this time, the computer becomes infected.

- A fault with a PC or its access permissions prevents it from downloading antivirus software updates.

- An engineer or support technician sets up a new PC, installs the antivirus software, then connects it to the corporate network to download the latest Windows security patches and antivirus updates. Before the updates can be installed, the PC gets infected.

- One or more computers become infected by a new virus that the antivirus software is not yet able to detect or remove.

Let's take each of these in turn, and see how we can avoid these common situations occurring within your company.

First, visitors. Never allow visitors to connect their computer to your network unless you can be sure that it's fully loaded with all important Windows security fixes and up-to-date antivirus software. If you fail to do this, you risk infecting one or more of your company's machines within seconds of the visitor's machine being plugged in. There's always a risk that one or more computers on your employees' desks won't yet be running the latest updates, and these will be easy targets for a laptop which is continually attempting to contact other machines on whatever network it happens to be connected to.

If you trust your visitors' honesty and technical abilities the authorization process might require nothing more than asking a question and blindly accepting the answer. If you need proof then a software solution is called for. One easy answer is to make up a CD-ROM or a read-only USB flash drive containing basic antivirus software and the Microsoft Baseline Security Analyzer. Use this to check the computer. A Web search for McAfee Stinger will lead you to a useful free utility that will detect and remove many of the most common viruses.

Next, computers that haven't yet had antivirus software installed. Computers without up-to-date antivirus software must never be connected to the network. This is easier said than done, as it is clearly convenient when setting up a new PC to install the standard utilities such as antivirus software from a CD (which might well be out of date) and then to connect the computer to the internet so that it can update itself. You should never do this, and never allow any employee or technician or engineer to do it, because the computer will be at increased risk from infection until the updates are installed and active.

All antivirus companies provide their updates in stand-alone form that can be downloaded via another computer and transferred via CD or a USB flash drive. If you use McAfee, for example, you need to download the latest SuperDAT file from the company's Web site and run it on the new computer. Once you have done this, the new machine can be connected safely to the network and will keep itself up to date from now on. Although this adds maybe 10 minutes to the time taken to set up a new PC with your standard collection of application and utilities, it will save a great deal of time in the long run.

Faults that prevent a computer from updating its antivirus software are common, especially in corporate environments where access permissions are usually configured so that most staff are unable to install new software or tinker with the workings of the computer. I have seen cases where this has led to problems with antivirus updates because the installation of the software didn't have the necessary permission to install updates. Most big-name antivirus software vendors have corporate versions of their software which are designed to get around this problem, and also provide additional reporting capabilities so that your IT support people can easily check when each PC in the company last had its antivirus signatures updated. Some include 'push' technology so that, if a new dangerous virus is discovered, you can force all of your PCs to update their antivirus software immediately rather than waiting for the next scheduled update. These corporate editions are essential if you are managing more than a few dozen PCs, otherwise it becomes impossible to keep track of whether each PC is running the correct version of the software and is free of viruses. Major players in this arena include ePolicy Orchestrator (ePO) from McAfee and the Kaspersky Administration Kit. There are others too – you can read about them, and much more besides, on the excellent www.itsecurity.com site.

Sometimes a new PC can become infected between the time that it is first connected to the internet and when it finally downloads all the critical Windows updates that it needs. This is a real problem that causes trouble in most companies, and it will affect yours too if you don't actively take steps to avoid it. A good example of why such precautions are needed is the Blaster virus, which was released in early 2004 and affected millions of computers around the world. Very few antivirus products were able to prevent infection by this virus, even after it had been identified and the antivirus vendors had updated their software, because it exploited a bug in Windows to spread. The only way to prevent infection was to install a Microsoft security patch, which had actually been issued six months beforehand, but which had been ignored by many companies who had failed to realize its significance.

This event spurred Microsoft into action, and the current version of Windows XP (Service Pack 2) changes the default settings so that updates are automatically downloaded and installed unless the user chooses otherwise. This was not the case in the original XP release. This is good news, but there are still occasional problems in a corporate environment if users don't have the necessary access privileges to install software (and thus security patches) on their computers. If this is the case in your company then it should be fixed as soon as possible, and not by granting increased privileges to users. Check out, for example, Microsoft's Server Update Services (previously known as Software Update Services), which is a free add-on to Windows 2000 Server or Windows 2003 Server that allows you to host your own master copy of Windows updates on your own network in such a way that users don't need administrative privileges to keep their machines up to date.

All major antivirus products work by using a virus signature database, and the ability of the product to detect and remove viruses will only ever be as good as this database. The database tells the program how to recognize each virus and how to remove it. Most antivirus vendors also include heuristic detection techniques in their software, which attempts to spot and block virus–like behaviour (such as a program trying to send email or access the computer's address book). Heuristics rarely works as well as using a signature database, but it does provide a useful extra layer of security so you should not disable the feature if it's available.

Additional Actions

There are other things that you should consider to help keep your company's computers virus-free. After all, it's not just your organization that will suffer. Consider the consequences of someone within your company inadvertently sending out a virus to one or more of your largest customers. At best they will be fairly unhappy. At worst, they'll want legal redress and will stop being a customer.

Ironically, one useful tip is to disable one of Windows's security features that were originally designed to help users stay safe. System Restore is a feature of all recent versions of Windows that automatically restores any key system file if it is accidentally deleted by the user. An amusing side-effect of this feature is that, if a virus is detected in a key file and your antivirus software attempts to remove the virus, System Restore will notice that the contents of the key file has changed and will helpfully put back the virus. This catches out a lot of support technicians who can't understand why their efforts to remove a virus infection are continually failing.

Testing Antivirus Software

How can you be sure that your antivirus software and procedures are working? Clearly you don't want to risk the deliberate introduction of a virus into your network. The answer is to use the EICAR test virus, developed by the European Institute for Computer Antivirus Research. This is a file that, while totally harmless, will be detected by most major antivirus programs. The test file was specially designed to contain no special characters. This makes it easy to reproduce in printed form, so here it is:

```
X5O!P%@AP[4\PZX54(P^)7CC)7}$EICAR-STANDARD-ANTIVIRUS-TEST-FILE!$H+H*
```

Type this file using a text editor such as Notepad (or download it from the Web by typing 'eicar test' into your search engine). Save the file as eicar.com and you should find that your antivirus program springs into action whenever you subsequently attempt to open, run or copy it. Not only does this test that your virus detection is working, you can also test additional features such as deleting or quarantining infected files, or ensuring that email warnings are correctly sent to your administrators. If you're feeling particularly devious, you may also wish to try emailing it to some of your users as an attachment and see just how many of them decide to report that their antivirus software has detected something.

Hoaxes

While some cyber-vandals get their kicks by programming and releasing viruses, others enjoy causing panic or inconvenience by creating hoaxes. For example, one of your staff might receive an email along the lines of:

> "Microsoft and AOL today warned all customers that a new, highly dangerous virus has been discovered which will erase all your files at midnight. If there's a file called hidserv.exe on your computer, you have been infected and your computer is now running a hidden server that allows hackers to access your computer. Delete the file immediately. Please also pass this message to all your friends and colleagues as soon as possible."

Of course it's a hoax. Despite its suspicious name, hidserv.exe is actually part of Windows. It's the Human Interface Device Service, which looks after various hardware items such as the special function keys on certain keyboards. But in their eagerness to help keep this 'virus' at bay, and because you've educated your staff in basic security awareness techniques, employees will try to be helpful and will forward the hoax to as many people as they can think of.

You can help avoid the inconvenience caused by such hoaxes by informing all staff that they must forward warnings to the IT helpdesk and no one else. If the help desk staff are unsure as to whether a message is genuine, there are some useful Web sites which can provide guidance. One is at www.symantec.com/avcenter/hoax.html. Also, www.virusportal.com contains lots of useful information about viruses.

If you're not sure whether something is a hoax, select a phrase from the email and type it into a Web search engine such as Google. This will point you to any sites on which the message is being discussed. This technique is also useful for dealing with unknown error messages produced by any software application – type some key words into a search engine and you'll probably find that someone has encountered the error before you and worked out what it means.

A Word about Platforms

The great majority of computer viruses are written specifically to infect Windows-based desktop and laptop computers, because virus-writers tend to dislike Microsoft's domination of the operating system market and want to damage the company's standing among its customers. Plus, the typical virus-writer is more likely to have access to a Windows-based computer than one which runs anything else.

Viruses for other platforms do appear. A handful of examples exist for most of the smartphone and PDA platforms, and there are a few native Linux and Macintosh viruses. Some viruses manage to infect across multiple platforms too. Those which are written in the form of Microsoft Word macros can infect not just PCs but also Macs. And even Linux machines, if a Windows emulator such as WINE is being used to run the Windows version of Word under Linux.

Many of the major antivirus software vendors market a version of their product for platforms including Linux, Palm OS, Mac, and Microsoft Windows Mobile. If you use such devices within your company, your antivirus strategy should include ensuring that all of these machines are equipped with antivirus software and that it is regularly updated . . . even if only to prevent infected files travelling between PCs on mobile devices.

The Future

As the internet continues to govern our lives, there is no limit to what future viruses might do in order to annoy or defraud victims. It's probably only a matter of time before viruses start using our credit cards to book holidays or order groceries without our knowledge. To protect against the constant threat, ensuring that all your computers and servers use antivirus software is essential.

FUNDAMENTAL FIVE

Your action points for this chapter:

1. Make sure that every workstation, server and laptop has up-to-date antivirus software installed. ☐

2. Make sure that all your antivirus software is configured to update itself at least once per week. ☐

3. Ensure that your antivirus software is configured so that you will receive immediate notification of any virus that is discovered on one of your company's computers. ☐

4. Configure your antivirus software so that you can verify that all computers are being updated properly. ☐

5. Ensure that you have procedures in place to prevent someone with an infected machine, or a machine that doesn't have antivirus software installed, connecting that computer to your company network. ☐

Spyware, Adware and Rogue Diallers

Windows is a multi-tasking operating system, which means that it can run more than once program at once. In the case of a machine with a single CPU this isn't technically true, of course. The reality is that the system switches rapidly between each application thousands of times each second to give the impression that multiple applications are running. When Microsoft's marketing people boast about multi-tasking, the implication is that each task is a major application such as Word, Excel, Photoshop, Internet Explorer and so on. There's a further implication that, if no applications are running, Windows is merely twiddling its tiny electronic thumbs in anticipation and doing little else. In reality, this is not true.

Press Ctrl–Alt–Del and select the Task Manager, then click on the Processes tab. This will list all of the background programs currently running to keep the system operating correctly. As I write, there are 32 of them, each competing with my word processor for the attention of my single Pentium 4 processor. Discovering the details about each of these is not easy, as the name of the process as displayed by Task Manager doesn't always provide sufficient clues to identify its purpose or the name of the application with which it is associated. The Web can help here, and `www.liutilities.com/products/wintaskspro/ processlibrary/` is well worth a look if you're trying to play the process detective.

Of the applications and processes that run on PCs without the knowledge or permission of the computer's user or owner, viruses are the most dangerous and the least desirable. But spyware and adware must also be considered. We will consider them together because they originate from similar sources and the techniques for removing them are similar.

Like viruses, spyware and adware come under the umbrella heading of malware. That is, software that you wouldn't install if you actually had the choice. But crucially, because spyware and adware are not true viruses (they don't attempt to copy themselves to other computers) they are not detected by traditional antivirus software. Therefore you need to obtain and install (and keep updating) separate software on all your company's computers to avoid the quite considerable risks that these programs can pose.

Spyware is the generic name for software that spies on the computer user's activities. Some spyware is designed to provide information and feedback for marketing purposes. For example, when a user installs a printer driver, an additional spyware component might send regular reports via the internet to the manufacturer of the printer to report how many pages have been printed. Lexmark was discovered to be doing just this in 2004 (type Lexmark Spyware into your Web search engine for the full details). Although such information can be incredibly useful for marketing purposes, it is also intrusive, and too much spyware on a computer can start to slow down the machine as it struggles to cope with all the additional programs that it is being forced to run.

Another sign of a PC full of spyware or adware, in addition to a possible slowdown, is that settings sometimes appear to change without warning. A common adware tactic is to change the user's internet home page to that of the company being promoted, and to install a small program which ensures that the new setting is put back even if the user notices it and resets his home page to his preferred choice. Other symptoms include unexpectedly high levels of network activity on a modem or broadband connection as the spyware 'phones home' to report its results or to download additional components, additional sites being added to the user's list of bookmarked sites, and the hijacking of results from search engines in order to display sites other than those which might have been expected.

Some spyware is even more intrusive than a curious printer driver. It might, for example, monitor all of the Web sites that a user visits, or examine all the applications that are installed on the user's PC, and feed this back to all the companies whose marketing people have paid the makers of the spyware for regular reports. Even more dangerous is spyware which monitors the passwords that you type into online banking Web sites and transmits the details to hackers, who can then empty your accounts. Such programs are the key tools of those who engage in identity theft.

Some companies wrongly assume that adware and spyware is harmless and that, if anyone's going to force their staff to read ads, those ads might as well be relevant. Such an attitude is ill-advised, because the statistics gathered by adware can be highly detrimental to a company's reputation. A few years ago, for example, playboy.com revealed the name of the company whose employees were making the most visits to its Web site during working hours. The answer was IBM.

Differences

Adware is generally less dangerous than spyware, but still a nuisance. Adware programs monitor activity on the affected computer to display advertising at various times (mostly, but not always, while the user is using the Web). They don't 'spy', as such, because no information is sent back to the adware supplier.

For example, if the adware program notices that the user frequently visits online bookstores, it might pop up adverts for other book stores on the user's screen. It silently downloads these adverts via the internet and then displays them on the screen whenever it judges that this will have the most impact. Or if the user frequently downloads MP3 music files from illicit sites, the adware might display ads for legitimate providers of downloadable tracks.

Adware and spyware doesn't magically appear. At some point the user has to be duped into initiating the process of running the installer or setup utility in order for the adware or spyware to be installed on their computer.

One method is to send the program as an email attachment or via an instant messaging client (i.e. a Trojan horse). But if the adware or spyware can be bundled into another program, namely one that the user actively downloads and installs, the spyware or adware has an easy ride. And this is generally what happens. Whenever one of your users installs free software, there's a high chance that they will also be choosing to install one or more spyware or adware programs too. Sometimes this is made clear in the licence agreement that the user clicks on to indicate that they accept the terms, although the details rarely appear near the top of the document so remain unseen except by those who have the foresight to scroll down to the end.

Among the categories of programs that include spyware or adware, clients for accessing file-sharing networks come top of the list. After all, those who run the networks have to make their money somehow, and generally they do it by selling advertising and promising the advertisers that their ads will be carefully targeted. Yet another reason not to allow staff to download software and install it without permission.

Spyware is also prevalent in browser plug-ins, such as custom toolbars or animated cursors. Some spyware programs even take the form of installers which use your internet connection during idle time to download and install additional programs once the small initial program has been activated.

While most spyware can be deleted by simply removing one or more entries from the PC's registry, some are deliberately programmed to be much more difficult to kill off. Among the most notorious of these is CoolWeb-Search, which masquerades as a handy browser-based toolbar but which hijacks the user's Web browser in order to display advertising at every opportunity. While manual removal of CoolWebSearch is tricky in the extreme, there are a multitude of programs that can do the job automatically. Just search the Web. As always, beware of using programs from an untrustworthy source as some of them could contain viruses or additional spyware.

Research carried out by makers of anti-spyware and anti-adware products suggests that at least 70% of the world's PCs are affected by these particular strains of malware. Such infections are not always easy to detect by hand. There may not be an obvious entry, or indeed an entry at all, in the Task Manager's list of currently executing processes. But if you don't run anti-spyware and anti-adware software on all your company's computers it can be almost guaranteed that many computers are suffering.

I was once asked to sort out the computer of a friend of mine, and discovered 378 separate spyware programs in residence. Attempting to remove them all caused so many further problems that the only sensible option was to reformat the hard disk and start again. In July 2005 a survey by Sunbelt Software (**www.sunbelt-software.com**), which markets enterprise anti-spyware products, found that 68% of corporate IT administrators reckoned that spyware was the biggest problem currently affecting their employees' PCs, and that 42% of companies admitted to being unable to control the proliferation of spyware within their organization.

Thankfully, keeping spyware and adware off your company PCs is easy and, even better, cheap. Unlike the antivirus sector, where the market-leading programs all cost money, some of the best-known removers of adware and spyware are free. AdAware (**www.lavasoft.com**) and Spybot Search & Destroy (**www.safer-networking.org**) are used world-wide by millions of satisfied customers, and don't cost a penny. Also highly regarded is PC Tools Spyware Doctor (**www.pctools.com**), although this isn't free.

Unlike viruses, spyware and adware don't corrupt or otherwise alter any files on the hard disk, so removing spyware and adware is much easier. Normally it's just a case of deleting a file from a particular directory and/or removing the entry from the registry that causes that file to be loaded each time Windows is started up. But like antivirus software, spyware and adware removal tools depend on a database of signatures so you must ensure that the software is regularly updated. This is just a case of ticking a box during installation, or manually clicking on the Update Now button before initiating a scan.

Both AdAware and Spybot require some additional configuration if your company's internet access is via a proxy server, otherwise they will attempt to make a direct connection from the PC to the software vendor's update service and this will fail. The documentation supplied with the programs explains how to do this. It's not difficult, but be aware that simply installing the software on users' computers without carrying out this additional stage of the process will result in software that never gets updated.

A small amount of caution is required when you're using anti-spyware programs. Although deleting spyware usually improves a PC's performance, some companies take a dim view of people who remove the revenue-generating component from their software but still wish to continue using it. This sometimes results in certain ad-supported programs refusing to run if the accompanying spyware has been deleted.

Some anti-spyware tools are a little over-zealous in their definition of spyware. Spybot, for example, will warn you about 'Windows Security Center.FirewallOverride' and ask if you wish to remove it. In reality, the program is simply reminding you that you have turned off the Windows XP firewall because the computer runs inside a corporate firewall. This will be a common situation within many large companies, and is perfectly acceptable. Placating Spybot by re-enabling the Windows XP firewall would be a mistake as it's not necessary, and might prevent other features from working (such as existing network shares).

Love it or hate it, the fact is that the internet makes market research easy and more sophisticated than it has ever been, and spyware is at the heart of this. Although intrusive, it's legal in most countries and generally goes undetected. Where once companies had to spent large amounts of money conducting surveys among customers in order to receive results which were far from reliable or trustworthy, now the research can be carried out in much more detail for free and with 100% accuracy. There's no need to telephone the owner of a printer and ask them to estimate how many pages they printed last month, or whether they use the printer's built-in scanner, because the driver software can record this information automatically and send it straight back to the vendor for automatic inclusion in a database.

Developers of Web sites use similarly advanced technology to track the way that visitors use their sites. Through advanced use of staple html technologies such as cookies, they monitor the precise path that visitors take when navigating the site's pages. They can find out not only which pages have been accessed, and how many times, but in what order the stories were read. If the majority of hits to the online sales page for a book come via the reviews page rather than from the publisher's official description, the site's operators will capitalize on this and promote the reviews more heavily. And by continually tweaking the order of the menu items on main menus and measuring the resulting changes in the hit rates, marketers can make sure that their sites are as profitable as possible. Much as we dislike being manipulated and monitored in this way, there's little that we can do to stop it.

Logging and Grabbing

One of the most dangerous classes of spyware is the keystroke logger or screen image grabber. As the names suggest, these programs record all keystrokes typed by the user or regularly grab a copy of the image on the screen. The program then sends these details to a remote site used by hackers, or creates a back door on the infected computer that allows the hackers to access the PC remotely and retrieve the information that has been gathered.

Keystroke loggers and screen grabbers are widely used by technical support and IT security personnel for legitimate purpose, such as troubleshooting problems or investigating staff who are suspected of misusing their computer. One such well-known example is TrueActive (www.winwhatwhere.com). This program costs around £70 and is widely used in the corporate world by investigators. It can record keystrokes or grab screen images, and can record continually or in response to a trigger event. An event can be, for example, the user visiting a specific Web site or receiving an email from a specific person. Needless to say, the makers of TrueActive go to great lengths to ensure that the existence of the program is not obvious to the user of the computer that is being monitored. The program can be installed with a single click (or remotely by network administrators), and doesn't show up in the Windows system tray. It frequently changes the name of the process under which it runs, so anyone looking in the Task Manager for signs of such a program will find nothing suspicious. The sequence of keystrokes required to invoke the program's menu is totally configurable rather than being a known standard.

While such programs have their legitimate uses, hackers obviously have a use for such technology too. It makes identity theft easy, for a start, and because the program captures information before it gets sent to a secure Web site, it gets around the problem of SSL and other forms of encryption that are supposed to prevent our online banking secrets from being accessed by criminals.

One malicious keystroke logger of my acquaintance is so sophisticated that, if you run RegEdit (the Windows registry editor) in an attempt to look for signs of the program's presence, it will remove its entries from the registry so that all appears to be clean. As soon as you exit the registry editor, the keystroke logger puts back its data so that the logger will continue to run when the computer is next restarted.

Where the hacker can gain physical access to a computer, even for just 10 seconds, he has another option available. Rather than installing a keystroke logging program, he can plug in a hardware device instead. To do this he simply unplugs the keyboard cable from the back of the computer, plugs in the device (which looks just like a slightly elongated keyboard plug), and then plugs the keyboard cable into the device. From now on, everything typed on the keyboard will be recorded within the chip that's built into the logger. It's totally undetectable by any software because there's nothing running on the computer. The device simply records the information that passes through it, because it is connected into the cable which links the keyboard to the computer.

These devices (see **www.keyghost.com** for an example) can store up to 2 million keystrokes before they start overwriting old data, which is typically sufficient for up to a year's typing by the average computer user. Once the device is full, the hacker requires another 10-second visit to retrieve the device. He then plugs it into his own computer, starts up a word processor or text editor and types the special password. The key logger recognizes the password and displays the contents of its internal log, ready to be saved to the hacker's hard disk.

In March 2005, the London offices of Japan's Sumitomo Bank were the scene of an attempted £220 million robbery. Rather than donning balaclavas and attempting to hold up a van while brandishing pistols, the robbers chose an altogether more hi-tech route. With the help of a friendly insider, they installed keystroke loggers on some of the bank's computers. This allowed them to find out the passwords used by senior staff for accessing customers' accounts and transferring money. Sadly, the precise details of how the attempted robbery was foiled have not been made public.

Diallers

Rogue dialler programs are neither adware or spyware, but they are certainly malware. They typically arrive on a user's PC in the same way as an adware or spyware utility, but they have a specific purpose that is nothing to do with displaying ads or doing any spying. As the name suggests, the dialler is programmed to instruct the user's modem to dial one or more telephone numbers. These are generally premium-rate numbers, costing upwards of £1 per minute, of which the owner of the number receives a large cut. It is the owners of these numbers who produce and distribute the illicit dialler software, purely for the purposes of generating revenue.

Some dialler utilities re-program the user's internet settings so that all subsequent access to the internet is routed not through their normal service provider, but through a provider which happens to use premium-rate lines. In other cases, the dialler waits until the computer and the phone line are idle and then silently dials the expensive number. It generally takes a month or two for the victim to realize that they have a dialler installed, and this is only when the phone bill arrives. Which in some cases has resulted in a family receiving a bill for thousands of pounds instead of an expected 30 or 40.

Telephone companies are sympathetic to victims of dialler malware, but don't always write off the charges. And nor should they, as it is clearly not their fault. Some, though, offer free software to detect and remove dialler software, and to generate a warning when a program attempts to dial a new number for the first time. In the UK, for example, BT offers such software as a free download from its Web site.

Diallers tend not to affect corporate users, because most large organizations don't use modems for internet access. However, if you do have any PCs with modems (such as ones used for sending faxes) you should ensure that your spyware software is capable of detecting rogue diallers too.

Messenger Popups

Windows includes a facility called the Messenger Service, which allows applications to pop up messages on the screen of any computer. Despite the misleading name, this is nothing to do with MSN Messenger or any other instant messaging system. It's designed for use by software and by network administrators. For example, an antivirus program running on a server might detect a virus in an email message that was sent by a specific user, and wish to alert that user quickly. Or a network administrator might need to shut down a server at short notice for urgent maintenance, in which case he could use the messenger service to pop up a warning on all his users' screens so that they were aware of the impending downtime.

Unfortunately, the messenger service works over the internet and spammers use it to send advertising in the form of popups. These popups then appear on users' screens, regardless of what application they happen to be using at the time. So long as they have an internet connection available, there is no need for them to have a Web browser open in order to see the ads.

Preventing messenger popups can be done in two ways. The sledge-hammer approach is to disable the messenger service on the computer, which can be done via the Task Manager in Windows. However, this is not always recommended because, in addition to blocking advertising popups, it will block legitimate ones such as the aforementioned warning about network downtime. A better way is to configure your company's firewall so that messages that originate outside of your company are blocked but those that are generated inside your firewall will still reach their intended destination. See `www.stopmessengerspam.com` for more information on this.

▶ FUNDAMENTAL FIVE

Your action points for this chapter:

1. Make sure that all your company's workstations have anti-spyware software installed. It's quite safe to install more than one program on each computer – they don't normally conflict with each other, unlike antivirus programs. ☐

2. Ensure that you, or your users, update their anti-spyware program and perform a full scan at least once a week. ☐

3. Educate users so that they know to contact the IT security department if they suspect that they have some spyware on their computer. ☐

4. To avoid falling prey to rogue diallers on computers that have modems installed, don't connect the modems to the telephone line unless you need to. ☐

5. Familiarize yourself with details of the tasks that appear on the Processes tab in the Windows Task Manager, so that you are prepared if you need to identify a new task that appears on a user's computer. ☐

21

Piracy

I n today's technology-based economy, the content of our computers is more valuable than the contents of our filing cabinets or bank accounts. Digital content and intellectual property is the new currency. Although we own the copyright to much of the data and software that's held on our company's computers, much of it is the intellectual property (known as IP) of other organizations, and we merely have a licence that allows us to use it according to the owner's stipulations. Failure to adhere to those stipulations is generally known as piracy and, in almost all countries, illegal.

Most companies tend to equate piracy with traditional software applications such as Windows, Microsoft Office, Adobe Photoshop, and so on, but in truth it can apply to any computer file. Some examples of such files include:

- Custom fonts

- Graphics or text obtained from someone else's Web site

- Music tracks ripped from CDs and distributed as MP3 files

- Films copied from DVDs and distributed as DivX or XVID files

- Mailing lists licensed for one-time use but illegally re-used

- E-books purchased for a single computer but copied to others

- Web applications licensed for a single site but used on more than one

- Software licensed for use on a single-processor machine but used on a multi-processor computer without payment of the extra fee.

Offenders have always come up with multiple excuses as to why they had no option but to use illegal copies of software within their companies. A common reason was that they needed to evaluate the software but the product's manufacturer didn't offer evaluation copies. The internet has put paid to this as a valid excuse, as just about every software product can now be downloaded in 30-day demo form from the Web.

Another common excuse is that 'Microsoft can afford it'. Which, for a company with a quarterly turnover (revenue) of $10 billion and a profit (income) of £3 billion is undoubtedly true. But, as anti-piracy campaigners point out, that doesn't make it right, and it conveniently excludes all of the smaller companies which can't. Most software companies turn over less in their entire lifespan than Microsoft does in a day.

The software industry spends a great deal of money educating consumers and companies as to the harm which software piracy can bring. They point out that pirated software often contains viruses, doesn't come with any support or guarantee, and can result in both end users and the company's directors being prosecuted. Plus there's the negative publicity and humiliation as the offending company is hauled through the courts and ordered to hand over a large sum of money to the companies that it cheated.

For sound business reasons, major software companies go out of their way to avoid being portrayed as the bad guys, so the anti-piracy education and associated prosecutions are carried out by bodies such as the Business Software Alliance and the Federation Against Software Theft. These are independent industry bodies that are funded by their corporate members. Who are, of course, most of the major software companies.

Preventing Piracy

As with so many facets of IT security, preventing piracy within your organization must be a combination of training and technology. Use training (perhaps as part of your security awareness programme) to explain to users that piracy is illegal, that it is strictly forbidden, that the company takes a very dim view of it, and that anyone caught doing it could bring legal action and associated bad publicity upon themselves and the company.

Providers of licensed material, especially in the corporate market, can now be relatively certain that all users have an internet connection available, and many companies now use this to prevent and/or detect piracy. For example, recent versions of Microsoft Office and Windows require activation within 30 days of installation, otherwise they cease to function properly. Activation involves the program contacting a central server at Microsoft HQ and sending it details of the program's serial number plus a unique ID code to identify the particular PC on which it is installed. If someone else subsequently attempts to register the same copy of the software on a different computer the request will be denied. Similar procedures are employed by other major software companies, including Macromedia and Adobe.

Interestingly, Microsoft doesn't require activation in the case of copies of its software that are used under site-wide licences. It's only designed for consumers and small businesses. Microsoft has admitted to me that this is because it's aware that its larger customers simply wouldn't stand for the inconvenience.

One strange fact about Microsoft's product activation system is that, if you uninstall some software, the record of the installation is not removed from Microsoft's database. If you subsequently reinstall the program on the same computer the system will allow this, but attempts to install it somewhere else may require you having to contact the activation centre by phone and explain that you are not actually a criminal. Thankfully, the latest version of the activation system no longer assumes that a machine with an upgraded hard disk or sound card is a new computer. In the early days, those upgrading their machine were horrified to discover that wiping the hard disk and attempting to reinstall Windows caused the activation system to falsely believe that the operating system was being installed onto an entirely different computer in contravention of the licence agreement.

A trendy buzzword in copy protection right now is DRM, or Digital Rights Management. This is technology that allows the creator of a document or other file (such as a music track or movie) to control how it can be used. Adobe has built DRM into recent releases of Acrobat that allow creators of PDF files to restrict the way that those files can be used. Since the early days of the product, it has been possible to restrict a user's ability to print or amend a PDF file. Nowadays it's also possible to prevent a PDF file being copied, which has allowed Adobe to use Acrobat as a distribution medium for e-books, financial reports, and similar documents. Current versions of Microsoft Exchange have similar facilities, which allow you to send confidential email to people, but to stipulate that it can't be forwarded (except to specified people), printed, and so on.

While the MP3 music file format has no DRM capability, later formats such as Microsoft's .WMA files (Windows Media Audio) do include it. As do .AAC files downloaded from Apple's iTunes service.

Sealed Media (**www.sealedmedia.com**) is a company that specializes in providing advanced DRM for electronic documents. Once you have created a secure document file you can distribute and publicize the encrypted version in the safe knowledge that no one will be able to open it without your electronic permission. To open the file, the recipient has to connect to a 'licence server' every time. The licence server verifies the user's identity through a digital certificate, and then permits the user to use the document in whatever ways you have specified as being valid for that user. For example, you could allow certain users to view the document but not print it, and another group of users to both view and print it. And because the user must contact the license server each time he wishes to view the document, you can retrospectively lock documents by revoking a user's rights. Someone who obtains a copy of the document from a legitimate user will not be able to open it because they won't also have the necessary digital certificate stored on their computer.

In 2005, Microsoft unleashed its latest weapon against software pirates. Those without a properly licensed copy of Microsoft software are denied the ability to download updates and enhancements via Microsoft's Web site. The company makes an exception in the case of critical security updates that could otherwise facilitate the spread of a virus, but all other downloads (including non-critical security enhancements) require verification.

This move by Microsoft, considered as ill-advised by many, means that users of pirated software will fall rapidly behind owners of licensed versions in terms of the facilities available to them. This is yet one more reason why you should urge your users not to make or use unauthorized copies of programs. However, Microsoft's method for ascertaining whether a copy of Windows is genuine (known as Windows Genuine Advantage) was cracked by hackers within 2 days of its launch. The hackers posted a page on the Web that explained how to defeat the system and thus download updates even on a computer running a pirated copy of Windows. This amusing tale highlights an important point: most hackers don't like Microsoft, and most hackers target Microsoft software more than software from any other company. It is therefore a sad fact of life that you need to be extra careful if you use Microsoft software on your servers, especially those connected to the internet.

Indeed, many security consultants specifically advise clients against using Microsoft's Web server software for this reason. It is certainly true that the Web server software market is one of the few sectors that is not dominated by Microsoft (around 20% of Web sites run on Windows servers, compared with around 70% on Unix). The Web site at http://news.netcraft.com is of interest if you want to know more about Web server market share – its Web server survey results are automatically updated each month and there's also a facility that allows you to interrogate any Web site and find out what brand of server software it's running.

Microsoft tries hard to persuade consumers and business users to verify the authenticity of their software and, if they suspect that they have received a pirated copy, to report it to Microsoft. Under the deal, if the user of the suspect software also provides Microsoft with details of where the software was acquired from, and if they certify that the pirated software was acquired unknowingly, Microsoft will replace it with a genuine copy without charge. Those who are unwilling to provide details of the source will be charged a fee for their genuine software.

Installation Keys

While internet-based product activation is becoming common in the software industry, the most prevalent method for protecting software against misuse is still the installation key. Unless the key is checked via the internet (and in most case they are not) there is nothing to prevent the same key being used more than once in order to install a program on more than one computer. Furthermore, those who download evaluation copies of programs from Web sites but who lack a valid registration key in order to remove the restrictions can often find registration keys via certain illegal Web sites. In some cases, they can also download a 'keygen', or key generator, which is a program written by hackers that can generate valid registration keys for a particular product. Or, they can download a small 'crack' program which, when run, disables the part of the program which checks to see whether a key or serial number has been supplied.

You should alert your users to the danger of using keygens, dubious serial numbers and cracks. Not only are they illegal, but the Web sites which host them are notorious sources of viruses and spyware. Intentionally accessing such sites should be regarded as a serious disciplinary offence.

Preventing users from being able to install illegal copies of software is yet another reason why you should never allow users to have administrative access to their Windows PCs. Software installation should be carried out only by authorized personnel, who should be required to verify that the software they install is correctly licensed and logged.

▶ FUNDAMENTAL FIVE

Your action points for this chapter:

1. Ensure that you are aware of all the different types of intellectual property in use within your company, such as software, fonts, graphics and so on. ☐

2. If you allow staff to bring in MP3 music files that they can listen to while working, make them aware that the presence of illegally-copied music on company networks will not be tolerated. ☐

3. Ensure that all staff are aware that software piracy is illegal and that it can cause severe harm to the company's reputation. ☐

4. Ensure that all software installation is performed via a central IT helpdesk function rather than by individual staff, to help in keeping track of software licences. ☐

5. Make staff aware that downloading pirated software, music, e-books, fonts etc from the Internet will lead to immediate and severe disciplinary action. ☐

DANGER**22**

File Sharing and 'P2P'

I n 1999, an 18 year-old student in the US called Shawn Fanning designed and programmed an internet site called Napster. This was the first of a new generation of systems designed to allow users to share files between themselves. The timing was perfect. Music on CD was outselling vinyl, and most computers were equipped with CD-ROM drives which could be used to copy tracks from music CDs and save them on the computer's hard disk as a standard .WAV file. With so many people wanting to store their music in this way, and with most of them rapidly running out of hard disk space, the MP3 compression system was proving a boon – it could compress the typical .WAV file by at least 90% without any noticeable loss in audio quality.

Napster quickly became one of the most popular sites on the internet, as it provided something for which there was a ready market (music) at an attractive price (free). Anyone who wanted to participate could download the Napster software, install it on their PC, and then search by title or artist name from a worldwide database of tens of millions of music tracks. Click on the entry in the search results list, wait a few minutes, and the track arrives on your computer ready to play direct from the hard disk at will.

Shawn Fanning always claimed that his site was not doing anything wrong. He was merely making available a facility to allow users to share files among themselves, he said, and it was not his responsibility if all but a handful of those users chose to use his system to swap copyrighted material rather than items of their own making. The lawyers and the music industry vehemently disagreed, and eventually Napster had no option but to shut down.

A key factor in Napster's downfall was that the site acted as a central database. When a user installed the Napster software on his computer, he was asked to nominate a folder (directory) on the hard disk which would store shared files. Each time the user logged into the system, the software sent details of the contents of that shared folder (file names, artist details, track title etc) to the central server. When another user wanted to search for a track, he would search that central database and, if he then selected a track to download, Napster would copy the track to the person who requested it from the computer of the person who currently had it in their shared files folder.

The lawyers and the music industry successfully argued that, because Napster was acting as a central directory, it could be held responsible for the material being copied. It was impossible for Napster not to know what its system was being used for. In a compromise, Napster agreed to filter its master directory to exclude material from any band that requested the facility. This merely delayed the inevitable full-scale closure.

Napster used a peer-to-peer (P2P) system. Users would download files from each others' computers, in matches that were arranged by the Napster software. Napster could not claim to be ignorant of the type of files being copied. The illegal systems that operate today still use P2P sharing, but manage to avoid the wrath of the lawyers because they no longer operate a central database. Instead, when a user searches for a specific music track or other file, the client software contacts the computer of each logged-in user in turn, in an attempt to locate a match. There is no central database, hence no one for the recording industry to blame. Except individual users.

The recording industry fights back by regularly launching a handful of highly publicized prosecutions against people who have downloaded, or made available for download, large quantities of files using file-sharing sites. Those sites go under names such as eDonkey, BitTorrent, LimeWire, BearShare and Kazaa. Those who prefer to download music without fear have the choice of a number of legitimate providers including Apple's iTunes and, ironically, a new incarnation of Napster. But despite the immense popularity of legal music download sites, and their very reasonable pricing structures, illegal downloads continue. Connect to a site such as Kazaa at peak times and it's common to find upwards of 3 million people online, with half a billion songs available for download.

Scaremongering by the recording industry has deterred few users, and DRM (Digital Rights Management) technology is one good example of why. Illegally-downloaded files can be used as the recipient wishes – they can be played from the computer's hard disk or transferred to a portable MP3 player. In some cases, files downloaded from legitimate services include DRM technology to prevent the files being transferred between multiple devices, or from being copied more than a couple of times. If you stop paying your monthly subscription to the new Napster service, all of the music that you have downloaded becomes inaccessible. A very profitable business model, but also a clear incentive for users to shun legal sites in favour of the illegal ones.

File Types

The illegal file sharing pioneers restricted their activities to audio. But the current crop of file-sharing sites is not so fussy, and allow users to share (and to search specifically for) files that contain video clips, Word documents, PDF files and so on. The market for sharing video over the internet was created almost overnight with the invention of DivX, a compression system which does for video what MP3 did for audio. It allows a full-length movie to be squeezed into a data file of just a couple of hundred megabytes, which can be downloaded in an hour or two by anyone with an unlimited broadband connection at home. Or even more quickly if they do it at the office. DivX allows internet users to swap porn movies, feature films, and TV programmes. It provides a way for fans of TV series to see new episodes of their favourite shows before they become officially available – for example, if a US show is aired in the US many months before it officially airs in Europe.

Bad for Business

Allowing your staff to access file sharing sites from the office is bad for business, regardless of whether the sites are legitimate or not. Employees who spend time downloading files when they should be working will reduce your company's productivity, and there are security issues if they then wish to connect their personal MP3 players or other devices to their office PC in order to transfer the files that they have downloaded. If those files are actually illegal pornography or other undesirable material, both the downloader and the company whose network they were temporarily stored on (i.e. yours) are liable to prosecution. Remember too that one of the most common sources of spyware and adware comes from installing file sharing software.

The nature of the internet means that it will always be used to disseminate information which might otherwise be difficult for people to obtain, perhaps because the decency laws or public opinion differs between countries. Some European countries, for example, include images on late-night television programmes that, if shown in certain middle-Eastern countries, might lead to riots and condemnation. When terrorists beheaded a British captive in 2004, the video was quickly available via the internet for those who knew where to look. But in 2005 a man in Glasgow was jailed for 6 months for causing distress to a woman to whom he showed similar footage. Such unlawful and unethical use of the internet is best kept away from your company, and as the person responsible for IT security it is up to you to do so.

Preventing staff from accessing file sharing sites has other advantages too. It helps to ensure that your internet bandwidth is used sensibly. A handful of users who continue downloading large files will slow down internet access for all other employees. Also, prohibiting employees from storing large downloaded files on corporate hard disks, even if those files were legitimately obtained, will help to reduce the need for additional network storage. When servers become full it's often cheaper to simply plug in another hard drive rather than trying to work out whether all of the files on the existing drive are absolutely necessary to the business. But I know of companies who have gone down this route, only to discover subsequently that a large proportion of the server's storage was actually filled with users' MP3 collections to which they would listen while working.

Possibly the most important reason for banning the use of file-sharing software from your company's computers is the ease with which it can lead to security breaches. Many file sharing programs allow users to search for files by type. Kazaa, for example, lets searchers specify audio, video, images, documents or software. A tick in the 'documents' box and a search for the word "confidential" will bring up all of the private documents which users have inadvertently left in the folder on their hard disk that is configured to be shared with the world.

Downloading software applications from unreliable sources is a dangerous activity, as there is a strong possibility that the downloaded file will contain a virus. Anti-piracy groups such as the Business Software Alliance are not slow to point this out as part of their awareness campaigns. But MP3 and DivX files are safe. They do not contain any executable code and it is thus very difficult to infect them with spyware, viruses and other unwanted programs. This has made the job of educating users as to the dangers of downloading such files much more difficult.

Closing the Doors

As with any prohibited activity in the workplace, implementing and upholding a ban on file sharing sites requires a carefully administered combination of good management and effective technology. Good management means ensuring that everyone is made aware of the ban and, crucially, being told why it is necessary. Explain the risks and consequences to the business as well as to individual staff members if the software were to be inadvertently misconfigured or exploited by hackers.

The technology available to you comes in many forms. First, ensure that your firewall is correctly configured. File sharing programs use a variety of ports to communicate, and if you have followed the golden rule of firewalls (only open ports on an as-needed basis) then these should already be blocked. If you're not sure, now might be a good time to check. Plus, by denying users administrator rights to their desktop PCs you can help to prevent them from installing file sharing applications without your knowledge.

You might also want to scan users' hard disks, as well as the drives on your file servers, to check for suspicious content such as MP3 files. Of course, not all such files are illegal so be careful not to jump to conclusions. Your user might have downloaded a video or audio presentation from a product vendor's Web site.

One useful software tool is Digital File Check, available as a free download from the Web site of the International Federation of the Phonographic

Industry (IFPI), an organization which campaigns against music piracy. The program can locate and delete a range of well–known file sharing programs. If it finds such programs, Digital File Check also examines the contents of the shared folders that they were configured to use, and lists any audio or video files that were found inside them.

▶ FUNDAMENTAL FIVE

Your action points for this chapter:

1. Make sure that your firewall is configured to block employees from accessing P2P file sharing sites unless there is a good reason not to. ☐

2. If you allow staff to copy MP3 files to their computer in order to listen to during working hours, make it clear that these must be legally obtained (e.g. copied from CDs that the employee owns). ☐

3. Do not allow the installation of file-sharing client software on employees' machines. ☐

4. Scan your network server and workstation hard drives occasionally, to look for unauthorized audio or video files. ☐

5. Consider using the Digital File Check utility to detect and remove illegal audio content and to block access to file-sharing software. ☐

23

Backups and Archives

A user just accidentally deleted an important document from his area on the file server? Just recover it from the backup. A hacker replaces the contents of your corporate Web site with porn? No problem – just reach for your backups. A disk crash corrupts your personnel database? Just restore from a backup. The email server stops working after someone makes some changes to its configuration files? No problem. Or is there? Done properly, backups might just save your company's life. Get it wrong, and you'll regret it.

What To Include

A crucial component in any backup strategy is deciding what to back up. Sadly the answer isn't as simple as 'everything' – it depends on the nature of the computer and the information it contains. One early decision is whether to perform a complete or partial backup. A complete backup means copying every file, including hidden areas such as the Windows registry, in such a way that the entire contents and behaviour of the machine can be recreated in the case of total system failure. Such a backup strategy is tempting, because it means that a critical computer can be back up and running quickly with all required connectivity and installed software if, say, the hard disk fails. A useful option in the case of, say, a file or mail server.

But there are drawbacks to this approach. If the machine fails beyond repair, or is stolen or damaged, restoring the contents of a complete Windows installation onto new hardware may well result in the operating system complaining that the hardware has changed and things not working as they should. At the very least, drivers for items such as network cards will need to be reinstalled. At worst, the system will be unusable.

Therefore, consider two very different types of backup, namely a data backup and a full system backup. Data backups involve backing up important files only, rather than an entire working system. This is a more flexible way of working, because you end up with files that can be copied onto any computer once it has been set up with an operating system and some applications. This is preferable for staff workstations, where you are more concerned with protecting against accidental loss of a document rather than the loss of the entire computer.

When developing a backup strategy, remember that the definition of 'data' is a wide one. It does of course include all document files, and these should be located in the computer's My Documents directory. But other important files may be more difficult to track down. These include items such as Internet Explorer bookmarked sites (known as Favorites), email account settings, and so on. If Windows is configured correctly, and all applications are recent versions designed for modern versions of Windows, then it's a fair bet that such information will be stored in the Documents And Settings directory within a folder named after the user's username and/or domain. This can't always be guaranteed, though, so it's important to check. Custom fonts, for example, are not stored in this location. Some programs even store their information in the Windows registry.

Remember, too, that there's rarely any point in backing up the folders containing installed applications (normally the Program Files directory) because, without their associated settings in the registry and the numerous. DLL and system files which get installed elsewhere on the computer, the applications will not run when they are restored from a backup. Personally, I store copies of the installation CD-ROMs of all my important applications on my hard disk in a folder called Software Masters. This folder is included in my backup strategy so that, should a disaster befall my PC, I simply need to obtain replacement hardware and a copy of Windows and I can then reinstall all my software and data from the backup without the need to hunt for installation CDs. I also keep a text file in the Software Masters area containing all the relevant serial numbers that may be required during installation.

If your company uses network-based storage for employees' data files, and a standard corporate Windows image containing all required applications, the backup procedure for desktop and laptop computers is much easier because, in general, backup of the workstation is probably not required. If data files are lost, these will be on the server (which of course needs to be backed up regularly) rather than the workstation anyway. And if a hardware fault develops, the workstation's hard disk can simply be re-imaged with a pre-installed operating system and standard set of applications.

If you don't already use standard Windows images, you may wish to consider it. Such systems allow you to install Windows and a set of applications and then create a precise copy of the entire installation on a CD, DVD, portable hard drive or network partition. Rolling out that installation to one or more computers then takes around 30 minutes, rather than requiring a technician to spend hours installing the operating system and the required applications. The best-known product in this arena is Ghost, from Symantec. Be aware, however, that such products work best when the source and destination hardware platforms are near-identical. Creating an image on a PC produced by, say, IBM and then trying to install it on a Dell computer won't always work correctly because of incompatibilities with drivers and other low-level components. And of course you need to ensure that you comply with all software licensing issues regarding the applications and operating system contained on the master image.

Choosing a Medium

Over the past few years, the rapid growth in the business and domestic market for PCs capable of processing photos, music and video, plus the market for personal video recorders, has driven down the cost of hard disk storage. Desktop PCs in the home and office with 200 GB of storage are commonplace, as are portable MP3 music players with around 80 GB of storage. But as companies and home users have rushed to upgrade PCs and servers in order to store more data, they have come to realize that the backup industry has not kept pace so well. Although hard disk storage is cheap, fast and capacious, traditional backup media such as tape drives are still relatively slow, expensive, and limited in capacity. It is quite common for a modern network file server to contain more hard disk storage than can fit on a single tape, thus making unattended backups difficult.

Most desktop PCs now come as standard with recordable DVD drives, allowing around 4.7 GB of data to be recorded on a single inexpensive (less than $1) disc and double-layer disks provide double the amount of storage for just a dollar more. Although not large enough for a complete system backup, a single DVD is probably sufficient to store a data backup of the typical PC or small server and it is well worth considering mass-market technology such as recordable DVD rather than top-end products such as tape where possible. If 4.7 GB is not enough, the latest generation of DVD technology, using standards known as Blu-ray and HD-DVD, squeezes up to 60 GB onto a double-layer disk. Still not as much as tape, but very useful and cost-effective nonetheless.

Although space can be limited, recordable DVD has one major advantage as a backup medium when compared with tape drives: files stored on DVD disks can be accessed from just about any PC in your organization.

Another option when choosing backup media is to exploit the benefit to be had from the relatively low price and excellent reliability of hard disk storage compared to tape. Where logistics permit (for example, where there is no RAID array), install a second hard disk in the machine within a removable caddy. Once the backup has been completed, the caddy can be removed so that the backup drive can be stored off site. For small servers or other key machines, with storage capacity around the size of the typical hard disk unit, this method is cost-effective and simple. One drawback, however, is that the computer normally has to be powered off to remove or insert the caddy. External hard disk units that connect via USB get around this problem, as USB is hot-pluggable (i.e. you can connect and remove drives while the PC is powered up, and Windows will instantly recognize the change).

Another option is the latest drives from Iomega. The company revolutionized the high-capacity removable drive market in 1995 with the Zip drive, which stored 100 MB on each cartridge. The latest incarnation, known as Rev, stores 35 GB (or 90 GB if you use the optional compression built into the software). For backing up servers there's an auto-changer unit available which holds 10 cartridges rather than just one. Those who have replaced their tape backup solutions with Rev technology tell me that they are delighted with it.

How Often?

As part of your backup strategy that determines which parts of which systems get backed up, and to where, you must also consider how often the backup operations should be performed. The simple answer is, of course, as often as is practical. This will be dictated by a number of situations that are unique to your company, therefore it is not possible to give specific advice. But you will need to bear various things in mind. If a backup operation will require a change of tape, for example, arrange the timing so that there is someone in attendance to do it. For computers or folders where information changes infrequently, don't waste time doing daily backups. Conversely, if information changes often and it is important that nothing is lost as a result of having to restore from a backup, performing a backup once a day or even more frequently might be required

Storage

Having created a backup, whether to tape or DVD or indeed any other media, the question arises of where to store it. Most companies store backups on the premises, and this should always be in a fireproof safe (and you must make sure that the safe is always kept shut, as no one will want to stop to check if there are smoke and flames lapping at the door).

While keeping backups on-site is convenient, it is also seriously flawed. Not all fire safes offer total protection from the most severe of fires and, even if they do, few will survive an explosion such as a terrorist attack or landslide (these things happen, and it pays to be prepared). Secondly, if you are forced to evacuate your premises because of a major crime nearby or some environmental danger (e.g. asbestos is discovered), law enforcement personnel or some other department might prevent you from entering your building in order to retrieve the backups in order to transport them to your new temporary location.

This situation was graphically illustrated in Manchester, in northern England, in the summer of 1996. Two huge bombs, planted by Irish republican terrorists, severely damaged the centre of the City. Most large organizations in the affected area did of course have backups of all their important data, and these were in fireproof (and in most cases bomb-proof) safes. However, because of the need to preserve the scene of crime for forensic investigation, and because there were fears for the structural safety of some buildings, it was many weeks before some companies were allowed to retrieve the contents of their safes.

More recently, a series of bombs was detonated by terrorists in London in the summer of 2005. One suspect was traced to Hammersmith, in west London, a few yards from the offices of a friend of mine. As the police began closing roads and evacuating the area, my friend and his colleagues were instructed to leave their building immediately. There wasn't even time to close the windows, lock the doors, or retrieve the backup tapes from the safe. The police informed them that, because of the nature of the forensic examinations that would be required, it would be at least four days before anyone would be allowed back into the building. Although the staff could in theory all work from home, they had no laptops (these were still stranded in the office) and no data.

An on-site backup isn't a backup at all – it's merely a copy. So said Alan Solomon, inventor of Dr Solomon's Antivirus Toolkit about 15 years ago. Many business people in Manchester and London now agree with him, and fully appreciate the subtle difference between the two.

Unless there is a specific reason not to, all backups should be moved off-site as soon as possible and a procedure should be in place to indicate that the backup has arrived safely. If your company has multiple buildings that are a comfortable distance apart (but not on the same site), the solution is simple. Otherwise, serious consideration should be given to employing the services of an off-site storage company that will collect backups at regular intervals and store them until required. You will also need to decide on the total length of your backup period, and whether tapes are subsequently returned to you or destroyed after they become officially obsolete.

A cheaper option is of course to store backups at the homes of key staff. A modern backup tape occupies the same amount of storage as a deck of cards and is easily transported by pocket or handbag, and thus shouldn't be a physical burden. Many small and medium companies manage their backups in this way, and it's a perfectly acceptable method of ensuring that information is held off-site rather than near to the original source. If you opt for the home-based choice, ensure that a careful record is kept so that you know who has which tapes and, if necessary, instruct staff as to how tapes should be stored and handled. For example, keep them out of hot locations and away from sources of magnetic fields.

Another option is to set up a reciprocal arrangement with a company of roughly the same size, in your town or nearby. You agree to store their tapes in your safe, and they store yours.

Down The Line

Yet another option for creating off-site backups, and one that is becoming increasingly common, is to use an internet-based backup service. Instead of backing up to a physical medium such as tape or disc, simply install some software on your PCs or servers that will automatically copy selected files to a remote server at predetermined intervals. The backup software automatically detects where files have changed, and sends only the changes rather than the entire file. Therefore the process of keeping a backup current is fast, although the initial backup can take many hours or even days over a standard broadband link.

Internet-based backup services are available from many ISPs and business telecoms suppliers, and prices start from a couple of dollars per gigabyte per month. Data can be returned electronically if the loss is just a single file or two, or on tape or CD or DVD if a full restore is required. This normally costs extra, over and above the cost of renting the backup space.

You can of course use the internet to implement your own backup strategy without buying a conventional remote backup service. A PC in a remote location somewhere which runs some ftp server software and which is connected to a fast internet link is all that's required. There are a number of programs available which will automatically back up a PC to a remote ftp server, and which can be scheduled to run regularly in order to keep the backup current. For example, check out HandyBackup (`www.handybackup.net`) and APBackup (`www.avpsoft.com`).

If you have a WAN, and thus the ability to easily copy information between computers in separate buildings, you can also use data replication facilities that automatically synchronize the contents of one PC with another. Second Copy, for example, is a cheap software product for the PC that will instantly copy any file to a second computer if that file is edited. SyncToy, a free download from Microsoft, offers similar facilities.

If you want to experiment with internet-based storage and your capacity requirements are relatively modest, here's a tip: rent some space on a Web server rather than with a service provider that is geared up to sell space for storing backups. Because the market for Web space is so much larger than that for online backups, space is much cheaper. And so long as you store your files in a directory above the Web server root (i.e. above wwwroot or docroot), your files will be out of reach of the Web server and thus inaccessible to a hacker who tries to retrieve them with his Web browser simply by typing in their URL. If you're still worried about hackers retrieving your backups, encrypt them first.

Retention

An important consideration when storing backups is the decision as to how long they should be stored before being destroyed or overwritten. This is relevant whether you use tapes or other physical media, or down–the–line facilities – the only difference is that destroying a down–the–line backup simply means overwriting a file rather than securely erasing a tape. In some cases, local legislation or other regulations may govern retention of backups. For example, accounting data normally has to be kept for a number of years in case it is needed as evidence for or against your company in a fraud investigation. Anti-terrorism legislation may also require you to keep copies of email and telephone usage logs for six months or more. Check with your company's legal advisers as to the precise situation in your industry.

For data that is not covered by legal procedures, the retention period will obviously depend on your area of business and the amount of data being backed up. A common scheme, for both PCs and servers, is to back up daily (five days a week). Overwrite four of the backups each week, but keep one of them (i.e. a weekly backup) for six months. If this results in too many tapes, because there are too many machines being backed up, then recycle three of the four weekly backup tapes so that you always have five daily backups, four weekly backups and, say, six monthly backups.

Note that tape is not the most robust of media, and that tape backup software is notoriously unforthcoming when it comes to providing details of how many errors have been discovered and worked around on a tape. Discard any tape that reports errors as soon as possible. If the number of errors increases, discard the tape immediately.

The Restore Process

Very few organizations or consumers ever have any problems when making backups. The backup software runs, everything appears to go according to plan, and it is generally assumed that the process was successful. It is only when retrieval of one or more backed-up files fails that it is realized, too late, that the backup didn't actually go according to plan at all.

There are many reasons why restoring data from a backup fails. Among the ones that have befallen myself, my colleagues or my clients in the past have included:

- The tape drive was broken but the software was unable to detect that no backup was ever being made.

- A tape was stored incorrectly and got wet or was damaged by magnetic radiation from a nearby loudspeaker.

- A tape was lost or stolen.

- Critical files were not backed up because they were open at the time. Most backup software is unable to copy open files, such as shared databases.

- The backup media is an obsolete tape or diskette format and the drive has long since stopped working. No replacement can be found.

- The new system onto which the backup must be restored is incompatible with the backup file format. This commonly happens with database servers, which run on many different hardware platforms. If you back up the binary database files rather than exporting them to plain ASCII text format first, you will end up with backups that are not portable between platforms.

- A virus infection is discovered, so data is restored from a backup. It is subsequently discovered that the virus infection predates the earliest backup that is available, so none of the backups can be trusted to be clean and uncorrupted.

- It is discovered that the backup program has been copying the wrong set of files, because no one updated the backup schedule when the location of key files was changed.

- The backup program is incorrectly configured and didn't have the necessary permissions to access the files that needed to be backed up.

- Backups were set to run automatically overnight but an error on the remote server meant that this has not been happening for the past few weeks.

- Information on the source machine was encrypted with EFS, the encryption facility built into Windows, but no one had thought to back up the encryption keys too. When it became necessary to restore the encrypted data onto a new computer, Windows refused.

- There are errors on the tape that have developed since the data was recorded. According to Microsoft, in a press release in July 2005 that accompanied the release of its Data Protection Manager (see below), 42% of attempted recoveries from tape in the past year failed. These figures were compiled from a survey undertaken by Microsoft among its own customers.

The moral here is simple: test the restore process regularly to ensure that, should you need to recover data in anger, you can do so within the necessary timeframe and without error.

Wherever humanly possible, never test the procedure by restoring information on top of the copy that was originally backed up, or you risk replacing good data with bad. If you're restoring a complete system backup, restore onto duplicate hardware if you have it. This will of course be more likely if the backup is a PC or small server rather than a large mainframe, as few organizations have spare mainframes on standby.

If you're restoring one directory or a single file, ideally restore it onto a spare computer. If one is not available and you have to restore onto the machine that was originally backed up, restore into a different directory on the hard disk and then use a file comparison program (there are plenty of free ones available for download from the internet) to verify that the restored copy matches the existing one. Another way to do this is to use a checksum program on each of the two directories – most ZIP compression programs have such a facility, or you can download a CRC comparison utility from sites such as **www.download.com**.

Enterprise Backup Solutions

For the larger organizations, recordable DVDs and external USB drives clearly aren't sufficient for the backup needs of large numbers of staff workstations and file servers. In such cases, some form of enterprise-level backup solution is required, and a browse through the Web or a chat to your normal hardware supplier will unearth many possible contenders for your shortlist if you don't already have a suitable system in place.

One such product is Microsoft's Data Protection Manager, or System Center Data Protection Manager as it's more formally known. This is a disk-based backup and recovery solution. It runs under Windows Server 2003 or above. Notice that Microsoft refers to recovery rather than restore, which illustrates the markets into which Microsoft clearly wishes to sell the product.

DPM uses Active Directory to automatically discover file servers, and adds them to the backup schedule. Whenever changes to files are detected, DPM backs up the files. Only the changes to a file are copied to the backup server, thus reducing network traffic. Administrators of the DPM system can configure the software to specify how often a changed file is backed up, and can set thresholds for traffic so that backups in progress at peak times of the day don't slow down the entire corporate network.

In addition to backing up files as they change, a snapshot of a particular group of files, or of entire machines, can also be taken on demand or at predetermined intervals. These can be used, for example, to return a machine to a known state, such as that which existed before what turned out to be the unsuccessful installation of some new software or a security pack.

End users can browse their own permitted part of the DPM server from within Windows and easily select the files they wish to recover. This can even be done from within Windows applications such as Excel or Word, so there's no longer any need for them to contact the company help desk if they need to recover a file.

For companies which operate a WAN, the DPM systems allows servers in remote locations to be automatically backed up to a single central resource, removing the need for each location to maintain its own tape library. And for long-term archiving, there's the facility to copy information from the DPM disk-based server to tape. DPM backs up file servers, database servers (Microsoft SQL Server) and email servers (Microsoft Exchange).

Recovering Lost Data

When a backup proves unreadable (it happens) or if some important files are lost and there's no backup available (it happens even more often), all is not necessarily lost. There are a variety of specialist companies and products available that can, in most cases, recover some or all of the information.

If the problem is one or more corrupted or overwritten files on a hard disk that hadn't been backed up, there's one golden rule. If you think that you might have to use a specialist recovery service or product, stop working on that particular computer immediately. The more that the computer is used, the lesser the chances of successfully recovering information from the corrupted or overwritten files.

Among the software products that claim to be able to recover information from corrupted files, overwritten files, hard disks that are beginning to fail, and so on, is Spinrite (`http://grc.com/spinrite.htm`). It's relatively cheap, at around $90, and is aimed primarily at consumers. An IT support professional of my acquaintance swears by GetDataBack (`www.runtime.org/gdb.htm`) which is slightly cheaper than Spinrite and very effective (although he says that it can take the program up to 48 hours to recover everything from a highly corrupted drive).

GDB is one of a handful of programs that can recover files from a drive that has been accidentally formatted. Therefore, if you are disposing of computers that have previously contained highly confidential information you should remove and physically destroy the hard drives. Anyone who tells you that a formatted drive is an unrecoverable drive is mistaken.

If you don't consider yourself sufficiently competent to perform a data recovery, or if the problem is more severe (such as a hard drive which appears to be completely broken), then you need the services of a data recovery company. These companies can work miracles, but they are fully aware that most of their clients are desperate and so their services never come cheap. Recovering a few key files from a dead or corrupted hard disk will typically cost two or three times the price of the computer that the drive comes from. The price increases if you want it tomorrow, or if you want lots of files recovered. Most companies can recover files from a variety of data formats: hard disk; tape; memory cards; even PDAs and mobile phones. One of the best-known data recovery companies is Vogon (**www.vogon.co.uk**), but there are also others.

Archiving

Backups are designed specifically to provide protection from lost or corrupted data. To be useful, a backup must be updated frequently to reflect any changes in the working copies of the files. Data archiving is different. It involves making a one-off copy of information that represents a snapshot of that time, and is not subsequently updated.

Archiving is normally performed for one of two reasons, the most common being legal or regulatory considerations. You may, for example, be required to create and retain an archive copy of your sales and purchase ledger files from your computerized accounting system at the close of each financial year, prior to the files being wiped in preparation for the next year's trading. You may also choose to archive your firewall logs every month, rather than wiping them and starting again, in order to assist in the investigation of a crime that comes to light subsequently. Also, you might (indeed you should) wish to keep archive copies of outgoing email in case a dispute arises as to whether a message really was sent or whether its content was illegal.

The other reason for creating an archive is to move data from a relatively expensive and vulnerable medium (namely a hard disk in a PC or server) to a cheaper, safer medium such as a safely-stored tape. For example, copies of outgoing correspondence can be archived to tape after a year or two to free up hard disk space, because they won't be needed very often, but it is unwise to simply destroy them completely.

The processes and caveats involved in archiving are very similar to those of backups, and you may wish to consider expanding your backup strategy to include archiving too. Remember that archives are designed to provide a snapshot in time and therefore there is no need to update them. If an archive needs to be updated then there's something wrong with your archiving policy.

If you are archiving material in order to free up disk space, then it is crucial that you test the archived copy before deleting the original files. If the data being archived is important (clue: it is, or you wouldn't be archiving it), create two archives on two different formats (say, tape and a Rev drive) and store them in different places.

If it's done properly, storing information in electronic form is much more sensible than storing printed papers. The computerized version takes up less space, can be searched very quickly, can be protected by encryption and, most importantly, can be easily copied for safety. Paper has none of these advantages.

A few years ago, I went to a London hotel for a meeting with a client of mine who lived and worked many hundreds of miles away. He'd come into London to stay for a few days, partly to meet with me and partly for the annual meeting with his accountant. He'd brought with him a year's worth of bank statements, purchase receipts, and all the other legal documentation that needs to be handed over to an accountant for the preparation of a company's annual accounts. The documents were in half a dozen plastic carrier bags, all lined up neatly under the desk in his hotel room. Which, to the girl who made the bed and cleaned the room, looked like any other half-dozen bags of waste paper. So she threw them all away while my client was having a pre-meeting breakfast. By the time the loss was discovered, the content of the hotel's bins was in the back of a dumper truck on its way to the tip. It's stories like this that make me glad that I run an almost paperless office. Everything is on disk, copied to multiple locations.

The current leader in archive storage is a disk format called Ultra Density Optical, or UDO. Disks typically hold around 30 GB, and the format has the distinct advantage of being available in a WORM version. WORM stands for 'write once, read many'. That is, once you have written data to a UDO disk you can't subsequently write any more data or change what's already been written. This ability to provide confidence that data has not been tampered with since it was written is what differentiates a true archive from a mere backup. You can find out more about UDO at www.plasmon.com.

Deterioration and Obsolescence

Technology changes so quickly that there's a real chance of your archive data format becoming obsolete during the lifetime of the archive. Anyone whose archives are stored on 3.5 inch floppy disks is shortly going to find that it's impossible to buy new drives that can read that particular media. Those whose archives are even older, on 5.5- or 8-inch disks, are already out of luck. Therefore your data and archiving policy should specify that the media format should be reviewed at least every two years, with the suggestion that the archived files be moved to a newer format if it's considered necessary.

Whatever digital media you choose, whether CD, DVD, tape, hard disk, Rev drive and so on, remember that magnetic media deteriorates over time and has only a finite shelf life. Although companies often claim that their media has a shelf life of 50 years, this is calculated purely by simulation and extrapolation. No one knows for sure if old CDs or tape will spontaneously burst into flames after a few years, as has been found to happen with old cinema film. Review and test your archives regularly.

Shortcuts, Links and Virtual Folders

A Windows shortcut looks like a file or directory but is actually just a link to one. For example, if your personnel database is stored in

C:\PERSONNEL\CURRENT\STAFF.MDB there might also be an icon on the desktop called Personnel. To all intents and purposes, the desktop icon is the personnel database – clicking on the icon allows you to open the file. But in reality it's just a tiny text file which points to the real data elsewhere.

Visibly differentiating real files from shortcuts can be tricky. Windows normally adds a small white arrow to an icon if that icon is actually a shortcut, although it's possible to turn off this feature via a change to the registry using the Windows Power Toys (a useful set of free software that's downloadable from Microsoft's Web site).

personnel.xls   personnel.xls

I often come across cases where users have religiously followed a weekly backup regime, dragging icons from their original location to the backup drive without fail, only to discover that they've been backing up a collection of useless shortcuts rather than the information to which those shortcuts point.

```
Prompt
 Volume in drive E has no label.
 Volume Serial Number is D8AE-9B74

 Directory of E:\Personnel

24/10/2005  21:51    <DIR>          .
24/10/2005  21:51    <DIR>          ..
24/10/2005  21:48            13,824 personnel.xls
24/10/2005  21:48               495 personnel.xls.lnk
               3 File(s)        14,319 bytes
               2 Dir(s)  181,424,463,360 bytes free
```

One simple way to locate shortcuts in Windows is to look for files that have a. lnk (for link) extension. If your staff back up their files to a network drive, you might wish to check the drive for large numbers of .lnk files.

▶ FUNDAMENTAL FIVE

Your action points for this chapter:

1. Identify all the important data in your company that needs to be backed up. ☐

2. Implement a policy to ensure that those backups are made, as often as necessary. ☐

3. Ensure that backups are stored safely and securely. ☐

4. Test your backups occasionally to ensure that they can be restored correctly, that you are backing up the right files, and that no important files or folders are being missed. ☐

5. Consider whether you need to implement an archiving policy and, if so, how you can be sure that archives are not tampered with once they have been created. ☐

24

Preventing Internet Misuse

I n many companies, all employees' computers have access to the Web as a matter of course. Such access is rapidly becoming ubiquitous, and new staff now expect it of their employer. As a research tool the Web is second to none. It's the biggest encyclopaedia on the planet, and invaluable to just about everyone.

Unfortunately it's so useful and so addictive that almost everyone misuses their internet access during working hours for personal purposes. A few minutes at lunchtime or during a coffee break for staff to check their personal email is normally tolerated, and all helps contribute toward a pleasant working environment and good staff morale. Sometimes, however, employees overstep the mark. For example:

■ They spend extensive periods pursuing personal interests instead of carrying out the work that they are paid to do;

- They look at inappropriate sites such as pornography;

- They access illegal material such as pirated software or child porn;

- They download copyright material such as music and films;

- They waste time in online chat rooms or looking for holidays;

- They do their grocery shopping online;

- They use internet banking facilities;

- They buy and sell on eBay.

Unconstrained, misuse of the Web by employees can have a serious impact on your company. Those who access illegal material are potentially liable to prosecution and, depending on the type of material, so is the company whose computers were used to store it (i.e. yours). Excessive Web use also consumes bandwidth, slowing down access for legitimate users. But most importantly, staff spending time on the Web for personal entertainment are costing you money in terms of lost productivity. If someone on a 35-hour week spends half an hour every day using the internet for non-business tasks, you're wasting 7% of their salary. In a recent survey conducted in Europe, more than 40% of respondents said that they do indeed spend more than 30 minutes each day using the internet at the office for purposes unconnected with their job.

Given that most people nowadays have access to the internet from home, why do they want to do it at work too? For many people, internet access at their place of employment is much faster than what they have available at home, even if their home connection uses broadband. Further, not all Web usage fits neatly into non-work hours. A good example is someone who is in the process of bidding for an item on an online auction site such as eBay where the auction closes during working hours and thus must be accessed regularly from the office in case a higher bid needs to be placed. Similarly, someone who dabbles in online share dealing as a hobby, or who enjoys watching live sporting events that are taking place on the other side of the world, might have no option but to use the Web during office hours in order not to miss the result or to take advantage of a good deal.

Banning all Web access is one possible solution to the problem, but it's not ideal because you restrict users from accessing material that is of use to them. Including terms in employees' contracts explaining that personal use of the Web to access illegal material is prohibited is a start, but both the staff member and the company might still be liable if the staff member breaks the rule. And an employee who downloads offensive material and forwards it to someone who is less broad-minded can land themselves and their employer in legal hot water if, for example, the material is grossly offensive on religious grounds.

As always, technology comes to the rescue here in the guise of Web filtering software. Install the software on your network servers, configure it appropriately, and you can control users' access to Web sites easily. Many programs include reporting facilities so, if someone is making repeated attempts to access banned sites, the system manager can be alerted.

Web filtering software generally works in one of two ways. Some programs use a keyword scanning program which pre-examines every Web page that a user requests and, if it contains one or more prohibited items, blocks the user from seeing the page. Although such software works well, and requires little configuration or regular updating, it can cause problems by blocking access to legitimate sites. For example, the software might be configured not to allow access to pages where the title or content includes the word 'breasts' or 'testicles'. Which works perfectly well until an employee fears that they might have breast or testicular cancer and finds themselves banned from looking at Web sites that could offer useful information.

Some Web filtering software employs a database of Web sites that are classified into categories by the software vendor. Categories might include hardcore pornography, softcore pornography, gambling, auctions, entertainment, educational, technical, TV listings, audio streaming and so on. You can then configure the software according to a series of rules, which can be as complex as you wish to make them. You might choose to ban all access to hardcore porn sites, allow all access to educational and technical sites, and to ban all access to audio streaming except before 9am and after 6pm.

There are many companies offering software to monitor, filter, manage or control employee's Web access and typing any of those words into your favourite search engine will help you start compiling your shortlist. One well-known company of my acquaintance is WebSense, but there are many others too. Net Intelligence (www.netintelligence.com) is also worth a look.

Whichever product you choose, handling the installation and rollout can be a difficult management challenge and should be carried out with sensitivity. It is all too easy to inadvertently brand all employees as lazy perverts, so take care to 'sell' the concept to everyone before the software is installed. Stress the benefits to employees, such as them not accidentally encountering unpleasant internet content during the course of their work. The fact that it will save the company money might well be of interest to senior managers, but most employees will simply see it as yet another example of the company's mean spirit if you mention this as a benefit.

Make it clear that log files won't be routinely scanned in order to catch and discipline those who attempt to continue looking at banned sites. Explain that logs will only be examined if someone is suspected of a serious disciplinary offence, and that the records will be seen only by senior managers.

Image Investigation

While traditional Web filtering software can block sites by analysing the textual content of the pages, a new breed of software product can now do the same with graphics. It's a technology that has been used in the law enforcement industry for a number of years, especially when looking for child porn. The same technology is now available to mainstream business, and one player is PixAlert (www.pixalert.com).

The PixAlert software installs on your servers, and filters Web pages by analysing the content of any images on the page. It attempts to discern whether the image is of a pornographic nature, which it does by looking at the shapes which make up the picture, and their colour. If PixAlert thinks that a user has requested a page which contains blocked content, it can take a number of actions depending on the way that the software has been configured by the administrator. It can remove the picture from the page, or replace it with a blurred version that can't be changed, or replace it with a blurred version which will be un-blurred if the user clicks it. There are full logging and reporting facilities so, if the software is configured to allow users to un-blur an image by clicking it, the administrator can request a report to find out which users have un-blurred which images.

Additional Techniques

The ways in which an internet connection can be misused are many and varied, and therefore your strategy and tactics to monitor and prevent such misuse must live up to the job. Plans will need to be revised occasionally, too, to cope with new technologies.

Who would have thought, for example, that we'd all be carrying multi-gigabyte USB data sticks on our key fobs, capable of smuggling a downloaded movie out of the company in order to watch at home on a multimedia computer? Just think about it for a moment. Remember those 3.5 inch 1.44 MB floppy disks? An 8 GB USB stick on your key fob holds around 5500 floppy disks' worth of information. A survey in 2005 by security company PointSec found that these devices are being used in 84% of companies and that, in the typical organization, more than 30% of staff own one.

Webcam Security

Ensure that your security planning includes some consideration as to the way that webcams are used. In the past, videoconferencing meant expensive dedicated hardware which talked via ISDN lines at a fairly high per-minute charge. Now, £20 worth of webcam linked to a PC on the company network running free MSN Messenger software is all that you need to talk to, and see, workers down the road or across the world. As is so often the case with internet technologies, where porn started so the corporate world followed.

The risks associated with Webcams are negligible but not zero. Most webcams contain no physical switches or dials – they are controlled solely through software. Therefore, someone who manages to gain remote control of a computer can also control the camera connected to it. So concerned are the webcam manufacturers about this, that at least one company now fits plastic privacy visors to its cameras which the user can slide down over the lens to guarantee that, even if the camera is enabled, no images will be visible.

Illicitly-obtained control of a camera can be exploited either to turn the camera on or off, and each has benefits for the hacker. Someone who manages to turn off a live camera can effectively disable a security monitoring system, and with so many companies now using network-connected cameras that plug into Ethernet sockets rather than into coax cable this is sure to become an even greater problem in the future. Ensure that you configure your camera software correctly to provide the required degree of access control, and use your firewall too to ensure that a connection to the camera's IP address can only be made from specified locations.

A hacker who manages to turn on a camera can also exploit it, or its owner, in unexpected ways. In 2005, a 45 year old man from Cyprus was charged with illegally hacking into the computer of a 17 year old girl, turning on her Webcam and taking illicit pictures of her alone in her bedroom. He subsequently contacted her and threatened to send the pictures to all of her email contacts unless she stood naked in front of the camera for him, but she contacted the police and he was arrested.

Antivirus company Sophos said in 2005 that more than half of all newly-released Trojan Horse programs which contained a back door facility included the feature to spy on the victim via their Webcam. To help reduce the risk of such an event, ensure that your firewall is correctly configured and that Webcams (especially those which include microphones) aren't installed in sensitive areas such as server rooms.

Sometimes, misuse of the internet doesn't involve misusing the office connection (or indeed using it at all), but is all about what someone says online. What does your employee contract and/or internet usage policy say about using online chat rooms, bulletin boards, forums, newsgroups and blogs for purposes which might bring the company into disrepute, divulging company secrets, or speaking on behalf of the company when not authorized to do so? In most organizations, such topics are not included in any policy documents, but these are actually very important situations which will arise more often than you think and you need to work out in advance what to do about it.

Take blogs, for example, the craze of creating online journals or Web-logs which anyone can read. Millions of people do it, through sites such as blogger.com, and while many blogs are rarely accessed by anyone except the author and their friends, some become cult sites that are devoured by hundreds of thousands of people across the world every week.

Most bloggers include material about their job within their blog. Sometimes the coverage is positive but frequently it's not. What would your company do if you discovered that an employee had written in their blog about their terrible day at the office, the dreadful coffee, their incompetent boss, the outdated equipment and the current dire lack of customers? If the material is true then it's not generally considered to be libellous, so legal action is not easy. Does the employee's contract forbid them from divulging such information? Could you legitimately dismiss someone for saying such things online and, even if you did, would it result in extensive bad publicity?

In 2004 Ellen Simonetti, who called herself 'Queen of the Sky' in her blog, was dismissed by Delta Airlines, her employer, on the grounds of bringing the company into disrepute. A couple of months later, Joe Gordon lost his job as a senior bookseller with Waterstone's in Edinburgh for similar reasons, after his blog referred to the company as Bastardstone's and to one of his managers as Evil Boss. Ensure that all staff know what they can and can't do online when it comes to referring to the company. If you don't want people acting as unpaid spokespeople in online forums, even in their spare time, and even if they're only trying to help, then make this clear. Regardless of whether you permit such activity, it's a good idea to ban staff from ever quoting their work email address in a usenet newsgroup or IRC chat channel because such places are frequented by spammers who use automatic programs to detect email addresses. Use a disposable account for such things instead, such as one at hotmail.com or googlemail.com.

Cuckoo Sites

It is far from uncommon for staff to misuse their employer's internet facilities to take advantage of hosting space or applications for their own purposes. Someone in the marketing department who has the ability and privileges to create and edit Web pages on the corporate server might set up a directory there in which to host their personal pages or perhaps a family photo album. Or someone with sufficient access to the email system might set up a mailing list for their club or society. Occasionally this practice goes further, perhaps using the company's ftp or Web server to allow software pirates or even paedophiles to exchange files. The key to stopping such activity is a combination of management and technology. Make it clear that this is not allowed, and use standard server management tools to keep an occasional eye on the log files and the contents of the publicly accessible directories.

You might also consider allowing a limited amount of personal space on a Web server where staff can create home pages for any purpose which fulfils a couple of basic principles (e.g. nothing obscene or libellous). Rather than allowing users to upload html files of their choosing, a content management system or a database-driven site will allow you to provide a small set of basic templates (news story, picture story, photograph album, blog, a list of interesting or useful links, diary of events etc) so that users can create pages by selecting a template and typing the information into a Web-based form from within their browser. Such a server will help users to resist the temptation of using the company's computing resources in an inappropriate or underhand way, and is generally seen as a useful perk.

Online Banking

Millions of people now use internet banking, and it's quite likely that some of your staff check their accounts or pay bills online while at work, i.e. while using your company's computers. This can pose particular security risks. Firstly, if your systems record all Web traffic then it's likely that your logs will include highly confidential information such as the details of employees' bank accounts and/or the passwords required to access them. Not only does this put a legal obligation on you to keep that information secure, but you risk being blamed if the employee's account is ever plundered or otherwise misused.

Secondly, an employee who receives a phishing attack via their email account at the office might be tempted to click on it, especially if it appears to come from the bank that holds their account. There is thus a real risk that Trojan software such as keystroke loggers might find their way onto your company's computers and that such software might be used to steal not just the employee's banking details but also confidential files belonging to your company.

Internet banking is perfectly safe so long as basic precautions and common sense are used. This includes ensuring that the computer used for banking has antivirus software installed and that it is up to date, that the computer is fully patched against all current Windows vulnerabilities, that it runs some anti-spyware software, that it is protected by a firewall, and that users don't click on email attachments unless they are confident that the attachment is safe. Assuming that these rules are adhered to, there is no reason why you should not allow staff to access their e-banking facility from company computers. However, if you wish to avoid the risk and responsibility that might arise, you may wish to consider banning such activity or, at the very least, formally explaining to staff that you can't guarantee the privacy of their private information if they access such sites via the company's network.

⏵ FUNDAMENTAL FIVE

Your action points for this chapter:

1. Implement rules and/or technological solutions to ensure that staff do not abuse the Web or email system while at work, especially when using it for personal purposes. ☐

2. If you have rules as to how your internet connection can be used by staff for personal purposes, ensure that these are widely circulated to all staff. ☐

3. If you keep logs of Web and email access, ensure that these are not retained for longer than is necessary. ☐

4. Ensure that staff are aware that setting up Web or ftp servers on their computer at the office is not permitted. Block such services at your firewall to help enforce the policy. ☐

5. Inform all staff that their use of the internet must not do anything which brings the company into disrepute, and that they must adhere to your internet usage policy. ☐

DANGER

25

Document Security

E ffective computer security needs to be about protecting information, not electronics. Should a disaster befall the hardware of a typical corporate desktop or laptop machine, it can be replaced within the hour for a couple of hundred pounds from a local store. The contents of its hard disk, however, are generally worth many times more, and they must be protected from accidental and deliberate loss and damage.

Most companies operate networked file servers, and all employees' PCs are configured to store document files on the server by default. This removes the need for the user to back up his or her files but does nothing to guard against the fact that anyone with physical access to the user's PC and/or their network login details can access those files and, in all probability, view confidential information.

Where no central file store is available, and documents are stored on the local hard disk, the risk becomes greater because the onus is now on the user of that PC to ensure files are backed up and properly protected. Not only is this dangerous, but it potentially represents a legal and contractual minefield. Most employee/employer contracts and computer usage policies explicitly state that the employee's PC and its data is the property of the company, and that therefore the company has every right to restrict its use to legitimate company business and to monitor its usage. All of which makes perfect sense, until the company also tries to suggest to a staff member that he or she owns responsibility for the data and is responsible for ensuring that it is safely backed up and properly protected. Someone who finds themselves facing disciplinary action for not taking care of something they own, yet having signed a contract accepting that they don't own anything at all, will present an interesting challenge for all concerned if the case gets as far as a tribunal or a court. Therefore it makes sense to spell out clearly who is responsible for the security and safety of documents on your employees' computers, and to ensure that there is no inherent ambiguity.

Metadata and Markup

Modern programs for creating and editing information, such as Word and Excel, are powerful applications. Not only do they allow users to work on their files in a feature-rich environment, but they include collaboration facilities to allow multiple users to work together, add comments to documents, record detailed information about the content of a file, and track the changes that have been made to a file during its life cycle. But this all comes at a price. If you enable these features, anyone who receives an electronic copy of the file (perhaps by email) can view this additional information. Sometimes this can be done from within the program, such as ticking the box in Word to show the history of changes. But even if no facility exists within the application to access the additional data, it is often still visible to anyone who has the skill to load the file into a basic text editor such as Notepad rather than the correct application such as Word or Excel.

By using either the text editor technique or by simply ticking some boxes in Word, it is possible to find out a lot of information in addition to the actual visible content of a document. This includes:

▬ The name of the person who created the file;

▬ The names of the last 10 people to have edited the file;

- The serial number of the copy of Word that was used to create the file, and thus the particular PC that was used;

- Any comments made by the document's authors that were not intended for publication;

- A complete list of changes, including the recovery of all information that was subsequently deleted from the finished copy;

- The total time that the document file has been open for editing, i.e. precisely how long the file has taken to produce.

All of this information can be potentially damaging if your staff are inadvertently allowing it to leak out. For example, if you charge a client for 10 hours' work in producing a report but the document's hidden data clearly shows that it has a total editing time of just seven hours, expect questions to be asked. Equally, if your marketing people have deleted a couple of superlatives from a press release before distribution (presumably because they don't reckon that they are deserved), you would be ill-advised to allow the press to find this out. Journalists, incidentally, are well aware of this weakness in Word. Whenever they receive documents, press releases, white papers or product manuals electronically, their first step is often to view the document in a text editor and to turn on the View Changes feature.

This additional information contained in document files is known as metadata (the term means 'information about information'). If your company doesn't already have a policy about metadata, consider adopting one. This should include ensuring that all metadata is removed from documents before they are sent electronically to anyone outside the organisation.

Having taken notice of the bad publicity that metadata has brought, Microsoft now makes available a free software utility called the Hidden Data Removal Tool. Typing those four words into your favourite search engine will find the program and instructions on how to use it. It works on Word, Excel and PowerPoint files, and I strongly recommend that you use it on all three file types. If all staff save their files on your network server, you might wish to consider running the tool automatically every night on all files. If documents reside on individual users' computers then your job is slightly harder, but a combination of automatically-scheduled Windows tasks plus some user education in the correct use of metadata will pay dividends.

If you run Office 2003, then you can take advantage of a feature built into the applications that allow you to strip metadata automatically. In Word 2003, for example, in Tools, Options, Security, tick the box that says 'remove personal information from file properties on save'. You need to do this in your normal.dot document template to ensure that it will apply to all subsequent documents that you create.

Metadata is used extensively by IT forensic experts to help track down the perpetrators of computer crime. One virus-writer, for example, was caught a couple of years ago because his virus was written in Word's macro language and Word had embedded his name in the code without his knowledge.

The concept of metadata is not unique to Microsoft. MP3 music files use something called ID3 tags to embed details such as the name of the artist and the track, plus the name of the album that the track was taken from. Image files such as JPGs use a similar system, known as EXIF, to embed metadata in images. In the file properties window of the picture below you can see details of the camera that was used to take the shot, the exposure settings, and whether a flash was used. If you're a professional photographer such information might be regarded as trade secrets, yet if you put a collection of thumbnails on the Web as a showcase for your talent then you may be unaware that such facts are available to everyone.

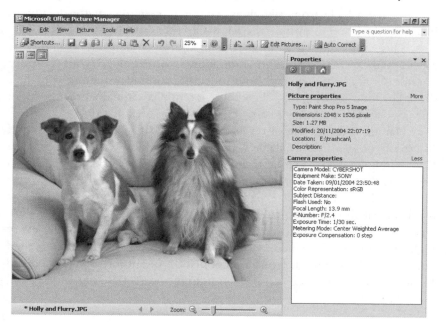

▶ FUNDAMENTAL FIVE

Your action points for this chapter:

1. Ensure that all staff workstations are configured to save documents by default in a location that is regularly backed up, such as a network server. ☐

2. If you don't have a central file server, ensure that you have some other way of backing up important documents stored on the hard disks of users' desktop PCs. ☐

3. Implement a policy to ensure that metadata is removed from documents that are distributed outside the company. ☐

4. Roll out Microsoft's Hidden Data Removal Tool to all staff. ☐

5. Be aware of the dangers of using the change-tracking facility in Microsoft Word. It could allow others to find out the complete revision history of a document. ☐

26

Data Theft

One of the favourite phrases of IT security consultants is that your company's data and information is its greatest asset. Accountants prefer to tell you that your greatest asset is the cash in your bank accounts, and HR people tell you that your greatest assets are your staff. Whatever the truth really is, there's absolutely no doubt that all those data files held on all those PCs and servers dotted around your organization represent a huge asset and that the company would suffer irreparable damage if those files found their way into the wrong hands.

An extreme example is the precise recipe for Coca Cola, which is said to be known only by two or three people, none of whom are allowed to travel together in the same plane. Should this recipe ever become widely known to those who manufacture cheaper colas, it's probably fair to say that the share price of Coca Cola Inc. could lose 50% of its value overnight.

Experts and surveys tend to agree that computer misuse and the theft of information by employees, rather than by outsiders, accounts for around 65% of all instances. This comes as a great shock to many, who assume that the greatest threat to their computer systems is from spotty teenage hackers operating from filthy bedrooms and college dorms on the other side of the world. Understanding where the threats come from is crucial if you wish to stop them becoming a reality – there's no point in blowing your security budget on a wonderful firewall if the crimes are taking place on your premises and thus beyond the firewall's reach. Instead, maybe some of your security fund needs to be diverted into ensuring that all new employees' references are properly checked.

Why do staff want to steal, or at least misappropriate, your information? The reasons vary, but include:

- Because it might come in useful in the future, for purposes as-yet unknown;

- For convenience, to work on at home even though this is not officially allowed;

- Because they wish to gather evidence of what they regard as illegal, immoral or unethical behaviour by the company or a colleague;

- Because they intend to sell it to a competitor;

- Because they intend to use it to their advantage if/when they move to a new employer;

- Because they are being bribed or blackmailed by someone who wants it;

- Because someone has offered them a large sum of money for it.

This final point (the large sum of money) is an important one. I am often asked how I'd go about breaking into uncrackable systems such as those belonging to banks, police forces or governments. My explanation is always the same. There's no point in hacking them because the security is always incredibly tight. The weakest link in such systems is always people rather than technology, and greed makes a weak link even weaker. So I explain that I'd hang around in local bars, get to know people who work for the organization and who have legitimate access to the information I need, and then offer them money. Lots of money, if necessary. It's relatively easy, and it bypasses all the standard security techniques such as firewalls. It might even be going on in your company right now. Would you be able to tell? Is anyone driving a brand new car that you reckon they probably can't afford? Have they just moved to a smart house or taken an expensive holiday?

Spies, Damned Spies

Is someone in your organization a 'plant'? Have they taken the job solely in order to find out information about you and to steal confidential files such as your customer database? Are they actually working for your biggest competitor? A study of 3000 CVs (resumés) by The Risk Advisory Group (TRAG) in 2005 found that a quarter of them contained incorrect information and that, on average, each contained not one mistake but three. The most common lies were in the areas of employment dates, academic dates, previous positions, academic qualifications and undeclared directorships. The survey also found that one in four companies had withdrawn a job offer after finding lies on a CV, while almost the same amount had also subsequently fired an employee who was found to have lied to get the job.

You should always take up references rather than simply relying on what someone says in their CV, especially when employing someone who will be in a position of trust. British Standard BS7858 (see **www.bsi-global.com**) contains some useful guidance on security screening of employees. For some fascinating real-world examples of what can happen if you fail to take up references, consider the tabloid journalist who applied for a job in the summer of 2005 at the military training centre where Prince Harry (younger son of the late Diana Princess of Wales) was based. No one thought to check applicants' references, resulting in the journalist exposing the lack of security within the pages of his paper. Needless to say, the Ministry of Defence issued the standard statement saying that they take security seriously and that they would take steps to ensure it couldn't happen again. Two months later, a reporter from another newspaper used precisely the same technique and it did indeed happen again.

Assessment

Before you can start to protect your company's data, you need to know where it is and, just as importantly, know how important it is. Which means that we're back to one of the first subjects that we covered at the start of this book, namely risk assessment. You also need to distinguish between data and information. Data is the raw log file from your cash tills that contains millions of impenetrable lines of transaction data. Information is the single-page management summary which tells you that the average spend per customer in your London store is currently £72 per visit, up from £68 last year, while the New York store has seen a 4% drop in average customer spend but also a 6% reduction in losses due to wastage. As you start collecting information about everything that's stored on your computers, think about whether it's raw data or usable information, and about who might want it (and what they'd be willing to do or pay to get it).

I quote the example of average customer spend for a good reason, which indicates just how difficult it can be to keep track of the information assets within your company. In the summer of 2005 I was on a train heading out of London when I noticed a few sheets of paper that had been discarded by a previous passenger and left on the seat next to me. Being the curious type, and always on the lookout for ways to occupy my mind on boring train journeys, I took a glance at the documents. There were six sheets, each of which had been torn into quarters – presumably in a primitive attempt to avoid anyone else reading them. The papers were the current month's trading summary for a large chain of fast food shops with around 120 branches in England. One sheet contained the current week's diary, printed from Outlook, of the person who'd been reading them. He was a manager with the company concerned. The others contained detailed information for each of the 120 branches. Money taken, loss through wastage, number of customers, average spend per customer, number of hours worked by staff and managers, and how the actual figures compared to budgets. It all made fascinating reading, such as comparing how much the average business customer spends on lunch in the affluent parts of central London compared to someone after a quick pre-departure snack at an airport.

I returned the papers, by post, to the company's CEO and also hinted that, should they require the services of someone to educate their staff as to the safe way to store and handle confidential information, I would be more than happy to provide it. His reply thanked me for the safe return of what would have been 'of immense value to our competitors' before going on to say that his company does not have any problems with data security.

It's unusual for a collection of data to be so identifiably beneficial to a specific group of people. Your task during your risk assessment, therefore, is to examine the type of information that your company holds and decide who it could benefit, in what way, and what it's worth you spending in order to stop that happening. Remember that not all information is of immediate use as–is, but might be a means to an end. Social engineers, for example, are skilled in filing away many tiny snippets which, in the future, will add up to something that's greater than the sum of its parts.

Compiling a list of all the data that you have is tricky, not least because it varies greatly between companies and business sectors so it's impossible for anyone to produce definitive checklists. However, your list might contain entries such as:

- Recipes

- Software source code

- Designs and plans for existing and forthcoming products

- Staff salaries, home addresses and telephone numbers

- Email addresses of senior management

- Computer and network configuration data

- Suppliers

- Customers

- Sales leads

- Accounting information

- Copies of email messages sent and received

- Research into techniques that could provide a competitive advantage.

Information can leave your premises in many ways, and you must ensure that the correct mix of policies, procedures and technology is in place to stop it doing so. Just as importantly, you need a method that will alert you if information does get out, so that you can act quickly. Encryption is your friend here. Wherever possible, confidential information stored within the company's systems should be encrypted. This will prevent, for example, any losses if someone steals a backup tape. But encryption is no panacea because it won't prevent the theft of information by someone who knows the password or who manages to discover it through means such as a keystroke logger or guesswork. Or the age-old standby of seeing it written down in some obvious place.

The ways in which information gets taken away from its home location are many and varied, and increases all the time. The easiest way for a staff member to copy information is to send it by email. If they have access to your company email system from home, perhaps via Outlook Web Access, then they can subsequently retrieve it. Alternatively, they can bypass your email system completely via an account with a Web-based email provider such as Hotmail or Gmail, and use this both to send and receive the files as attachments. While your email system's log files will help detect misuse of your own systems, such as someone sending information to a Hotmail account via your Exchange server, no such logs will exist if Hotmail is used both for the sending and the receiving. At best, your Web server logs will simply record that the employee visited the Hotmail site, but it's unlikely to contain details of what they sent during the session.

Programs and facilities do of course exist which will allow you to keep more detailed records of a user's Web surfing activity (see Chapter 24), but there are legal pitfalls here which really mean that you should seek specialist advice before deploying them unless the employee in question is under suspicion.

Just about everyone these days has a portable USB device which can be quickly plugged into a PC or server and to which files can be copied simply by dragging with a mouse. No special driver software needs to be installed – Windows will automatically recognize the device and make it available as soon as it's plugged in – so there's no need for the user to log in as an administrator in order to access it. The risks associated with USB pen drives (or memory sticks as they're sometimes known) are obvious, especially as the devices are so cheap and ubiquitous that they are to be found on the key fob of just about every tech-savvy computer user. In addition, don't forget portable music players such as the iPod and others, which contain large amounts of storage space (frequently in excess of 40 GB on a tiny hard disk) that can be used to copy any file and not just music tracks. USB storage devices can also transmit viruses, which could allow a virus from someone's computer at home to enter the office environment. Even mobile phones can now store data files, which can be downloaded either via a cable or often through a wireless Bluetooth connection.

Not all data theft is the result of dishonest employees, and it certainly doesn't always require physical access to a computer in order for the theft to take place. Hackers, thieves, competitors and the simply curious often try to persuade a Web server to disgorge its content database. For example, if your site provides a full-text search facility, what happens if you try to search for all articles containing the letter 'e' or the word 'it'? Will the system produce a list of every single article and, if so, will it allow the user to mark them all for downloading? Would this allow your competitors to download your entire catalogue or site and, if so, is this a security risk?

Even if your employees access data via thin-client systems such as Web browsers or terminals, rather than being given access to entire database files, it is still trivial for information to be copied from the system and removed from the company. Every Web browser has a menu option that will save the entire current page to the hard disk (or any USB device that's currently plugged in).

Windows doesn't make it easy to restrict the use of portable devices, but there are some third party products that can help. These include Device-Wall (`www.devicewall.com`) and DeviceLock (`www.protect-me.com`). Each provides system administrators with the means to prevent employees from connecting devices such as USB drives, WiFi devices, Bluetooth adaptors, PDAs and MP3 players to a computer without permission. Each has extensive configuration options so that you can specify different permissions according to the type of device, the current user, and sometimes even the time of day. There are also exception facilities that allow you to remove restrictions from certain devices only, which is ideal for use on computers that still need to be able to read smartcards or fingerprints for authentication.

The Need to Know

The most effective weapon in any serious attempt to limit the amount of information that is copied from your company without permission is to implement a 'need to know' rule. Use the facilities built into your network, firewall and desktop operating systems to ensure that staff have access only to the information that they need to use. No one should be allowed to see the database of sales leads except the sales team. No one should be allowed to update the company Web site except those who need to do so, and each department's area of the site should be protected with a separate password. Each server should have a separate administrator password, and only a handful of key technical staff should have access to the complete list.

As well as examining your log files regularly in order to find out who's been doing what, keep an occasional eye on your ACLs, or Access Control Lists. This is the configuration information that specifies who has access to what on a particular computer, be it Windows or Unix, workstation or server. A regular review of all ACLs will alert you to any access permissions that are considered unnecessary and can be revoked, and possibly to permissions which have been granted without the relevant authorization. Whenever a hacker manages to crack the account of someone with permission to grant access privileges or create new accounts, the first thing he does is to increase the privilege levels of other users so that, should the cracked account be discovered and shut down, he still has at least one other route back into the system.

A useful tool is AccessEnum (**www.sysinternals.com**). This free program for Windows creates reports on the access permissions on all directories and registry keys.

If you have a network file store where users keep their own files, rather than storing them on users' individual PCs, ensure that the permissions are set so that users can't see anyone else's files. Don't grant users the permission to give other people access to their files, because this will rapidly get out of hand. Instead, either implement a blanket 'no shared access' rule, or insist that all requests go through the IT support department or help desk. If you opt for the latter, requests should be in writing (email will suffice), a reason should be given, and ideally there should be an automated way of checking that the current state of the access control lists corresponds to the database of requests that have been received.

FUNDAMENTAL FIVE

Your action points for this chapter:

1. Investigate the different types of data that is created, stored and processed in your company. ☐

2. Consider how those different types of data need to be protected, and which types deserve your most urgent attention. ☐

3. Limit access to confidential data on a strict need-to-know basis. ☐

4. Ensure that you always take up references when employing a new member of staff. Investigate whether there are any current staff whose references were not checked at the time they joined the company. ☐

5. Ensure that you are aware of the various means by which a dishonest employee can smuggle confidential information out of your offices, such as ftp transfers and USB data sticks. ☐

27

Encryption

n 1981 Sony introduced the 3.5-inch floppy disk format, which went on to replace the 5.25-inch diskette. There are many reasons why the designers settled on a size of three and a half inches, one of which was because it would comfortably fit in a man's shirt pocket. For the first time, a businessman could carry a copy of his important computer files with him at all times – something that is still highly desirable, although achieved nowadays through a tiny USB pen drive with over 1000 times the capacity of a floppy. Being able to store and transport data on small, portable media such as USB drives and backup tapes is of great benefit to companies who need to keep information securely. It allows staff to ensure that the information they need is always to hand, and it makes off-site backups a piece of cake.

But remember that backup tapes are highly desirable to hackers because, by definition, a backup tape will contain up-to-date copies of all of a company's most important information. Where once a rogue employee or casual data thief could easily conceal 1.44 MB of data and walk out of a building unnoticed, he can now fit a 300 gigabyte tape cartridge in that very same pocket. Where companies have made the misguided decision to store backups in the desk drawer next to the computer that has been backed up, such a realization has often come too late. One such company, which came to my attention many years ago, is now one of the world's most successful suppliers of cellular phones. But the company very nearly went bust in its early days when the PC belonging to its marketing director was stolen from their offices. The computer had a tape drive fitted and backups were regularly taken. But the tape was kept in the drive and thus disappeared along with the computer. Recovering from this error of judgement was time-consuming and expensive.

It is essential that you encrypt all your backups, regardless of whether they are stored on or off site and whether they are on a physical device such as tape or sent down a line to a remote server. There are very few genuine instances in IT security where a certain procedure or product can bring you peace of mind, but encryption is perhaps the closest you'll get. If your information is encrypted you can relax in the knowledge that, if someone walks off with your backup tape, it will at least be a long time before they manage to decipher its contents. It also means that your backups are safe from prying eyes if they are stored in employees' homes, in the safe of a company down the road, or on a remote server which might be attacked by hackers or which might also boast your biggest competitor among its customers.

All of which came too late for three companies. In May 2005, CitiFinancial, a division of Citigroup, sent off a backup tape via courier company UPS to a credit bureau for processing. The tape never arrived, for reasons that no one quite understands. It was not encrypted. The company had to notify almost four million customers that their social security numbers, payment history and account numbers might possibly be in the hands of internet miscreants. A month earlier, US-based share dealing company Ameritrade discovered that the company which handles its backup data had mislaid four tapes containing information on more than 200,000 customers. And Iron Mountain, a company which handles data storage for clients, admitted in mid-2005 that it had lost track of four sets of customer tapes since the beginning of the year. Ameritrade later claimed that it had managed to locate three of its missing tapes. The fourth was assumed to be lost or destroyed.

Somewhat surprisingly, a survey in the US in 2005 found that 56% of companies with an annual turnover (revenue) of more than five billion dollars don't encrypt their backups. Yet all backup software includes facilities for creating encrypted backups, and if you're implementing your own procedures using external disk drives or ftp transfers then there are plenty of stand-alone encryption products on the market. But beware of any proprietary encryption algorithm that has been invented by the backup software's developers. Always use a recognized international standard algorithm such as DES or AES. And never, ever rely on the so-called encryption built into common Office applications – type 'microsoft office password recovery' into your Web search engine to see why.

Not Just Backups

Any data that is a possible target for hackers and other cyber-criminals should be encrypted. This includes, but is not limited to, backups. You should encrypt data held within your company's computers, and also data which is transmitted remotely such as email messages and attachments or when using facilities such as ftp to send information to remote offices or home-based workers. Remember that the internet is not a secure transmission medium – any information sent over the internet which is not encrypted can be intercepted (and possibly altered) by someone who has the necessary hacking skills.

If the hacker is connected to the same internet segment as the source of the information, this process is very simple indeed because the information will pass through the hacker's computer as it travels into and out of the computer on which it normally resides. All that the hacker needs to do is to program his computer, or specifically his internet connection, so that it displays all the traffic which passes through it rather than just the information that he has explicitly requested.

A fascinating insight into the competitive world of international aviation in 1993 illustrates neatly why encryption of business data is so important. BABS was the British Airways Booking System, a large mainframe-based system for planning various aspects of a flight. It was, as the name suggests, owned and run by British Airways. Amazingly, BA allowed one of its competitors, Virgin Atlantic, to rent space on BABS. Unsurprisingly, someone within BA soon realized that Virgin's data was too good to ignore and decided to examine it.

Virgin used BABS for two purposes. The first was for Weights and Balance Documentation. A pilot needs to know precise details about the load that a plane is carrying as this affects the aircraft's handling and its fuel requirements. Details of all passengers were recorded, including the weight of their luggage and the location of their seats. With access to this data, BA was able to find out just how full each Virgin flight was. By reference to the published price list they also knew how much each passenger had paid and could thus work out how much money Virgin was taking for each flight.

Virgin also used BABS to store backup copies of customers' names, addresses and telephone numbers, plus brief details about the flights on which they were booked. When the case came to court, BA actually admitted telephoning Virgin Atlantic passengers and attempting to persuade them to switch airlines but denied having obtained the phone numbers from Virgin's area on BABS.

You can't help but laugh at the foolishness of a company that stores its most sensitive information in unencrypted form on a computer owned and operated by its closest rival. Yet this type of arrangement, or ones just like it, are still commonplace, especially where companies don't run their own Web servers but use the services of a hosting company. Do you know what's in all the files and databases on your Web server, and who has access to them?

If further justification for the use of encryption were needed, here's a story from my days as a magazine editor. When we had finished producing a new issue of the magazine, we'd upload the PostScript files of the finished pages to our typesetting company's ftp server for processing so that they could be turned into printing plates. Despite my frequent warnings, the company never bothered to issue separate passwords to each of its customers or to fix the permissions on its ftp server. So I could download and view every customer's files, which included forthcoming issues of magazines as well as press adverts for as-yet-unannounced products. If only the uploaders had used some form of encryption software, I would have been unable to decipher the files once I'd downloaded them.

Every technology has its downside and data encryption is no exception. Encrypting files can add another level of complication for users, and can cause performance slowdowns. So there's no point in encrypting files or email the contents of which would, if disclosed to the world in general, cause no problem for anyone. Conversely, bear in mind that any data that is encrypted will immediately attract the interest of a hacker who happens to encounter it, so if you're going to encrypt anything it's important to do it properly or not at all. In the case of data encryption, doing things properly means using an algorithm and a product that is known to be secure. And this, sadly, is about as large a can of worms as you'll ever encounter in IT security.

The law enforcement community, including covert intelligence agencies, doesn't like encryption. While corporate bodies appreciate the ability to exchange confidential information in private between those who need to know it, some people are of the opinion that encryption is only used by paedophiles and terrorists. Until just a few years ago, encryption was classed as munitions and there were strict rules about including encryption facilities in software.

In the past, some well-known commercial encryption products have included back-doors that allowed intelligence agencies to snoop on whatever travelled through the device. One such instance came to light in 1992 when Crypto AG, a Swiss manufacturer of encryption devices that were widely used in industry and by many international governments, admitted that its products had contained a back door that had been installed at the request of the USA's National Security Agency. As to how many other back doors exist, those who know are not telling. In the words of David Herson, during his time as head of the Senior Officers' Group on Information Security at the European Union, "The fact that the algorithm might be good – in principle – does not guarantee secure cryptography".

Meanwhile, various governments are tightening the rules on the use of encryption. In the UK, for example, it is a criminal offence not to divulge the password to encrypted information if asked to do so by the police. To the great concern of civil liberties groups, claiming to have forgotten the password is no defence.

When it comes to trustworthy encryption algorithms, the best choice today is the Advanced Encryption System or AES. This replaced DES, the Data Encryption Standard, as the recommended algorithm in the financial and defence sector a couple of years ago although either will suffice in the vast majority of cases. You'll also come across 3DES or Triple-DES as an option in some systems, which means encrypting something with DES and then re-encrypting it twice more. Most encryption software and hardware products use DES or AES in varying strengths. When using products that offer a choice of proprietary own-brand encryption or worldwide standard, always go for the worldwide standard. PKZIP, for example, the world leader in data compression software, offers own-brand or AES encryption. Always go for AES. If there's a choice of key strength, the more bits the better. So 128-bit

AES is better than 64-bit AES. But the algorithm always comes first, so 64-bit AES should be regarded as better than 128 bits in some proprietary system.

How Encryption Works

To understand why you should always go for a known algorithm such as DES or AES rather than a proprietary system, you need to know the fundamentals of why encryption works. Good encryption doesn't work on the basis that it is considered totally uncrackable or that the workings of the algorithm (the formula) is secret. There is no such thing as uncrackable encryption, and secret algorithms are a bad thing, because they completely fall apart if the secret gets out. Instead, good encryption works on the basis that the algorithm is widely known and understood, that it is based on mathematical principles, and that even with today's computing power it would take a very long time to solve the mathematical puzzle at the heart of the encryption.

For example, take two prime numbers such as 3 and 17. Multiply them and we get 51. Mathematicians say that 3 and 17 are the prime factors of 51. No one has yet discovered a formula for calculating the prime factors of any given number – it has to be worked out by trial and error. Clearly that's not difficult if we start with 51. But if we start with a number that's hundreds or thousands of digits long, calculating the prime factors is a lot of work even for today's most powerful computers. And that is the secret of good encryption – everyone knows what is required to crack it, but no one can do so.

The benefit of this philosophy was ably demonstrated in 2005 by Cisco Systems, the world's largest manufacturer of routers, switches and other equipment which is used to connect companies' computer networks to each other and to the internet. Michael Lynn worked at a firm of security consultants and, as part of his research, discovered various bugs in Cisco's products that could be exploited by hackers. He felt that it was important to make the details public so that companies that relied on Cisco equipment could take steps to protect their networks from hackers, and he announced his intention to reveal the details at a security conference in Las Vegas known as the Black Hat Briefings. Cisco went to great lengths to prevent the information becoming public. It obtained a legal injunction barring Michael Lynn or the conference organizers from ever revealing it. The company also hired staff to remove the offending pages from the conference proceedings and to re-master the CD-ROM that was to be issued to attendees.

Lynn's presentation went ahead, suitably censored, during which he demonstrated to the audience how to remotely gain root-level 'exec' control of one particular router. But not before Cisco had suffered a major PR disaster in which it was described as 'thugs' by one of the world's best-known commentators on security and encryption.

The trouble with computers is that they keep getting more powerful. It's easy to create an algorithm that would take 1000 years for today's most powerful computer to break. But we know that today's computers are probably 1000 times faster than those of a decade ago, hence the need to keep coming up with more complex formulas on which to base our encryption. Because while encryption that still takes a year to crack might quickly bore the typical hacker, it is not beyond the interests and capabilities of the average intelligence agency which needs to investigate the contents of an electronic notebook found in the possession of a terrorist. So when you next read in the papers about a university or a power company taking delivery of a computer with 6,000 processors, to be used for mundane tasks such as simulating the effects of climate change, ask yourself whether it might also occasionally find itself being used for other less public purposes. Possibly without the knowledge of its owners.

When you're encrypting information, there's no point in using lots of computing power in order to protect something in a way that will take 1000 years to crack unless it's really necessary. An email message which contains details of a company takeover that is due to happen next week must obviously be protected from insider traders until the facts become public, which means that a less demanding algorithm that can typically be cracked within a month will suffice.

The length of time required to crack a known encryption algorithm is one of the reasons why experts specify certain definite time periods for the duration of a password. If your operating system or application encrypts passwords using an algorithm that is known to take at least a year to crack, it's a good idea to change your passwords every few months so that, by the time a hacker has cracked the password, it will already have been changed.

In practice, with today's encryption algorithms being so powerful, those who need to crack an encrypted file (both hackers and law enforcers) tend not to use brute-force techniques because it would simply take too long. Instead, they use keystroke-loggers and other Trojan horse software or forensic techniques in order to discover the password that was originally used to encrypt the information. Police officers have told me that they rarely have to attempt to crack an encrypted file that's found in the possession of a suspect – instead they simply ask the suspect to provide the password and carefully explain the legal consequences of him or her refusing to do so. In the vast majority of cases this does the trick.

Getting Lucky

Sometimes hackers get lucky when they wish to break into encrypted information. The most famous case in recent years involves CSS, the Content Scrambling System that was built into the DVD specification to prevent pirates from copying movies from the original disk and distributing them over the internet. Although you can copy a movie from its DVD to a hard disk, it won't play unless the original DVD is also in the drive.

In the early days of DVD movies, the only way to play a disk was on a player that hooked up to your TV and hi-fi. DVD drives in computers were not yet available. Breaking the CSS system, which was based on encryption, would involve decoding the information held in chips within the player, which was impossible.

When DVD drives started to appear in PCs, software was made available by the drive manufacturers to allow DVD movies to be played on a computer's screen. It didn't take hackers long to dissect the software and discover the encryption passwords that were at the heart of CSS. And so Jon Johansen created DeCSS, which finally allowed customers to create backup copies of DVD movies that they had purchased, much to the annoyance of the movie industry.

Portable vs. Office-Based

The days of the desktop PC tied to a single location by a mess of data cables and the requirement for mains power look numbered. Laptops were once priced so highly that they were available only to highly-paid executives. Yet nowadays it's far from unusual to be in a train carriage and see laptop computers being used by business people, tourists, students, and anyone else who wants to work, write, listen to music or watch movies while out and about. In addition to laptop PCs running Windows or Mac OS, other portable computing devices are also incredibly popular and affordable. These include smart mobile phones, PDAs, palmtops, handhelds, and so on. All of which are capable of processing and storing large amounts of confidential information. And all of which are eminently easier to steal than a desktop computer.

Despite this, most such devices are not supplied out-of-the-box with any form of encryption. So if the device is lost or stolen, its contents are available to everyone. In cases where encryption is available, such as on certain palmtops and PDAs, it's rarely enabled by default.

Stolen laptops are big business. The going rate, I'm told by those who know, is a couple of wraps of heroin or crack cocaine. And while many machines end up being wiped clean and used by anyone who wants a cheap computer, a large number are stolen by people who know that the data stored on them is, to the right people, worth more than the hardware. Much, much more. Your sales people, for example, probably have some or all of your customer database on their laptops, along with other commercially sensitive data and, I'd guess, the passwords necessary to access the corporate network from any payphone. And there's probably an offline dump of an Outlook mailbox on there too.

A few years ago, the BBC in London had to hire security personnel to accompany its staff for the few hundred yards between its Television Centre premises and the underground train station because so many people were being mugged for their expensive mobile phones and laptops. Not only was the BBC worried for the safety of its employees, but there was also concern that many of those devices contained confidential information about celebrities such as home telephone numbers and payment details. Were this to have entered the public domain, lawyers acting for those celebrities would almost certainly have sprung into action.

In the second half of 2004, a survey among licensed taxi drivers in the UK discovered that, during the period, 5838 PDAs and 4973 laptops had been left in cabs accidentally by passengers. Perhaps the most embarrassing case ever was in 2000, when a spy working for the British foreign intelligence organisation known as MI6 left his laptop in a Tapas bar in London. The news came just a few days after an officer at the domestic intelligence unit, MI5, had his laptop stolen at an Underground station.

In August 2004 Louis de Bernieres, author of the hugely successful *Captain Corelli's Mandolin*, had just finished the first 50 pages of *A Partisan's Daughter,* his latest novel. He had been working in a large shed in his garden, on a laptop, and forgot to bring the laptop into the house before leaving for Edinburgh where he was attending a festival. Upon his return from Scotland he discovered that burglars had taken various items from his shed, including his garden tools and his laptop. The computer had not been backed up so the unfinished novel was lost and he had to start work on it again. "It was going very well, I was on a roll. I mostly feel angry", he told a BBC interviewer.

By default, Windows, Mac OS and all of the PDA/smartphone operating systems don't encrypt data that is stored in their memory or on the hard disk. This means that anyone who steals or finds the device can access all of the information that's stored on it. If a BIOS password has been set to prevent unauthorized users from starting up the machine, programs are widely available via the internet which can bypass these passwords and allow the thief to start up the computer. And once he has done so, all of the files on it become visible.

Among the many companies offering encryption products for both laptops and many other portable hardware platforms such as smartphones and PDAs is Pointsec (see **www.pointsec.com**). In addition, popular PDAs such as those from Palm and HP do include encryption but it is not enabled by default.

Encryption for the Masses

With Windows 2000, Microsoft introduced its Encrypting File System or EFS. This adds automatic encryption to any selected folders on the computer so that, if the machine is lost or stolen, information stored on the hard disk will not be readable. EFS works on a per-user basis, not per-computer. So if multiple people share a computer and they each have their own login account, enabling EFS will provide an additional layer of security over and above that provided by the separate logins. Plus, if the machine is stolen, the thief won't be able to view the data unless he knows the correct password. Even if he boots from a new copy of Windows, the data will still be hidden.

Enabling EFS is simple under either Windows 2000 or XP. Just right-click the folder or file that you want to protect and select Properties. Then on the General tab, click the Advanced button and tick the 'encrypt contents to secure data' box. That's it. The file, or files saved in that folder (or in any folder within that folder) will be encrypted. There's no need to enter any passwords to retrieve the information, and any application that needs to retrieve information from that folder will seamlessly be able to do so. EFS only works if the hard drive is formatted as NTFS rather than FAT.

Indeed, many of the security features built into Windows don't work with the FAT file system so you should always format your hard drives as NTFS.

Although Microsoft doesn't publicize EFS as much as it should, most security professionals suggest that users or employers should always enable it for all folders that contain data rather than applications. And because domain administrators (or any other designated Data Recovery Agent user) can still access all of the information on a user's PC, including files in an EFS-encrypted folder, the risk in a corporate environment of a user being able to use EFS to conceal illegal or forbidden information on his or her office PC is non-existent.

If you are not currently deploying EFS, a browse through Microsoft's Web site will enlighten you as to the benefits of this excellent facility, which offers many more features than this brief introduction can provide.

If there is a fly in the EFS ointment, it's the way that encrypted files are handled when moved or copied. Depending on the capabilities of the target operating system and media, the encryption may be removed. Sometimes the user will be informed that this is happening, although sometimes the file will be decrypted with no warning. For example, the FAT file system doesn't support EFS and floppy disks don't support any other file system, so files copied to floppy will lose their encryption on the copy but the source file will remain encrypted.

While EFS can be used on USB pen drives, it will only work if the USB device is formatted with NTFS. This is not normally recommended by Microsoft, and indeed the default configuration of Windows XP will prevent a USB stick from being formatted in any other way than with the FAT file system. To be able to format a USB drive using NTFS, you have to change its properties from 'optimize for quick removal' to 'optimize for performance'.

Users who choose to enable EFS, especially on stand-alone systems without the benefit of a domain or network administrator to fix things if they go wrong, should be made aware of the consequences. Primarily, this is that encrypted files which are backed up to media that supports EFS won't be accessible from any other computer. This means, for example, that someone who copies some files from their office PC in order to work on them at home will be unable to do so. Further, if you back up your encrypted files for safekeeping and you subsequently need to re-install Windows from scratch following a system crash, the new installation will effectively be another computer and thus it won't be possible to restore the backed-up data onto it.

There is of course a way around this, which is to back up the EFS encryption key to a floppy disk. The key is automatically generated when a user first starts using EFS, and is used to encrypt all files on that computer that belong to the particular user. By backing up the key, encrypted files can then be accessed on a different computer, or on the same computer after a re-installation of Windows. A Web search for terms such as 'windows efs key export' will provide all the information you need on how to back up the EFS key. If you have any files protected by EFS and you are currently backing them up to external devices, you should investigate key export as a matter of urgency. Otherwise, there is a real risk that you won't be able to restore data from your backups.

EFS protects files by only allowing access to the information if the user who is currently logged into the PC is the user who encrypted the file, or a user who has been granted access by the person who encrypted the file, or a user who is logged in as what's known as a Recovery Agent. By default, the Recovery Agent is the administrator account for that computer or for the domain, so beware of allowing the admin passwords for your PCs to become widely known.

While EFS appears to restrict access to encrypted files only to those with one or more specific usernames, the reality is slightly different. It is not the usernames that are checked but the internal id number of those usernames, which Windows uses for its own purposes. There is a subtle but crucial difference here, which it is important to understand. If you delete a username by removing that account from the computer, and subsequently create a new user with the same username, the names will be the same but their internal id numbers will not. So any encrypted files created by the original user will not be accessible to the new user. Or indeed to anyone at all, unless there's an administrator account to hand or the EFS certificate was backed up beforehand.

For more tips on EFS, including a 'Best Practice' guide, search Microsoft's Web site for Knowledge Base article number 223316.

Encrypting Email

Internet email is notoriously insecure and unreliable. There is no built-in way of finding out whether a message has reached its destination, or of ascertaining whether the message was intercepted during the course of its transmission. Reading the contents of an email message as it makes its way around the internet between sender and recipient is more difficult than faking a message but is far from impossible.

Internet-based email is great for sending confidential information between people, whether they are in the same building or on different continents. In fact, email is so popular that estimates put the totally daily usage of email worldwide at around 40 billion messages (including spam, which is said to account for around 65% of all email).

Because the internet is not inherently secure, sending confidential information by email requires that the data is encrypted by the sender and later decrypted by the recipient. There are various ways of doing this, which will be discussed below. Depending on the encryption method that is used, your email communication becomes more secure and altogether useful in four different ways:

1. *Scrambling.* The information can't be read by someone who deliberately intercepts it or perhaps who is sent a copy of the information by mistake;

2. *Integrity.* If someone attempts to alter the content of the message during its transmission, or if the information gets corrupted because of technical problems, this will be evident because the decryption process will fail. When using the internet to exchange important information, knowing that the information has not been deliberately or accidentally altered is often just as important as knowing that it hasn't been intercepted;

3. *Non-repudiation.* The ability to prove beyond reasonable doubt that a particular message was sent by a particular person, even if that person denies having sent it. This is incredibly useful in business, such as when

email is used to agree to the terms of a contract or to initiate a sale. Non-repudiation is a by-product of public key encryption, which is discussed below.

4. *Digital signatures.* In addition to non-repudiation, public key cryptography also allows email to be digitally signed by the sender. Such a facility has become even more useful in recent years because, in many countries, digital signatures that adhere to certain technical standards are now legally binding and carry the same weight as a hand-written signature. In the past, this was not the case – a document that bore only a digital signature and no hand-written one was not considered in law to have been signed at all.

Sending encrypted information via email can be done in a number of ways, depending on the capabilities of your company's existing email systems and the skills possessed by those who operate them. A relatively simple low-tech option is to use a third-party encryption program to scramble the confidential information that you wish to send, which you then attach to a standard unencrypted email attachment. Lots of third-party encryption programs are available. You could even consider using a file compression utility such as WinZip or PKZIP, the latest releases of which support the new AES algorithm.

If you'd rather 'do it properly', and allow your employees to send and receive encrypted and/or signed messages without needing to manually encrypt the information beforehand, you need to use an email system which supports the S/MIME protocol. MIME is one of the standards for internet email, and S/MIME contains additions which support encryption. Among the programs that support S/MIME is Microsoft Outlook, which is the most widely used email program among medium and large corporations.

Microsoft Knowledge Base article number 286159 details the precise steps required to send and receive encrypted and/or signed messages with Outlook 2002 and 2003. You can find it via **www.microsoft.com**. Another option is to consider a program such as Enigmail, which is well worth a look (and it's free).

Note, by the way, that EFS is only of use in protecting information held on a Windows PC and to prevent it being accessible by anyone else who gains access to that PC. If you send an EFS-encrypted file somewhere by email, or copy it directly to another machine over your LAN or WAN, the encryption is removed from the copy. When copying over the network, this will normally be pointed out in a dialogue box but no such warning is generated when the file is attached to an outgoing email – the recipient will simply get an unencrypted copy and the sender will not be told that this is the case. A similar situation exists if you use an ftp program to copy an encrypted file to your Web server – the copy will not be encrypted.

Encryption on the Move

It's great to be able to carry files around with you, either as a backup or to allow you to work on other people's computers. But if you don't encrypt those files, anyone who manages to get hold of your portable storage device can ready or copy them.

A USB data stick formatted to the NTFS standard will allow you to copy EFS-encrypted files to the device without losing the encryption. But for added security, you can buy USB sticks and portable hard disk drives that include hardware-based encryption as standard. Anything copied to the device is automatically encrypted, and access to the files requires a special program to be run into which you need to type your password. External USB hard disks with encryption are available from a number of manufacturers, one such being the encryp2disk brand from Amacom.

Recovery Procedures

There are some important management and technical decisions that should be considered before deciding whether to implement encryption within your company and, if so, how to manage its use by employees. In the case of highly confidential data that needs to be stored on users' computers or sent by email, circumstances will dictate. But should you allow encryption to be used more widely? Should all employees be allowed to use EFS for their general files? What if certain staff or departments prefer to use a third-party encryption program?

Is there a risk that dishonest staff can store illegal or stolen material on their office PC and that your technical staff won't be able to monitor this? While this generally can't happen with EFS (assuming that you don't allow staff to use administrator passwords), it is very easy for someone to install, say, PKZIP or WinZip on their computer and protect a collection of files with a password that no one else knows. One way to avoid this is to ensure that accounts used by employees don't have sufficient privileges to install new applications. You should also consider adding a clause to your computing policy that prohibits staff from protecting information with encryption except via officially-sanctioned programs and procedures.

The Key Exchange Problem

Encryption as a concept is said to have been invented by Julius Caesar, some 2000 years ago. But the biggest problem facing cryptographers since Caesar's era was always that of key distribution, and it took until the 1970s to solve it. The problem is very simple to describe. Having encrypted your information with a password (or, in Caesar's case, a substitution), you then need to convey the necessary information to the recipient in order that he can reverse the operation. So how do you manage to securely transmit a password to someone without any chance that it could be intercepted? After all, if such a secure method existed, there would be no need to have encrypted the original information in the first place.

The solution was ingenious. Instead of finding a way to transmit the password securely, a new form of encryption was invented in which the password doesn't need to be transmitted. At least, not all of it.

In traditional private-key or symmetric encryption, a password (or key) has to be exchanged for decryption to take place. Public-key or asymmetric encryption works very differently. Both the sender and the recipient have two passwords rather than just one. These are known as the private key and the public key. Each person guards their private key and never divulges it to anyone. They give copies of their public key to anyone who wishes to send them an encrypted message. Indeed, you will probably have received email from people who include their public key in the footer of all the email that they send, in order to disseminate it as widely as possible.

To encrypt some information, the sender uses both his own private key and the recipient's public key. To decrypt, the recipient requires his own private key plus the sender's public key. Hey presto — no private keys need to be exchanged.

The mathematics behind public-key encryption is complex, but one useful analogy between public- and private-key cryptography is to think of encryption as sending someone a valuable diamond that is protected by a padlocked box. In private-key encryption, the sender puts the diamond in the box, attaches a padlock, locks the padlock, and sends the locked box to the recipient. The sender then has to find a way to send the key, so that the recipient will be able to unlock the box.

With public key cryptography, the sender puts the diamond in a box. The recipient then sends the sender an unlocked padlock, which the sender uses to lock the box prior to dispatch. When the recipient receives the box, he already has the key for the padlock so he can open it without needing to request anything further from the sender.

In practice, public-key cryptography doesn't require the use of padlocks. One simply obtains the necessary program, which will generate a public and private key for you in the form of a string of numbers and letters. You keep the private part private, and publicize the public part. You can then use the program to exchange information with anyone else whose public key you know. To exchange information with someone whose public key you don't yet know, you simply ask that person to send it to you by email.

The best-known program for implementing public-key encryption is PGP, or Pretty Good Privacy. You can download it from **www.pgp.com**. You can use it to encrypt files for subsequent transmission by email to anyone whose public key you know, and it will also search various online directories where users of the program can publish their public keys for automatic discovery by the software.

The maths behind public key encryption means that, if I encrypt something with my private key and your public key, the only combination that will successfully decrypt the information will be your private key and my public key. If the message decrypts successfully, this proves that the information must have originated from me. Such a feature is known as non-repudiation, which is incredibly useful in business. It allows you to prove that someone sent a message, even if they deny having done so.

But there's still a problem on the horizon. If you receive an encrypted message from me, using my private key, how do you know who 'me' actually is? How do you know that I haven't simply downloaded PGP or any similar program and created a public key in the name of Microsoft Corporation or His Holiness The Pope? The answer is that you don't.

The solution, thankfully, is relatively simple. Rather than generating your own set of private and public keys, you buy them from a company that verifies your identity before issuing the key. Such companies are known as Certification Authorities, and two of the leading such organizations are Verisign and Thawte. Once you have your keys, you can exchange information with others with the added benefit that the recipient of your encrypted information has a guarantee that you are who you claim to be, which gives us digital signatures in addition to non-repudiation.

Sadly, implementing public-key encryption within an organization is a complex matter. How do you issue keys to employees and, more importantly, how do you revoke those keys when the employee leaves? The technology for managing all this is known as a Public Key Infrastructure. A Web search for PKI will lead you to a wide range of products and companies that can help you.

SSL and VPNs

It is possible to ensure that all information which is transmitted between a Web site and its users is encrypted, using a technology called SSL or Secure Sockets Layer. This is used widely in electronic banking and online shopping, and a closed padlock symbol on the user's Web browser tells him that he is connected to a secure site.

Implementing SSL on your site is relatively straightforward – you simply need a certificate from a company such as Verisign and a server that supports it.

If you are considering allowing staff to work from home, a Virtual Private Network or VPN is a method for setting up an encrypted link between an employee's home PC and your company's network via the internet. Your employee can then work from home and connect to all of your company's network resources just as if he was in the office, but the link is encrypted so no one who intercepts it can access any confidential information such as the contents of private files or any passwords that the user types.

Windows includes software as standard for connecting to VPNs. To host a VPN your network server or router needs to support such a feature. Type 'vpn tutorial' into your search engine for more information, although be aware that setting up a VPN correctly is fraught with difficulty and you would be wise to seek professional advice if you intend to do this.

► FUNDAMENTAL FIVE

Your action points for this chapter:

1. If you wish to use encryption, set up a sensible policy. Don't allow staff to install encryption products and set their own passwords without the knowledge of the IT security department. ☐

2. Consider setting up EFS on all workstations, but ensure that it is done correctly so that passwords can be recovered by administrators and no-one else. ☐

3. Encrypt all confidential information, especially backups. ☐

4. If your encryption software offers a choice of algorithms, always use the strongest one. ☐

5. Always enable the encryption features on laptops and PDAs as these are most at risk from data theft if the machine is stolen. ☐

28

Employees' Own Computers

There are all sorts of potential security problems when an employee uses his own computer for company purposes. The employee will almost certainly have administrator-level access to the system, to install any software that he wishes. There's no guarantee that it will be free of viruses and spyware. It might be shared by partners, spouses and children for all sorts of dubious purposes such as file sharing, hanging out in chat rooms, and so on. You wouldn't permit one of your company's computers to be used in this way. But when it comes to computers that don't belong to you, you don't really have a choice. You have no legal or moral jurisdiction over such hardware.

The easy way to avoid problems is simply to impose a blanket ban and to decree that it is not permitted for someone to use their own computer at home to carry out company business. While this will help to solve problems, it also means that the company loses out on a great deal. Staff who want, or need, to work at home will simply not be able to, which is bad for business.

One option is to set up a 'sheep dip' computer. This is a PC running antivirus software that is not connected to the company network. Anyone who has been working on a document at home on a computer that might potentially be infected with a virus must scan the document on this computer before being allowed to copy it onto any other workstation in the company. This does of course require the document to be brought in on CD, floppy or USB stick rather than being sent by email or ftp. If email and ftp facilities are required then the sheep-dip computer will require a network connection, though ideally this should remain disconnected when not being used.

Although it's impossible to lay down rules as to how employees configure or manage their own computers, it's wise to offer some basic advice and to explain the risks involved to the staff member and to the company as a whole if the advice is not followed. Among the points that you should spell out are:

- Make sure that your home computer has antivirus software. The software should be the latest version and the virus signature database should be updated at least once a week. Ensure that it is configured to scan all files each time they are accessed, which will flag up a warning message as soon as you try to copy an infected file to another computer;

- Install some anti-spyware software and run it at least once a week. Download the latest updates from the internet before you run it. It's a good idea to use more than one spyware detection program, as they each have areas in which they perform less well than others. However, do not install more than one antivirus program as they tend to clash;

- You should avoid bringing in your personal laptop and connecting it to the company's network. If you need to do so, consult the technical staff first in order that they can verify it is free of viruses and other dangerous software;

- Ensure that your computer has a firewall. This is highly recommended if you are on a dial-up modem connection, and absolutely essential if you have an always-connected broadband ADSL or cable connection because your machine will be open to potential hackers all day and all night.

Perhaps the greatest problem with home computers owned by employees is that they are used not just by the employee, but also by their partners, children, the children's friends, and possibly many others. Where at all possible, stress to the employee that it makes sense not to allow non-technical users administrator-level access to the computer. Sadly this is not the default mode of operation with either the home or professional edition of Windows XP, but it can be configured with a little effort – see Chapter 9.

The dangers of not locking down a home PC are many and varied. Researchers from Symantec took a PC with a brand new unsullied installation of Windows and spent one hour surfing Web sites that were specifically aimed at children. By the end of the session the computer had acquired 359 assorted items of adware which had been installed without their knowledge, purely because the Web browser had not been configured to block such activity.

Firewalls

Firewalls for home PCs come in many shapes and sizes. If the computer uses a dial-up modem connection to access the internet, a software firewall is the most common solution and the best-known products are ZoneAlarm (`www.zonelabs.com`), the Norton Personal Firewall (`www.symantec.com`) and the McAfee Personal Firewall (`www.mcafee.com`). ZoneAlarm is available in a free version, which is perfectly adequate if you need something that performs basic port-filtering functions.

If the home user has a broadband always-on connection, the choice of firewall is wider but the need for one is greatly increased. An always-on connection is always-hackable, 24 hours a day, seven days a week, so basic protection from a firewall is essential. According to a survey carried out in 2002, a newly-connected broadband installation receives three attempted hacks within the first 48 hours of its existence. The current firewall on my own broadband connection at my office has, at the time of writing, been installed for just a couple of months. It is currently telling me that it has blocked some 42,000 attempted attacks.

Broadband is generally delivered via a cable TV provider or through a telephone line. If it comes through the telephone line it's often known as ADSL or DSL. DSL stands for Digital Subscriber Line. The "A" version is asynchronous, meaning that the upload and download speeds are not the same.

If the broadband comes via a cable TV company, the incoming line will be connected to a cable modem supplied by the provider. To use the broadband connection on a single PC, you plug the cable modem into that computer. To share it among multiple computers in the household, you connect the cable modem to a router and each PC then plugs into the router. The cable modem doesn't normally include a firewall so some additional product is needed. In single-PC mode, the easiest option is to install a software firewall on the computer. If you go for the router option, simply buy one with a built-in firewall.

If the broadband comes via the phone line as ADSL or DSL, almost all providers issue subscribers with a broadband modem that connects to a single PC via a USB connector and which does not include a firewall. The easy option is then to install a software firewall on the PC, but there's a better solution.

If you want to share the ADSL/DSL connection across more than one computer, you buy a box that contains an ADSL/DSL modem, router and firewall in a single package. Throw away the USB modem, plug the new box into the telephone socket, and plug each of the PCs into the other side of the box via an Ethernet cable. Each PC now has broadband internet access, the router means that the PCs are also now networked so can share each other's resources, and the built-in firewall provides better protection than would be achieved if you simply used a personal firewall. This additional protection is the result of the hacker encountering the firewall at the router rather than at the PC. That is, earlier in the chain. And a Trojan or other malicious program that might crash a personal firewall and thus allow hackers in will not manage to crash the router.

Routers with built-in firewalls are considered more secure than personal firewalls. Therefore, if you have an ADSL/DSL connection and just a single PC, it is highly recommended that you still abandon the USB modem in favour of a router, even if you will only ever be plugging one PC into a router that is capable of accepting four or more machines. Although USB modems are generally supplied free of charge, ADSL routers with built-in firewalls cost less than £50 and are well worth the investment. Major players in the market for consumer-priced devices are Vigor/Draytek, Netgear and Zyxel.

Getting NATted

One reason why a router with built-in ADSL modem is safer than a standard ADSL modem connected to the USB port is that routers offer the option of NAT, or Network Address Translation. Each device that's connected to the internet (i.e. every Web server, mail server, etc.) has an IP address, such as 212.104.169.227. To talk to a device you need to know its IP address and, assuming that there's something listening on the other end that isn't blocked by a firewall, your request will get through. The rules of the internet state that certain ranges of IP addresses are non-routable, which means that they can only be used to communicate between machines on the same LAN, and not across the internet.

To understand this, think telephones. Consider the telephone number 202 456 1111, which will get you the White House in Washington. This is the equivalent of a fully routable IP address, because you can dial it from wherever you happen to be. It will work from within the White House itself or from anywhere outside. Conversely, consider the telephone number 2285 which, for the sake of argument, we'll pretend is the extension number of the White House kitchens. You can dial it from within the White House, but calling it from anywhere outside simply won't work. In internet terminology, 2285 is a non-routable IP address. If you assign IP address 2285 to one of your computers, staff in your building will be able to access it over your LAN but it won't be reachable over the internet.

One well-known range of non-routable IP addresses is 192.168.0.0 to 192.168.255.255. Anything with an IP address in this range cannot be directly contacted over the internet, but can be contacted over the LAN to which it is connected.

If you connect a PC to the internet via a USB-based broadband modem, the PC will require a routable IP address and thus it can be attacked by any hacker who knows what the IP address happens to be. Or by any hacker who happens to stumble across it by trying IP addresses at random. But if you use a combined ADSL modem and router, it is only the modem/router which talks to the internet and so it is only the modem/router which needs a routable IP address. The PC or PCs to which the modem/router is connected can be given non-routable IP addresses because they don't talk to the internet directly – they talk through the modem/router.

So, a hacker who finds the IP address of the modem/router can attempt to connect to it but will find his way blocked by the firewall within it. Should he wish to connect to a PC rather than the modem/router, he'd have to connect to a machine that might have a non-routable IP address of, say, 192.168.0.10. Which simply can't be reached over the internet, in the same way that dialling 2285 from your home or office telephone won't get you through to the White House kitchens.

Incidentally, it's possible to buy ADSL routers that include a Wireless Access Point. So not only can you plug up to four computers into the device via network cables, you can also connect to the internet via the router from machines that have WiFi capability. If you have a laptop or palmtop, this is the way to go. But remember the advice in Chapter 13 about configuring the WAP so that you don't inadvertently provide free internet access (not to mention access to all the files stored on your other PCs) to everyone in the neighbourhood.

▶ FUNDAMENTAL FIVE

Your action points for this chapter:

1. Be aware that you have limited legal rights to specify how staff use their own computers, so your only option may be to prohibit the use of such equipment for company purposes. ☐

2. Advise all staff to ensure that they have antivirus software installed on their computers. ☐

3. All staff should have a firewall on their computer, especially if the computer has a permanent (e.g. broadband) internet connection. ☐

4. If staff use wireless internet technology at home, ensure they are aware of the security implications. ☐

5. Consider a total ban on staff connecting their own laptops to the company's network. ☐

How Hackers Use Search Engines

Most users of the Web rarely stop to consider just how powerful and important search engines such as Google are. Without them the Web would be unusable. Google's network of some 10,000 servers is among the most powerful computer installations in the world. Its Website receives around a quarter of a billion hits per day, yet it still manages to deliver the results of most searches within a few tenths of a second from its index of over nine billion Web pages.

But the power of search engines is often underestimated and this can pay dividends for hackers in two ways. First, search engines often add confidential files to their indexes without the knowledge of the owners of those files. Second, the search engine makes it easy for hackers to locate those files.

Keeping Search Engines Away

A search engine works by continually trawling the Web in search of pages that can be added to its index. Although all search engines have the facility for site owners (or indeed anyone else) to submit pages for inclusion in the index, the vast majority of sites find their way in as the result of regular trawling (or spidering, as it's generally called).

There are probably some files on your Web site that you'd rather the search engines didn't index. PHP and Perl script files, for instance, and access control files such as .htaccess and .htpasswd which contain lists of usernames and passwords. Not to mention all those documents which are intended for employees' or customers' eyes only but which, for various reasons, have been placed in directories which are publicly accessible to anyone who happens to stumble across the URL.

Stumbling across files that were inadvertently placed on public Web sites is something that search engines are very good at. Try typing 'company confidential' into your favourite search engine for an instant demonstration of just how good. Thankfully there's a way to prevent this happening. Actually there are two. The first method is to use a robots.txt file, which is a small text file that you place in the root folder of your public Web site. By convention, any search engine which visits your site in order to add one or more pages to its index will start by checking for the presence of a robots.txt file and, if it finds one, will obey the commands within it. Those commands allow you to specify which folders or directories are out of bounds to the search engine. You can even specify search engines by name, if you want to prevent pages from being indexed only by one specific engine.

The format of a robots.txt file is fairly simple. For example, here's a file that will prevent all search engines from accessing any files in three named directories on your server.

```
User-agent: *
Disallow: /cgi-bin/
Disallow: /tmp/
Disallow: /private/
```

Note that you are only allowed a single robots.txt file on your site, and it must be in the root directory of the public site (docroot or wwwroot, as it's often called). So if your site is **www.mysite.com**, the file's URL must be `www.mysite.com/robots.txt` and not, say, `www.mysite.com/files/robots.txt`.

The other way to keep search engines away from your pages is to use a special META tag in your HTML files. Consider the following simple HTML document:

```
<HTML>
<HEAD>
<META NAME="ROBOTS" CONTENT="NOINDEX, NOFOLLOW">
</HEAD>
<BODY>
This file will not be added
to any search engines.
</BODY>
</HTML>
```

When a search engine scans an HTML file, it adds the contents of that file to its index. It also follows any hyperlinks contained in that HTML file, and adds those destination pages to its index too. The special META tag in the head section of the above HTML document tells search engine robots not to index the page, and not to follow any of the links within it either.

Although this META tag technique only works for HTML files, and not, say, for Word documents or PowerPoint presentations that may be downloadable from your site, it does have the advantage that it can be implemented by anyone who creates HTML documents. Conversely, because robots.txt must reside in the root folder of your Web site, it normally requires action by the site's administrator to maintain this file (if all of the staff who maintain your Web site have access to the docroot directory rather than being confined to the directory that holds the pages for their particular department or product area, then this is something that demands your urgent attention).

Through use of both the META tag and a robots.txt file you can ensure that information which is not intended for public consumption does not end up in the hands of the public. Or, worse, in the hands of hackers.

How Hackers Use Search Engines

The job of a search engine is to make things easy to find, and hackers use this to their advantage in order to retrieve files from the deepest recesses of those search engines. The practice even has a name – Google Hacking. By understanding how Google Hacking works, and some of the techniques employed, you will be able to ensure that your own site doesn't fall prey to such an attack.

First, make sure that you don't inadvertently upload files to your Web server which contain ftp password information. I mentioned in Chapter 5 that if you accidentally upload your ws_ftp.ini file to your Web server, anyone who retrieves it via a Google search will have details of all the passwords that you use when uploading files to your Web servers. Although the data in ws_ftp.ini is encrypted, the protection is trivial to crack and programs to do it are freely available on the Web. Locatable by Google, of course.

To locate ws_ftp.ini files, hackers use Google's **inurl** keyword. This allows them to search for words that appear within the URL of a Web page rather than within the content of the page itself. It's a fair bet that a URL that includes the word ws_ftp.ini is actually a ws_ftp.ini file. You can see for yourself by typing **inurl:ws_ftp.ini** into Google.

Make sure that any directories containing files for internal use only are protected by a robots.txt file and/or a META tag (see above). To see what happens if you don't, type **internal use only** or **company confidential** into Google. You can use Google's filetype keyword to narrow down your search. For example, type **internal use only filetype:ppt** into Google and it will return a wealth of interesting PowerPoint presentations.

Hackers often combine the inurl and filetype keywords, and the results can be truly frightening. A search for **inurl:admin filetype:xls password** will return links to Excel spreadsheet files which have been placed within admin directories on the Web server and which contain the word 'password'. You might assume that no one would be mad enough to store a list of passwords on their Web server, but sadly this is not the case.

Next, we'll use Google to look for Web-accessible directories that don't contain an index.htm file. If you fail to put an index.htm or default.htm file in a directory, anyone who points their Web browser at that directory will be shown a directory listing rather than an html page. The directory listing allows them to view and download any file, and to view the entire list of files in that directory and in any directories below it.

Directory listings which appear as a result of missing index.htm files generally start with a line of text such as 'index of /www'. The first entry in the listing is usually Parent Directory. So, by searching Google for sites containing 'index of' and 'parent directory', we can locate directory listings easily. The phrase that you need to type into Google is:

intitle:index.of "parent directory"

Next, a very simple technique that helps you find out whether hackers are currently targeting your company, discussing the possibility of doing so, or merely spreading unfounded gossip about the quality of your products. If this is the case, there's a fair chance that the discussion is taking place on a Web-based forum, chat room or news group. So use a search engine to help track down those discussions. The key to effective Web searching is to predict the words that might be used on those forums and chat rooms. For example, search for phrases containing your company name plus combinations of words such as sucks, hack, security, servers, crap and so on.

Beware of insecurities that happen as the result of deep linking. Say you have a public Web site for your company at www.mysite.com. You have a collection of files for employees only which resides in the /employee directory (i.e. www.mysite.com/employee). When a user follows the official link from your front page to the employees section, they are taken to a page that runs a special program that requests a username and password and, assuming this is correct, the index page for the employee mini-site is displayed. But what happens if the user goes straight to www.mysite.com/employee/documents.htm by typing the address into the browser? In this case, because the user has not entered the employee area via the official route, he or she will not be asked for a password.

In the case of legitimate employees, this isn't really a problem. If an employee bookmarks a page that they've visited in the past, and wishes to get back to it quickly, maybe it doesn't matter that they take a short cut. But Google, and indeed other search engines, make it possible for hackers to find those protected pages too.

For a simple example, type intitle:employees.only into Google and you'll find various pages containing that specified phrase in the page title. Some contain a username/password login box so you'll get no further, but many don't. During my research for this chapter I encountered the Web site of a company in the aviation and defence industry whose employee section was easily located via a Google search. From their employee pages I could download copies of commercial fonts that the company had purchased. I could also download logos and template files for all their letterhead, fax cover sheets, user manuals, Web pages, sales presentations and product brochures. A social engineer's dream.

▶ **FUNDAMENTAL FIVE**

Your action points for this chapter:

1. Use the major search engines to look for instances of your company and its products, so you are aware of what is being said about you in chat rooms, forums, newsgroups, blogs and so on. ☐

2. Use a robots.txt file on your Web server to control the information that search engines add to their index. ☐

3. Ensure that there are no confidential files inadvertently left on your Web server, such as private document files or ws_ftp.ini files. ☐

4. Try out some simple google hacking, targeted at your own company's Web site, to find out just how much a hacker could discover about your organization. ☐

5. Ensure that all directories on your Web server have an index.htm file, otherwise hackers can browse the full list of all files in that directory. ☐

30

Denial of Service Attacks

A Denial of Service (DoS) attack is a frightening concept because it doesn't require the defeating of any security obstacles such as passwords or firewalls. Instead, it simply requires the hacker to make use of publicly available facilities on the target computer.

Any computer system has a limit to the amount of requests it can handle at one time, and those who design systems spend much time and effort ensuring that these limits are never reached. Further effort is put into ensuring that, if the limits are about to be reached, remedial action can be taken. For example, the www.defeatingthehacker.com site will probably receive no more than a few thousand hits per day, which is well within the capability of the server provided by the company that hosts the site. In the unlikely event that traffic levels reach a few million hits per day, the current server should still cope. And if it doesn't, the hosting company offers faster servers to which the site can be moved in just a few hours with nothing more than an exchange of email messages and credit card numbers.

But what if the site were to receive a million hits per second, for days on end? It clearly couldn't cope, and would almost certainly crash. Which, in the case of a Web-based business, means a total inability to trade. The only real option is to pull the plug on the servers and wait for the attacks to stop.

This is the reality of a DoS attack, and they are very common because perpetrating such an attack is as easy as downloading the necessary tools from the internet and choosing a target. Thankfully, disabling someone's computer through a DoS attack is still covered by computer misuse legislation, even though no password cracking or firewall breaching is involved, because the law generally recognizes the effects of the hacker's actions rather than the methods he employs.

Many large organizations have been hit by DoS attacks in the past, including the likes of CNN, Yahoo and Amazon, causing huge amounts of lost business and a significant degree of adverse publicity. In some DoS cases, victims have seen usage levels on their servers increase to such a degree that the machines were receiving the equivalent of a month's traffic every second. That's an increase of around 267,000,000%.

In traditional DoS attacks, all of the increased traffic originates from a single source. Clearly this limits the hacker's ability to cripple a large server because it requires him having at his disposal an even larger server. However large the hacker's server, the victim can mitigate the problem by installing a filter which blocks all traffic from the hacker's IP address. The hacking community therefore needed something more powerful than traditional DoS, and it wasn't long before they found the solution to their problem in the form of DDoS (Distributed DoS). Now, instead of firing the spurious requests from a single location, the hackers employed thousands of computers around the world to join forces to attack the target. Most worryingly, the owners of those computers had no idea that they were being exploited in this way.

The hackers came up with Trojan software and viruses which, when installed on the computer of anyone who was gullible enough to click on the email attachment, would turn that computer into what's become known as a zombie or bot (short for robot). These zombie computers would appear to function normally so their owners would have no idea that the Trojan was installed. But they would be continually listening for commands, at which point they would spring into action.

The hackers would continue sending out Trojan-laced emails by the million, until a team of several thousand bots was in place (the bot was programmed to send a message back to its creators, so the hackers always know the size of their network of bots, or bot-net). Once the bot-net is large enough, the DDoS hackers are ready to pounce. They send out an electronic wake-up call to the army of listening zombies, each of which immediately joins the DoS attack on whatever company was specified by the hackers when they sent out the wake-up call. Within seconds, the victim organization is now receiving millions of times its normal levels of traffic, from tens of thousands of locations around the world.

Protecting Yourself

By their very nature, DoS and DDoS attacks are very difficult to protect yourself from. However good your firewall and IDS, and however complex your passwords, these techniques will offer no protection from a denial of service attack. Instead, you need hardware products that can filter out DDoS traffic before it reaches your network, or you need to rent a filtering service from a third-party supplier through which all your incoming traffic can be routed in the event of an attack. Such protection is aimed mostly at large organizations and doesn't come cheap – do a Web search for DDoS Attack Protection and you'll find a multitude of suppliers eager to help you survive an attack.

Possibly the best protection for small and medium companies is to accept that running and protecting your own servers on your own premises is fraught with all sorts of problems, and that this is a job best left to the experts. If your key public-facing servers (i.e. those which provide Web and email facilities) are hosted elsewhere rather than in house, then protecting against DoS and DDoS attacks is one less thing for you to worry about. Maintaining servers, especially those which are accessible to the world via the internet, requires time and skill which is often best left to others.

Accidents will Happen

Most DoS situations arise as a result of the deliberate actions of external hackers. However, some are accidental. A simple error in the configuration file of a new network server, or a broken cable somewhere, can result in total loss of your network at very short notice.

If everything grinds to a halt without warning, be prepared to accept that this might be the cause and that the culprit might well be unaware of the consequences of their actions. In one organization where I once worked, network access for 1000 staff suddenly stopped because someone plugged their printer into the wrong network socket after it came back from being serviced and cleaned. It took an hour of frantic effort by a lot of people to track down the source of the problem, during which time none of those 1000 employees could do any work because they couldn't log into the system or access their networked file store.

▶ FUNDAMENTAL FIVE

Your action points for this chapter:

1. If a DoS attack happens, you won't have much time to consider how to respond. So think about your options now. ☐

2. To help prevent attacks, ensure that you install all security patches on workstations and servers as soon as possible after they are announced. ☐

3. If you host your Web site or email on other companies' servers, talk to your provider to ensure that they have a strategy for handling DoS attacks. ☐

4. Not all DoS incidents are deliberate attacks by hackers. Some are accidental. Ensure that your planning takes account of this. ☐

5. Use a product such as the Microsoft Baseline Security Analyser to detect missing security patches on critical Windows servers. ☐

Provisioning and Identity Management

E ffective IT security means keeping tight control over all of your company's systems and assets and the people who have access to them. Unfortunately this is easier said than done. How many different accounts and passwords allow files to be uploaded to your Web server, and who has them? Who knows the administrator passwords for your employees' desktop PCs? Do you subscribe to any commercial Web-accessible databases or information systems? If so, who knows the passwords? Do you allow staff to dial into your network from home? If so, who has access to the system? Where are your key assets such as customer and product databases held, and who knows how to access them? What about the passwords for connecting your LAN to the internet or performing maintenance on your email servers or firewall? Or for changing the Web site to which your company's domain name

points? And the code for disabling the intruder alarms that allow access to your offices, warehouse, store rooms, server rooms and so on.

Then there's the hardware that you probably issue to staff. A desktop PC, perhaps a laptop, a mobile phone or PDA, external hard drives or USB drives, and other specialist devices that they may require such as ID tokens. Once you're on top of all this, then it's time to consider the assets which aren't particularly related to IT, but which are still assigned to staff and which must be accounted for. Company cars, petrol accounts, membership of the local gym, discount cards for the canteen, ID badges, car parking passes, software licences, and so on.

Keeping track of the physical and non-physical assets to which an employee is entitled comes under the relatively new management topic of provisioning, and it's essential that you give some thought as to how you manage the process in your company. One option is to invest in a software package designed specifically for the purpose of helping you manage the provisioning in your company, from suppliers such as Thor (`www.thortechnologies.com`). Alternatively you can do it yourself via a straightforward database or spreadsheet.

At its simplest, a provisioning database will be a matrix of assets and employees, and the dates on which a particular asset was issued to a particular employee. You should also record the reason why the asset was issued, the person who issued it, and the date by which the asset is expected to be returned. In the case of physical assets such as a laptop or an ID badge, the process of returning it is straightforward. Logical assets such as passwords can't be returned, so should be disabled. When an asset is returned or cancelled, record this in your provisioning system. Don't simply delete the record, as it may be useful at a later date if a dispute arises or an investigation is launched into a current or former employee.

Consult your provisioning system regularly, and ensure that it has the facility to produce reports by asset type or employee. For example, you might want to compile a list of everyone who has a company-issued laptop, or of all the assets that are currently issued to people in the marketing department.

Automated provisioning systems can save you money, especially if they also provide the function of an asset register. If a new employee needs a licence for Microsoft Office, for example, or a subscription to an online marketing database, the asset register might highlight the fact that there are already some spare licences and subscriptions available which were previously used by staff who have since left the company.

Roles

A two-dimensional provisioning system based on a matrix of assets and employees can quickly become unmanageable. Adopting a role-based method can bring some order to the proceedings, and this is the way that most commercial provisioning systems operate. Role-based provisioning involves defining a number of roles and the assets that accompany them, and then describing a person in terms of their role rather than the long list of assets that they require. Role-based provisioning has major benefits. First, it simplifies the processes involved. The role of marketing executive might be defined as requiring a mobile phone, low-spec laptop, a password for the Web server and an ID badge. If the specification changes, such as allowing a high-specification laptop or the addition of a gym membership card, updating the role definition can update all relevant employees' records.

The system will often also integrate with your other servers and domain controllers, to allow the automatic creation of new user accounts based on those defined roles. So when a new marketing executive joins the company, all of the necessary usernames and passwords associated with that role are created without the need for any manual work.

Role-based provisioning can automatically alert you to undesirable situations. A buyer with the necessary privileges to issue purchase orders should be prevented from being able to access the system which allows users to sign off purchases or pay suppliers, for example, as this would make it temptingly easy to commit fraud. A role-based provisioning system can therefore be configured to automatically issue a warning if a member of the buyers group is given access to the sign-off system.

Another benefit is that it becomes very easy to deal with short-term employees and contractors. In most companies, network and computer access for such people is handled by the establishing of one or more generic temporary or contractor accounts, the password for which is given to whoever happens to be doing the job at the time. Rarely are records kept as to who is using those temporary accounts. Clearly, this is an undesirable situation, because any misuse of the system cannot be undeniably linked to the actions of a named person. Not only will this hamper any subsequent investigation, but the user of the account will probably be aware from the start that his actions are not traceable.

Finally, role-based provisioning makes it easy to amend the database when someone moves to a different job function. Simply change the role associated with that user, and the system will produce a report which details the differences between them and thus the necessary actions that need to be taken (e.g. which passwords must be disabled, which can be retained, which items must be returned and so on).

Risk Avoidance

Formal management of provisioning, whether done manually or with an automated home-grown or commercial system, can seem like an unwelcome chore. Surely it's quicker and easier not to bother? After all, just about every computer system can produce reports as to who has access to it, so the information is always available if we need it. A central record of provisioning can certainly be complex to set up, but it will pay for itself through improvements in security and accountability.

Even the smallest companies can benefit from having a provisioning system in place, because automating your provisioning brings with it a benefit known as identity management. It allows you to control all of the assets and benefits which define someone as being part of your company, and thus makes it possible to control how those assets are used. Time and time again, companies which fail to control assets and identities discover, often too late, that those assets and identities are being abused or misused.

The misuse takes many forms. At the not-so-serious end of the scale, a former employee might still be able to enter your premises and take advantage of cheap meals in the staff restaurant because no one remembered to request the return of his entitlement card when he left the company. At the other end of the scale, a former employer might be able to access your confidential files because he had two passwords for the file server and, when he left, he only declared one of them and so the other one was not disabled.

When I am asked to present a paper at security conferences and seminars, I always make a point of asking the audience of security professionals whether they have discovered, after leaving a job, that the passwords for their previous employers' systems were still valid. It's not uncommon for a quarter of all such people to say that yes, this has been the case. In one instance, a password to a highly confidential file server was still valid five years after the employee had moved to another company (which, as it happens, was a direct competitor).

▶ FUNDAMENTAL FIVE

Your action points for this chapter:

1. Ensure that you have some form of provisioning facility in place, so that you know which equipment and privileges has been allocated to each staff member. ☐

2. When a staff member changes roles, review their entry in the provisioning database. ☐

3. If a staff member leaves the company, use the provisioning system to ensure that all equipment they were allocated is returned. Deactivate all logins and passwords immediately. ☐

4. Consider the use of a proprietary provisioning system rather than designing your own. It might well save you time and money in the long term. ☐

5. Whatever technology and database systems you use to record staff entitlements, adopting a role-based rather than person-based approach will be more efficient. ☐

32

Data Interception

Being hacked is at best unpleasant and at worst can spell the end of your company. But the silver lining, albeit a small one, is that you almost always know it's happened and can therefore take steps to limit the damage. Sometimes the signs of the attack are obvious, such as a defaced Web site or an empty bank account. Other attacks may be harder to spot but, if you follow the advice given so far about proactively keeping an eye on log files and using firewall software and other such tools, the clues will eventually materialize.

Data interception is different because it's very difficult to find out whether it's happened. If a hacker installs a keystroke logger on your email server there will be telltale signs that it's there. If the hacker prefers to tap into your network cabling or sniff unencrypted WiFi traffic out of the air, you'll probably never know precisely what he did or how he managed it.

The symptoms will still be there, of course, such as the broken Web site and the empty bank account, but no amount of post-event investigating is likely to reveal the tricks. And if the hacker is smart enough to resist the temptation to cause large-scale disruption, you might never find out that it's been going on. All of which is why your IT security regime must give some consideration to line-tapping, WiFi sniffing and all other types of data interception.

To help make the hacker's job as difficult as possible, restrict details of your network cabling and layout (technically known as the topology) and other sensitive information on a need-to-know basis. If you are proud of your new network it's tempting to tell everyone about it, and to put fancy diagrams on your Web site which tell everyone how many servers you've got, what each one does, and how they are linked together. But the sad truth is that most people don't care, and a fair proportion of those that do will misuse the information. If you want to impress your competitors and potential customers, do so by explaining why you don't make such information public. Those who understand will think much more highly of you. Those that don't need not concern you anyway.

Remember, anyone who stumbles across an unguarded network socket can plug in a laptop running a network protocol analyser and view the traffic that is travelling through that cable. Depending on the layout of your network, they might well be able to view all the data that is travelling over the entire network, including any passwords that are being typed and any confidential information that is being viewed. Protocol analyser applications are widely available on the internet and some of the best are even free. Check out www.ethereal.com for one of the most well-known examples. Then make sure your IT security policy expressly forbids staff from installing or using such programs without written authorization.

Although external hackers do use protocol analysers, this is one technique that is ideally suited to the proverbial disgruntled or dishonest employee because it only works if the perpetrator is on-site. To protect against the unauthorized use of such devices, ensure that you enable all of the possible encryption options on your network. Some protocols, notably ftp and telnet, do not support encryption and so anyone using these methods to communicate between machines on your network can potentially have their session sniffed by someone using a product such as ethereal. The solution is to use the safer, encrypted versions, namely Secure FTP (sftp) and Secure Shell (ssh).

Even an industrial-strength encryption system and heavily guarded network hardware won't necessary bring you 100% protection from hackers. Those who are really determined to steal your data still have other means at their disposal, albeit using methods that are risky, expensive, and practised mostly by the likes of MI5 and the CIA rather than disgruntled employees or curious students. For example, researchers at the University of California have developed software which can analyse the sound of someone typing on a keyboard and, from the tiny differences in the sound that each key makes, piece together what has been typed with around 96% accuracy. Another technique, codenamed Tempest, involves picking up the radio waves generated by electronic equipment such as display screens. Ultra-sensitive computer installations such as political headquarters and defence agencies often have their most secret computers installed in rooms that have metal cages embedded in the walls to prevent leakage of signals that can be picked up in this way. Not that hackers always have to go to such lengths. I've known some practitioners manage to steal sensitive information from computer screens simply by peering into an office from across the street using a pair of binoculars.

WiFi Tapping

Tapping into an unprotected cabled network is often easy, especially as the software to monitor the connection is readily available free of charge. Performing similar operations on a wireless network is, sadly, just as easy. As mentioned in Chapter 13, most wireless networking equipment includes facilities for encrypting all traffic but the default setting, especially in equipment made for home and small-company use, is to disable it. This means that anyone with a laptop and the right software who happens to be in range can monitor everything that happens on the network. And yes, you guessed it, the software to do this is available for free on the Web. The best-known example goes by the name of NetStumbler (`www.stumbler.net`).

Hackers use NetStumbler to look for unprotected WiFi networks that they can monitor. The software is also widely used by those who simply wish to find an unprotected wireless network that they can use, perhaps because they are away from home and need access to the internet to check their mail. By ensuring that you enable encryption on your wireless hardware, and take into account the other recommendations made in Chapter 13, you can ensure that travellers in need of a Web fix steal someone else's bandwidth rather than yours.

Many places offer public wireless access to visitors, including many hotels, bars, conference venues, shopping centres and railway stations. Some offer it for free, while others require payment on a per-day or per-hour basis. But remember that not everyone has read this book and not every public-access WiFi network is set up correctly, so think twice before using such facilities to send or read confidential files. If you're sending a private file to the office via a public link, whether wireless or not, consider encrypting it first with a stand-alone program and then attach it to an email message. After all, you can never be entirely sure of the motives or the technical skills of those who set up such systems.

Experiment

If you are genuinely concerned that hackers could intercept information on your network, you should seriously consider looking for vulnerabilities on your systems before anyone else does. To test wired network ports, download Ethereal onto a laptop and experiment. Use NetStumbler on a WiFi-equipped laptop to probe your company's wireless networks in similar ways. If your company doesn't have any wireless networks as far as you're aware, try NetStumbler anyway – you may be surprised. Make sure that you have permission to carry out the investigation. If it's not an accepted part of your job description, i.e. if you merely help out with IT security issues on an unofficial basis, ensure that you don't place yourself in a position where it could be argued that you were hacking. And if you come across any sensitive information, such as administrator passwords with which that you are not normally entrusted, inform the owner of those passwords in order that they can be changed. This avoids any subsequent misplaced suspicion if those passwords are ever misused in the future.

FUNDAMENTAL FIVE

Your action points for this chapter:

1. Use anti-spyware and antivirus software to look for unauthorized interception software on your computers. ☐

2. Make occasional physical checks of computers and cabling to check for the presence of devices such as keystroke loggers. ☐

3. Ensure that network sockets in unattended public locations are disabled when not required. ☐

4. Use a laptop and a copy of Net Stumbler to find out whether a hacker could intercept your company's wireless network traffic. ☐

5. Use a network protocol analyser such as Ethereal to try tapping your wired network. If you can do it, so can a hacker or dishonest employee. ☐

33

Out of the Office

Not everyone works in the office all the time. Sometimes they work at home, from an hotel, from an internet café, a library, a train, a client's site, or just about anywhere else. Sometimes the equipment at the remote location belongs to the employer, such as a laptop supplied by your company. Other times the equipment belongs to the user, such as when a staff member works at home on a document over the weekend or in the evening and uses his or her own PC to do so.

Allowing information to be taken off-site and subsequently re-introduced into corporate systems is a modern-day necessity but is fraught with problems. Not only are there risks to confidentiality, caused by someone who fails to appreciate the value of the information that they have taken home for the weekend, but there's also a real risk that a virus on an employee's home PC could find its way into your company's network.

This chapter deals with the use of computer equipment that is not owned by the employee, i.e. it belongs to the employer or, perhaps, to a third party such as a hotel or client.

Viruses

A reliable antivirus policy requires that a computer should run up-to-date antivirus software and that its database of known viruses should be updated at least weekly. This policy should extend beyond those computers that are permanently based on your premises, and should encompass those which are used away from base. This includes laptops and any other handheld computers issued to staff.

Assuming that the computer is connected to the internet regularly, either at remote locations or when brought back into the office, the antivirus software should manage to keep itself up to date if it is configured to update automatically. If a scheduled update is missed because the computer wasn't connected to the internet at the time, most software will remedy the situation as soon as an internet connection next becomes available. You should verify this occasionally by clicking on the About button in the software and checking the version number or date of the virus definitions database that is installed. If it becomes apparent that updates are being missed, do something about it as soon as possible. To maximize the efficiency of the updating, configure the software to update daily rather than weekly.

If it is intended that a laptop should be regularly moved between networks, such as a user's home network and the employer's system, it is likely that a small amount of reconfiguration will be required each time the switch is made. For example, the corporate network might require the laptop to be set up with a specific IP address while the home network or broadband router might insist on being automatically allocated an IP address via the DHCP standard. Equally, the company network might require that all internet access goes via a proxy server, yet attempting to use this proxy server from external locations may not work. All of which can cause problems if laptops are connected to different networks.

Although the solution is relatively simple from a technical point of view (just change the settings) it normally means that the user of the laptop will need to be given sufficient access privileges to do this whenever required. Changing a computer's IP address or details of its proxy server requires what Windows XP refers to as Power User status rather than Normal User.

On the subject of laptops, be aware of the security vulnerabilities of hibernation mode. In many cases, a laptop that is not fully shut down but is merely hibernating can be restarted at the press of a button or opening of the lid, often without the prompts for passwords that would appear if the machine was being started up from cold. If this is the case with your company's laptops, ensure that staff are aware of the risk and that they don't leave laptops unattended if they are in hibernating mode.

Transferring Files

Probably the most common uses of a computer for business purposes outside the office are to work on a document or presentation, or to present a PowerPoint slide show. These tasks require that files be transferred from an office-based computer to a different system and, in the former case, copying the revised file back to a system at the office.

An employee who needs to copy a file to work on it elsewhere can do so in a number of ways. Common techniques include the use of a USB stick, emailing the file to an external account, or uploading the file to an ftp server for later retrieval. All of these methods are perfectly safe and will result in the file being copied as required. Assuming that the user actually has permission to copy the file, all should be well. But bear in mind that these methods also make it very easy for an employee to smuggle information out of your company without your knowledge or consent. Staying on top of this problem can be done through technical means or simply by making it clear to staff that copying files without permission will be considered a serious disciplinary offence.

To prevent the copying of files onto USB sticks, check out products such as DeviceWall and DeviceLock, mentioned earlier in this book. Access to ftp sites can be controlled and limited through your firewall. Preventing staff from emailing files to a personal account on, say, Hotmail or Google Mail can also be done via your firewall if required, by prohibiting access to those sites and others that offer similar facilities.

Consider the use of encryption if confidential files are taken off the premises. However, as discussed in Chapter 27, remember that a file which is protected by the Windows Encrypting File System will lose its encryption if copied to a floppy disk, external email address, ftp server, or a USB stick that is formatted as FAT rather than NTFS.

PDAs, Palmtops and Handhelds

Portable computers, especially small devices such as palmtop PCs, are lost and stolen with frightening frequency. Yet it's common for sales staff who use such machines to carry around with them their employer's customer database, trade price list and other confidential information as a matter of routine. If this is the practice in your company, ensure that the information is encrypted so that, should the device be lost or stolen, its value to the finder will be no more than the cost of the hardware. Most portable devices offer encryption nowadays but it's rarely turned on by default – ensure that you enable it and make it clear to the user of the machine that they must not disable it. I know of one particular case where a laptop containing highly confidential data was mislaid in London and, although the machine had some top-quality encryption software installed, the user had disabled it because he couldn't be bothered to type in the password every day.

Shared Computers

Sometimes we access the Web from a shared computer while away from the office, in a hotel or internet café or at a customer's site. This is usually to check email messages, stock prices, or perhaps to view other documents on public or private areas of a Web or extranet site. Should your employees find themselves in such a position, you should point out the following to maintain security:

■ If you type a username and password into a Web page on a shared computer, it's possible that subsequent visitors can take advantage of that information after you have left. For example, if you go to www.securesite.com and enter a username of robert and a password of secret into the box, someone who visits the same site on the same computer and merely types an 'r' into the username box may find that Windows helpfully retrieves the remainder of the username and the full password from its cache.

■ Some Web sites specifically ask whether you are using a shared computer and, if so, will ensure that your login credentials aren't stored on it. Equally, some shared computers are specifically configured to prevent this – many internet cafés have a policy of wiping the Web browser cache each time a different user logs in. If you're not sure, assume that there could be a problem and consider whether you want to risk entering your details.

■ A computer which has been set up specifically to offered shared access, such as in a hotel or an internet café, is normally safe to use. A computer which has been temporarily pressed into service as a shared resource at an event such as conference or seminar, but which normally gets used as someone's regular desktop computer, is almost certainly not secure.

■ It's possible that the shared computer is infected with a virus or a keystroke logger, which will record everything you type on it. It is not unknown for unscrupulous operators to install such software deliberately on their shared computers. If in doubt, don't browse secure sites or send confidential data.

Remote Access

There are various software solutions which allow you to access a PC remotely over the internet or a telephone line. Generally, you see the remote computer's desktop on your screen and can interact as if you were in front of it. Everything looks and feels exactly the same as if you were there, except that some things (notably the screen display) will be slower than normal.

Remote access to a computer can work in a number of ways, each of which has benefits and weaknesses regarding security, complexity and flexibility.

Possibly the simplest option is to use a Web-based service such as Log Me In (`www.logmein.com`) or GotoMyPC (`www.gotomypc.com`). Log Me In, one of the simplest to use, requires the download and installation of a free application on the computer that you wish to access remotely. Once installed and running, you can connect to that computer over the internet using nothing more than a Web browser. This means that you can access your PC from just about anywhere, including an internet café. And because the program communicates over port 80 as a standard Web application, it won't be blocked by a corporate firewall.

Although the facilities offered by such programs can be incredibly handy, the security risks are obvious. Anyone who knows your password can connect to your PC via the internet and control it remotely. They can use any application installed on it, and access all your files. You should consider your options carefully before deciding to use it. Perhaps set up a separate computer in your company to which the Log Me In system is allowed to connect, and which contains only the bare minimum facilities that a remote user requires.

Keep a careful watch on any copies of remote access software such as Log Me In which are installed in your company. By restricting your Windows users to standard accounts rather than Power User or Administrator, you can prevent them from installing this or any other application without permission. You should certainly prohibit the installation of such programs without good reason.

The second option for providing remote access to a PC is to use a dedicated commercial application. The best-known program in this sector is PC Anywhere, which allows access over the internet or via a direct 56 k modem connection on a telephone line (slower, but clearly more secure). Although it can work over the Web with a standard browser, access is generally via dedicated client software which is supplied with the product. For security over the internet, PC Anywhere supports many of the more recent encryption standards.

You can download a free 30-day trial of PC Anywhere from www.symantec.com. If you require the facilities of PC Anywhere (albeit not the direct modem link) but would rather not pay at all, VNC is a very popular and highly regarded alternative that offers similar facilities but is free of change. A recent version can be downloaded from www.ultravnc.com, and counts technical support staff among its many fans.

Another option for remote control/access is also free, and is built into Windows XP Pro (but not Home). The facility is known as Remote Desktop. Once you have activated the feature on the computer that you wish to access remotely, you can then access it via the internet (not a dial-up line) using the free client software supplied by Microsoft. Any administrator account on the remote computer is automatically permitted to connect to that computer remotely if the feature has been enabled.

Access by any other user account must be explicitly enabled on the remote computer. Accounts without passwords are prevented from connecting. Detailed help in setting up and using Remote Desktop can be found on the Web – just type Windows Remote Desktop into a search engine.

The three options covered so far for remote access to a PC all have one thing in common. The client side, whether using a dedicated application as in the case of PC Anywhere or whether using a Web browser, simply displays the screen image of the remote computer. All processing takes place on the remote computer, and any mouse or keyboard input that happens on the client is sent to the remote computer. If you use Word to edit a remote document, Word runs on the remote computer and you are merely seeing a 'spy camera' image of what's happening on it. The document file never leaves the remote computer.

And so to the fourth option, which works somewhat differently to the previous three. This is the Virtual Private Network or VPN.

A traditional office network, whether LAN or WAN, uses dedicated cables or wireless links to connect all the computers together. Each user on the network can, assuming they have the necessary access permissions, access other resources such as hard disk drives and printers as if those resources were connected to the user's own PC. Editing a Word document that's stored on a network drive works just the same as if that file were held on the local hard disk, except for a possible slight delay as the file is transferred over the network into the memory of the user's PC for editing, and a similar delay once the editing is complete and the file goes back across the network to be re-saved on the remote network drive.

A VPN is a way of connecting a remote computer to an existing LAN over the internet so that it works just like any other computer on the network and can share any resources to which the user has access. Because the dedicated cabling has now been replaced with the public (and intrinsically insecure) internet for this particular limb of the LAN, VPNs use encryption to ensure that any data which is intercepted can't be decoded. The end result is that someone using a VPN connection can connect to your LAN or WAN from hundreds of miles away without the need for you to install a dedicated Ethernet cable to that particular location.

Learning how to set up VPN connections can be tricky, but thankfully the Web is full of useful tutorials. A search for 'VPN tutorial' will bring up lots of examples. Windows XP ships with a VPN client as standard, allowing users to connect to any network that has been configured to accept them and which has the necessary hardware or software installed.

If a staff member needs to work from home and he or she has a broadband connection linked to a VPN-capable router, the VPN might be the best option for allowing easy remote access. The remote user will be able to access your network as if they were in the office, sharing drives and other resources very easily. And assuming that you set up the link correctly, VPNs are generally regarded as very secure.

Using a VPN can have occasional unexpected drawbacks. A friend of mine started using one to allow him to work from home at the weekend rather than driving to the office. Having created a document, he decided to print it over the VPN to the remote printer so that it would be ready for him to pick up from the printer's tray on Monday morning. Within minutes of initiating the print job he received a call from the police to advise him that the intruder alarm at the office had been triggered – which turned out to be caused by the heat generated by the printer.

Bear in mind that a VPN connection works just like a network drive. If someone on the remote end of a VPN wishes to edit a Word document that's stored 'back at base', the document travels over the VPN link to the remote user and Word then runs on that remote user's computer. Compare and contrast with the previous technologies (Remote Desktop, PC Anywhere, etc.) where Word runs on the computer at base, the document never travels anywhere, and the remote user is effectively watching the results on a remote camera that's pointed at the screen of a computer far away. If the Word document is actually a large database file rather than a small document, this will have speed implications as well as security ones.

VPN links are often surprisingly slow, because so much processing power is required to handle the encryption. However, a VPN is by far the most secure way to link computers over the internet, and you should certainly consider using one if you require the facilities they offer. Although they are fairly impractical when used over 56 k modem links, broadband links of 512 Kbps and above provide perfectly acceptable performance.

Resist Temptations

In the age of the internet, everything seems to come with remote control or remote access capabilities which allow you to manage the particular device from home or indeed from anywhere else in the world. The TiVo is actually a video recorder with built-in hard disk, but its reliance on an inbuilt operating system based on Linux has allowed white-hat hackers to develop some useful additional software for it. One such utility is a Web server, allowing you to control the device over the internet from anywhere in the world. Useful, but insecure.

It's very tempting to enable all the remote-control features that are built into software and hardware, or not to disable those that are enabled by default. After all, what's the harm in being able to connect to your corporate Web server via telnet or ftp from home in order to be able to sort out any emergencies that happen out of hours? Windows 2003 Server has a Web-based administration mode that allows you to manage all aspects of the server via a password-protected Web page from wherever you happen to be. In the Linux environment, products such as Webmin (**www.webmin.com**) offer similar facilities, allowing you to manage your Linux-based server (including creating new user accounts) from any location where a Web browser is available.

But every silver lining has a cloud. Although such facilities can be incredibly useful, it's critically important that you consider the security implications before opening up any aspect of your company's IT infrastructure to potential abuse. If you can administer your Unix server via Webmin, then so can anyone else who knows the password. If you activate the telnet server to allow your technical staff to gain command-line access to your systems, then a hacker who manages to crack the passwords or social-engineer them from one of your colleagues can do the same. And someone with command-line access can wipe your entire server hard disk with a single command.

A firewall can help in such situations. If you really need to allow telnet access to a server, use it to restrict the range of IP addresses from which such access is permitted. Valid addresses should be the home locations of key staff. Similar rules apply to all other types of remote access. And check regularly as part of your audit procedures to ensure that no remote-access client software has been installed on PCs or servers without your knowledge or permission. Installing such software should be a serious disciplinary offence and staff should be under no illusion that this is not the case. Such behaviour is also a criminal offence in many countries.

FUNDAMENTAL FIVE

Your action points for this chapter:

1. If you're using a public computer in a hotel or an internet café, don't assume that the machine is free of viruses or spyware. ☐

2. If you connect to a public wireless network in a restaurant or hotel, bear in mind that your communications might be being intercepted by a hacker in the same building. ☐

3. Users who regularly take their company laptop off-site will probably need additional privileges to allow them to connect to different networks. Ensure that you are aware of the implications of this. ☐

4. Never leave laptops unattended in hibernation mode unless they are configured to require a password when they wake up. ☐

5. Don't use a shared computer to access confidential information that requires passwords to be entered, as it is possible that your keystrokes are being recorded. ☐

34

Social Engineering

While most hackers use technology to carry out their acts, sometimes they fall back on their wits. As a youngster growing up in a Jewish household in the early 1970s I occasionally spent family holidays in kosher hotels. Not content with denying me the luxury of a proper full English breakfast, the hotel owners also stuck rigidly to the rules about not activating electrical switches during the Sabbath. So, during the 24-hour period that started every Friday at sunset, metal cylindrical locks were placed on the dials of the telephones to stop them being used to make outgoing calls. I quickly discovered that I could still make calls by tapping the cradle in a steady pattern – three taps to dial a number three, 10 taps for zero, and so on.

During the pilot phase of the world's first bank ATM machines, a bank branch in London was chosen as one of the first sites. A machine was installed in the wall, and a select group of customers were issued with cards that allowed them to withdraw cash from their account. Every morning the bank staff checked the contents of the machine, and every morning it was short of cash. Someone was clearly stealing, but the staff simply couldn't work out how. The mechanics of the machine were scrutinized, as was the program code and the electronics. Everything appeared to be working as designed, yet cash was definitely going missing on a regular basis.

Suspicion eventually fell on the customers. One of them must have found a way of withdrawing money without it being recorded. So the bank's security department set up an all-night watch to find out just what high-tech procedure the thieves were using to persuade the machine to part with additional cash. Eventually they noticed a van stop outside the bank branch. A man approached the cash machine, carrying a portable vacuum cleaner with a customized nozzle. He then poked the nozzle into the machine though a slot that was inadequately shielded and proceeded to suck up the money before making a quick getaway.

Although bank robbers rarely adopt such low-tech methods today, hackers often fall back on the proven old-fashioned techniques. The best known of these is social engineering, which involves persuading someone to divulge confidential information by pretending that you are someone who is entitled to know it. It can be carried out in person, face-to-face, or over communications media such as the telephone or email. No special software or hardware is needed – just a clever way with words. Social engineering is often a highly effective way of obtaining confidential information because it hits victims at their weakest points. Rather than having to try to break through a well-configured firewall, the social engineer simply contacts a gullible staff member and imparts a sufficiently believable story.

Social engineers deliberately try to blend into their surroundings, so those who do it well are therefore notoriously difficult to detect. Further, they tend to concentrate on targets where they are aware that traditional hacking simply won't work, such as financial or pharmaceutical companies that are fully aware of the risks of not having adequate security technology in place. Of course, the greatest risk to the social engineer is that he must carry out his crime in person, often in full view of the victim, rather than having the luxury of being able to perform remotely via the internet. This additional level of danger does deter all but the most determined, therefore it is reasonable to assume that anyone indulging in social engineering has decided that the risks are outweighed by the potential rewards.

In most cases, social engineering attacks are carried out against a specific target. This is for good reason. It's easy to install a port scanner on a computer and probe random IP addresses in search of a Web server that isn't fully patched. It's harder, however, to wander the streets of the financial district in some large city, entering dozens of buildings in turn while trying to find a security guard who really does believe that you work there. However, that's not to say that social engineering never happens at random or that it always takes places on the target company's premises.

This is neatly illustrated by an exercise carried out in 2002 on behalf of the organizers of an IT security exhibition in London. A team of bogus researchers was positioned at Victoria, one of the main commuter rail stations, on the pretext that they were interested in discovering attitudes to IT security breaches. Around 150 commuters were asked questions such as whether they would be able to resist looking at a data file containing details of their colleagues' salaries if they accidentally came across it in the office. Having warmed up the interviewees with such trivia, the researchers then asked about attitudes to passwords and how often they are changed. By carefully wording the questions, they managed to persuade 100 of the 150 interviewees to disclose their company passwords. The 'researchers' took care not to ask the interviewees to provide details of their employers, as this would have aroused suspicion. However, most of the respondents were already wearing their company ID badges by the time they arrived at the station.

In a similar scam a couple of years later, 'researchers' pretended to carry out a survey into people's attitudes towards the London theatre scene, with the added incentive of free entry into a prize draw for all who took part. Using a twist on the old joke about finding out one's porn-star name, the researchers told interviewees that they could work out their stage name from a combination of their pet's name and their mother's maiden name. Some 94% of those interviewed took the bait and happily divulged their mother's maiden name in return for possibly winning a pair of theatre tickets in a prize draw.

How it's Done

Social engineering is, in principle, very easy to do. Just say whatever needs to be said in order to pull off a confidence trick. In practice it's very difficult, and requires skills that are a world away from the typical hacker's mindset.

A typical social engineering attack might take place on the telephone. The attacker might call your switchboard and ask to be put through to a senior manager, knowing full well that he'll actually end up speaking to a secretary or PA who probably isn't very security-savvy. When he reaches this person, he'll make his apologies about having reached the wrong person, and request that the PA put him through to a different PA in the office of a different senior manager. In passing, the attacker will ask for the name of the first PA.

When the attacker's call is put through to the second PA, the social engineering is well underway. He knows the name of the first PA, which will come in useful later. Plus, because the second PA received the call via a transfer rather than from an outside connection, the ring tone will be different. The second PA will think that she's receiving an internal call. So when she answers, the attacker can immediately launch into a well-rehearsed script.

"Hi, I'm Andy, I just started in tech support today and I was given your name by Michelle [the first PA] as someone who can help me. I need to find a couple of minutes to come by your office some time today and fix that loose cable which has been causing problems with your PC. You probably haven't noticed any problem, but our systems have picked it up and your internet connection is definitely running more slowly than normal. Actually, you know, it might be that some hackers have managed to intercept your line so it's probably best if I move you onto the backup system right away, just in case. Give me your username and password and I'll do it for you now, and then I'll pop over later and fix the cable for you."

There are of course thousands of variations on the theme. For example, the attacker might call a junior marketing person and, in his guise as someone from the IT department, hurriedly point out that there's a problem with the company's Web site and that hackers appear to have filled it with porn. "I can fix it for you right now, if you want, but someone in your department seems to have changed the passwords since last week and the guy here who knows the master list is at lunch, so can you tell me what it is please?"

You'll notice a pattern here, which is very common among social engineers. First, they tend to pick on junior staff who probably won't be as *au fait* with company procedures as those who have been in their post for many years. Second, they adopt the guise of someone who the victim assumes they can trust, such as a fellow employee. And most importantly, they force the victim to make a decision quickly about a dangerous situation that will only get worse if they don't do something about it right now. A hacker in the wires who needs to be stopped, or a Web site full of porn, can't wait while the victim consults their superiors or refers to the rule book. As is the case with employees who use email to circulate and forward warnings about hoax viruses – they're only doing what they consider to be the best thing for their employer.

Psychology, rather than technical ability, is a large part of the social engineer's skill. Forcing people to make quick decisions is one aspect of this. Another common technique, which works very well with male targets, is for the attacker to be female, to flirt outrageously, and to hint at eternal gratitude (and perhaps a little more) if the victim does as she asks. If the attacker can manage to fake some tears, so much the better. "I really hope you can help me. I know I've screwed up, but if you can just lend me your administrator password for a couple of minutes I know I can fix it and hopefully I'll be able to save my job".

Kevin Mitnick, a former hacker who has written about his past in books such as *The Art of Intrusion*, talks of a particular psychological technique that social engineering attackers exploit, namely the desire to reciprocate if help is offered. During the period after the lunch break, he'll follow a group of staff back into the building. He'll walk closely behind an employee and, when they both reach the outer doors, he'll be sure to hold the door open for the employee. Both the hacker and the victim will then head together towards the security barrier that leads to the heart of the building. The hacker, staying close to the person for whom he's just held the door open, fumbles in his jacket pocket for his security pass which would, if it actually existed, allow him through the barrier. The fellow staff member, seeing the discomfort of the 'employee' who's just been polite enough to hold open the outer door, does the decent thing and lets the attacker follow him through the security barrier even though he still hasn't worked out which pocket holds his security pass.

Need to Know

Social engineering is a particularly dangerous form of computer crime because no firewall or other software product can detect or prevent it. The attack means exploiting the weakest link in your security chain, which is almost always a person rather than a computer or another technology. Protecting your organization from social engineers therefore means training staff in how to minimize the risks. This is the so-called human firewall.

The best form of defence is privacy and secrecy. Adopt a need-to-know approach, where information is only given to those who need to know it and whose identity is known. If a sales person calls and asks who supplies your telecoms capacity, or which brand of firewall you use, every staff member should have been pre-warned that such questions must not be answered. Any scrap of company information that could allow someone to pass themselves off as an employee of your company should be protected, even if that information appears useless in isolation. Items such as internal phone directories are much prized by social engineers because they contain directories of staff names, job titles and phone numbers. Not only can the attacker then contact these people directly, but he can refer to other people during the conversation to sound more authentic.

Any pages on your Web site that aren't designed for external consumption should be protected. Set up directories on the server that can't be accessed from IP addresses other than those owned by the company. Alternatively, you can set up your Web server so that users must log in before they can view protected pages, such as key admin contacts and internal telephone directories. There's no harm in allowing external users to look up the email address or telephone number of a single staff member or department, but don't allow the system to display the entire database. Also, ensure that all confidential waste paper is shredded before disposal.

One common goal of the social engineer is to request a password change. By posing as the legitimate user of an account, he calls the support department or help desk to explain that he has forgotten the password and requests that it be changed to a particular phrase of his choosing. Those staff members who have the necessary privileges to change passwords should be made aware of the correct procedure for changing a password, which should normally go something like this:

1. The user requests a password change in person, by visiting the help desk or IT support department. In exceptional circumstances, and if the user's voice is known to the person performing the password change, it can be done over the telephone but must never, ever, be done via email.

2. The user is given a new password, which is generated by the computer or chosen at random by the administrator rather than being specifically requested by the user. Assuming that the password is for a Windows-based network, the administrator who changes the password should tick the 'user must change password at next logon' box.

3. The user logs into the system with the new password, and is then forced to change it. This ensures that the password is known only to the user, and not to the system administrator who created it.

By forcing the user to change their password after it has been generated by the system or by an administrator, you ensure that the only person who knows the user's password is the user himself. Administrators can still access the user's data, using the administrator password rather than that of the user. This ensures that it is impossible for the user to blame an administrator if the user's account is subsequently implicated in any form of computer misuse.

▶ FUNDAMENTAL FIVE

Your action points for this chapter:

1. Ensure that everyone who answers the telephone in your company understands that the caller may not be who they claim to be. ☐

2. Instruct all staff not to divulge information to callers or visitors except on a need-to-know basis. ☐

3. Sales personnel who enquire as to what security hardware and software you currently use do not qualify as needing to know. ☐

4. Ensure that IT support staff do not reset passwords unless the identity of the person requesting the reset can be verified. ☐

5. Beware of personal visitors who arrive unannounced – all staff should be on their guard for anyone acting suspiciously in the building or around external areas such as waste bins. ☐

E-Commerce Fraud

I f you sell things on your Web site, then chances are that you accept credit cards and that this is handled via your merchant account with one of the major card processing organizations. Credit card fraud is big business for hackers and it's important that you examine this area as part of your overall effort to reduce your exposure to all aspects of internet crime.

Credit cards, introduced in the 1960s, were designed from the outset to be used in situations where the card and the cardholder are in the same place during a transaction. When consumers started shopping by post, telephone and fax, credit and debit cards were pressed into service to provide a function that the designers had never envisaged and to which the cards were simply not suited. Unable to check the signature on a card or examine the plastic for tell-tale signs of tampering, companies who sell via the Web in so-called Cardholder Not Present (CNP) transactions soon found themselves becoming the subject of large-scale attention from fraudsters.

Until relatively recently, the most widespread method for ensuring that a CNP customer was in physical possession of a card was to request (and occasionally verify) the card's expiry date. While security experts have always implored users never to write down PINs and passwords, retailers had little choice but to rely for authentication on four digits which were embossed on the card and which could easily have been glimpsed and memorized by a thief. The fraudster's life was made even easier because receipts for card purchases, frequently discarded by shoppers in car parks and domestic rubbish bins, often contain full or partial card numbers, expiry dates, and even signatures. Unsurprisingly, fraud levels associated with plastic cards grew quickly and continued to rise year-on-year. When the internet shopping revolution began at the end of the last century, levels of fraud rapidly risked becoming unsustainable and out of control.

Internet shopping made credit card crime a global phenomenon. With the online shopping industry understandably keen to take its share of the gift-buying market, few companies insisted on delivering goods only to the registered address of the cardholder. When e-commerce extended to mobile phones and WAP, potential exposure to fraud grew even more. Pay-as-you-go phones, difficult to trace if the unit has been bought for cash and not registered, are widely used by criminals who need to evade detection while placing orders.

The internet's adoption as a popular distribution medium for music, pornography, downloadable software, e-books and other non-tangible information also made yet another contribution to the plastic card crime figures. Shopping online for non-tangible goods removes the need for the fraudster to accept deliveries or arrange collection. As soon as the criminal has downloaded the file, or had it automatically emailed to the anonymous email address that he provided to the online ordering system, the crime has been committed and the loss to the vendor has occurred. The criminal has no need to make good his escape because he was never at the scene of the crime.

Losses on non-tangible goods are significant. A mobile phone ring tone or MP3 music file might retail for less than £1 and its cost price to the host Web site will be even lower, but if a criminal makes the product available on a pirate Web site then each download is £1 in lost revenue for the owner of that particular piece of intellectual property. If the IP in question is the result of an expensive market research analysis that the compiler had hoped to sell for many thousands of pounds per copy, the risks are even greater.

Yet another example of intellectual property is computer program source code. In February 2004, hackers got into Microsoft and stole the source code for much of Windows 2000, which caused the company to issue dire warnings to the Web-hosting community that anyone found to be carrying the code on their site, or even a link to it, would face serious consequences.

In a similar vein, try searching Google for 'Kazaa Lite' and note the message at the bottom of your screen. Kazaa is a well-known file sharing program, supported by advertising and spyware. An enterprising hacker produced a version of the software with the adware removed, and the program's owners took legal action to prevent anyone discovering sites that made the program available for downloading.

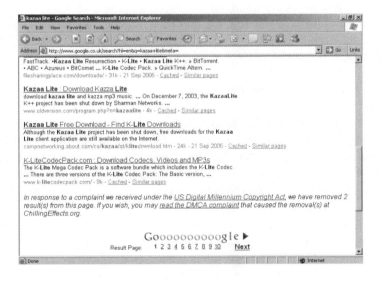

In many countries, cashless on-street vending machines dispense product by allowing the customer to pay via text message from a mobile phone. By the time a fictional card number has been discovered to be fraudulent, a criminal could have emptied the machine of its stock.

Introducing Chip and PIN

To help combat credit card fraud in retail premises, Chip and PIN is now widely used as a replacement for signatures during purchase. It prevents card cloning because the on-card chip, unlike a traditional magnetic stripe, is almost impossible to copy. While the writing on a typical signature strip is clearly visible to a thief, the secret PIN code encrypted onto the chip is not. In the UK, following widespread introduction of Chip and PIN during 2005, card crime in retail premises dropped almost 40%.

While Chip and PIN is working miracles on the high street, its effect on fraud in the global village has been less welcome. Chip and PIN doesn't work for CNP transactions, so those who sell on the internet can't use it. This situation is unlikely to change within the next few years, because the typical computer keyboard doesn't have the facility to read a credit card and verify that the PIN code on the chip matches the digits that the user has just typed. Until this time comes, Web-based retailers are highly vulnerable to credit card fraud.

In every country where Chip and PIN has been adopted, it has been noticed that fraudsters quickly desert the high street in favour of online retail, where the technology is not used. Therefore, you need to ensure that your Web site and the code behind it is able to detect fraud, or that you sign up with a card processor that has the necessary technology to do it for you.

AVS and CSC, while not as high-tech as Chip and PIN, are proven technologies that do work to reduce CNP fraud. AVS, the Address Verification Service, checks that the house number and the postcode specified in an online order is that of the registered cardholder. CSC, the Card Security Code (also known as the Card Verification Number or CVN) utilizes the additional digits on the reverse of the card to ascertain that the person placing the order is in possession of the card and hasn't simply picked 16 random digits and passed them through a card number verification routine.

Card fraudsters, whether one-off opportunists or organized criminals, are ingenious in their techniques and the internet makes it easy for them to share advice and warnings with each other. They use techniques such as identity theft and bin-raiding to gather personal information about other people. Particularly at risk are those who move house and fail to have their post redirected – the fraudsters intercept unsolicited invitations to open new credit card accounts, and then do so in the name of the departed householder. Once the account is established, the fraudster runs up huge bills with companies such as yours, which simply go unpaid.

Some e-commerce businesses are sufficiently lax in their credit card verification schemes that customers need only provide a valid credit card number and expiry date in order to be allowed to download intangible items such as music files and ring tones, or to obtain a licence key for software that has already been downloaded. Fraudsters exploit such systems by using programs downloaded from the internet which generate valid credit card numbers. Obtaining the expiry date is then a matter of guesswork. Fraudsters are well aware that most cards expire after five years or less, so having stumbled across a valid card number they need try only around 60 possible expiry dates (one for each month) rather than the 9999 possible combinations that would exist if the expiry date were a true PIN.

Many e-tailers simply write off the cost of credit card fraud because they incorrectly assume that this is a cheaper option than investing in combating the problem. It's not, though some care needs to be taken.

One strategy that may seem obvious is to 'get tough, and be seen to get tough' with fraudsters. However this can be fraught with problems. It is poor business practice for an e-commerce portal site to display numerous warnings about how harshly you intend to treat fraudsters, because legitimate and loyal customers will feel sufficiently intimidated to look to somewhere less oppressive to spend their hard-earned money.

A card transaction normally requires customers to provide little more than their name, address and card details. While it can be tempting to request additional personal information in order to be able to trace the customer more easily, it must be borne in mind that internet-savvy shoppers are generally averse to handing over more information than they deem necessary. Also, attrition rates increase greatly if customers are asked to fill in yet more forms when they merely want to place their order and leave the site as quickly as possible.

While it might be prudent to refuse to deliver goods anywhere except the cardholder's registered address, companies which adopt such a policy lose out on the gift market and the growing trend of delivering goods to a customer's workplace rather than their home address. Following some recent spates of CNP fraud involving high-value computer components such as processors, often sent in the form of spam to thousands of online vendors, many computer companies now refuse to deliver to non-registered addresses which can present difficulties for small companies needing to supply equipment to branch offices or home workers.

To avoid tarring both fraudsters and real customers with the same brush, it is clearly important that you identify criminals quickly, easily, cheaply and reliably. While this is possible to achieve with fairly good results by training staff and/or computers to make such decisions at the point of order, an integrated solution from an experienced service provider often produces much more reliable results. In such cases a third party is used to vet transactions, with criteria for which merchants can set individual importance and thresholds in order that a quick and accurate decision as to its *bona fides* can be made. By working with a third party, you gain from that company's expertise and, crucially, they also benefit from the huge knowledge base of data that the company has collected from all its merchant clients. This knowledge base is growing all the time, and significantly helps to spot trends in criminal activity and thus to ensure that decisions regarding whether to allow or deny a transaction are as accurate as possible.

Detecting different types of crime requires a variety of techniques. Where one technique is applicable to crimes perpetrated by a variety of offenders, detection thresholds will vary and the detection technology needs to be able to adapt accordingly. Attackers attempting to defraud a site that sells high-volume, low-cost goods behave in different ways to those trying to obtain low-volume high-value items. Therefore, effective fraud prevention must be based around a complementary range of techniques and the ability to tailor the algorithms to the business environment.

Various methods are available to help merchants detect and prevent card transactions that appear to be, on balance of probability, fraudulent. Some are commercial products and services, while others are procedures suggested by card issuers, financial institutions, industry associations or other advisory bodies.

Hot lists are an essential part of every business's fight against card crime. Where appropriate, staff should be made aware of the procedures involved in consulting the list or adding to it. This will probably happen automatically in all but the smallest companies. The IHCF (Industry Hot Card File) is a UK database of some five million card numbers which are registered as missing, stolen or simply made up, and more than 80,000 retailers currently subscribe to the list. In 2003, some 300,000 cases of attempted fraud were prevented by the IHCF. However, while such lists provide a quick and efficient way to detect the use of cards that have been reported stolen, they are not a complete solution to the problem of card fraud. They cannot, for example, detect against fraudulent use of a card that has not yet been reported stolen, or one which was obtained as the result of identity theft.

Another technique is the velocity check, of which there are two types in common use. Velocity of use is the first type. This involves checking whether a card is used for multiple sales within a short time, and requires monitoring not just the card number but also the delivery address, telephone contact number, customer name, and other common characteristics. By looking for recognizable patterns it is possible to detect fraud such as that committed by someone who is trying to use a stolen card as quickly as possible before the theft is discovered, or perhaps multiple criminals working together from different locations but each quoting the same card number when ordering goods.

Velocity of change is the second type. This involves looking for data that changes frequently through the initial order entry process, such as a customer of an online ticket ordering system who visits the site on three consecutive days and continually enters different yet incorrect expiry dates. This often indicates someone (or an automated computer program) trying to place an order by trial and error.

Although telephone verification of suspicious transactions is common, it's not always cost effective. Results from a survey by fraud prevention specialists Cybersource in 2005 found that 80% of orders selected for manual review are ultimately accepted, which makes for a significant and inefficient drain on human resources. It can also inconvenience and irritate customers, and lead to delays if the customer is not available to verify that they did indeed place the order.

If you sell goods or services, ensure that you are protected against credit card fraud. If your site is based on your own code, ensure that you take sensible precautions to detect and prevent fraud. For example, when your card payment processor automatically transmits a transaction report to your system, the record will include details of the product purchased and the amount that was charged to the card. Before you ship the product, check that the price is correct and that the purchaser hasn't amended it by hacking the HTML-based order form on your Web site and submitting his own version of the form instead of your original (a so-called form injection attack).

If you use a third-party to handle your card payments, check out their fraud detection systems and ensure that their terms and conditions regarding liability for fraud are acceptable to you. You can find lots of useful information about online card fraud at **www.cybersource.com**, which is one company that specializes in online fraud detection.

▶ FUNDAMENTAL FIVE

Your action points for this chapter:

1. Keep a close eye on reports from your payment handling company, so that you are always aware of the scale of the card fraud problem. ☐

2. If your company develops its own software for accepting online payments, consider employing external advisors to check that it is safe and secure. ☐

3. Keep a close watch on your Web server access logs to ensure that your site is not being targeted by hackers. ☐

4. Consider using a third-party company to vet all credit card transactions before shipping goods and services to online customers. ☐

5. The security of your transaction database is paramount, especially if it contains customers' credit card details. ☐

36

Intrusion Detection Systems

For any company with a connection to the internet, a firewall should always be your first line of defence. But despite what the glossy brochures promise, a firewall doesn't mean that you no longer have to worry about computer security.

Firewalls can be attacked through the use of social engineering techniques or by bribing someone on the inside. They can also fall victim to dishonest insiders, which is something that the firewall vendors rarely tell you. Also, most firewalls aren't particularly intelligent. They filter by IP address and by port number and are thus vulnerable to so-called tunnelling attacks whereby hackers use non-standard port numbers. If your firewall is configured to block incoming traffic on port 21 (ftp servers) but to allow incoming port-80 data (Web servers), what happens if someone writes a program that sends ftp traffic on port 80? The answer is simple, and is probably not the one you want to hear.

One way to plug these gaps in your security is to use an Intrusion Detection System (IDS) or Intrusion Prevention System (IPS). The terms are often used interchangeably, although the official differentiator is that an IDS tells you that someone is, or was, attempting to hack into your network while an IPS will try to prevent the attack from going ahead. In what follows, assume that all references to an IDS also include IPS products.

Although an IDS is a useful tool to have, they are mostly used by large organizations. Small and medium sized companies rarely install them. While it is quite normal for an organization without a firewall to be regarded as something of a pariah by the IT industry and just about every security consultant, those without an IDS are not judged so harshly. Hopefully this chapter will help you to decide whether you need the extra security that an IDS can offer, over and above the techniques and products already mentioned.

The Two Tribes

As with firewalls, an IDS can be hardware- or software-based. Some take the form of a dedicated appliance that connects into your network, while others are merely software programs which you install on a spare computer (or, if you wish to live dangerously, onto an existing computer that also has other tasks to perform). And as with firewalls, they are available in commercial and open-source (free) varieties, so a short session with your favourite internet search engine should help you track down lots of examples.

An IDS typically comes in one of two flavours, namely a network-based IDS or a host-based IDS, so let's start by examining the differences between them.

A network-based IDS monitors your network traffic in real time, and reports any irregularities to a central monitoring station. The system normally consists of a pair of components. The sensor comprises a computer that performs the analysis, and there might be multiple sensor devices on a large network. The management station receives the alerts and deals with them as required, such as by flashing a message on a screen or by sending a warning to key operations staff by email, pager, mobile phone, text message and so on. The management station software is normally capable of performing some analysis to indicate the type of problem that is occurring, rather than merely displaying raw streams of captured information.

Network-based IDS sensors are passive devices that start working as soon as they are plugged into the network and suitably configured. A major advantage of such devices, especially compared with firewalls, is that the network will continue to function normally when the IDS is attached. There's no need to reconfigure any other device on the network. You should, however, take care to install the sensor system somewhere where it can not be physically accessed by the curious, if only to prevent hackers from disabling it during their periods of mischief-making.

A network-based IDS can only act upon traffic which is on the same network segment as the sensor. In the case of large, complex networks, therefore, multiple sensors may be required. In addition, many network-based IDSes can't properly analyse encrypted data, such as that which travels across the wires during a VPN or SSL session. To help reduce the amount of data that a network-based IDS needs to analyse and store, most can react to certain trigger events in order to start and stop their work. For example, they might only start logging if a possible attack is detected, and might stop logging if no suspicious activity has been noticed for 10 minutes.

The other type of IDS is known as host-based. A host-based IDS analyses one particular network device, normally a server, and typically does this by scanning and interpreting the device's own audit and log files rather than performing any active monitoring of its own.

A host-based IDS is a powerful piece of software which, because the information available to it is of a higher, more intelligible level, can often produce extremely valuable and comprehensive reports that explain precisely what the hacker did (or is doing) and how he managed it.

While host-based IDSes tend to provide a better class of feedback, and fewer false alarms, than network-based IDS, they do have their drawbacks. Most importantly, installing the IDS on the necessary servers means that those servers might be out of action during the installation, and may require substantial reconfiguration (such as increasing the logging level to maximum) or hardware upgrades (adding hard disk space or memory). A major advantage, however, is that there is no increase in network bandwidth with a host-based IDS because everything happens locally on the server that is being monitored.

A further drawback of host-based IDS is that the increased likelihood that suspicious activity will be overlooked because it happens on a server other than the one being watched. Watching two servers means installing and monitoring two host-based IDSes. A corresponding network-based IDS would have multiple sensors and a single management station, allowing you to receive alerts from multiple sensors via a single point.

Additional Techniques

IDS systems allow you to keep a watchful eye on key devices in real time, and receive alerts upon which you can act instantly. Even a host-based IDS, which examines a server's log files 'after the event', can still act quickly enough to warn you of an attack that is in progress. And if your IDS is actually an IPS the system can take steps to prevent the attack, such as disconnecting the hacker's login, disabling the account that was being used, shutting down the computer (or at least configuring it to deny all further logins) and so on.

If an IDS/IPS is beyond your means and your requirements, there are other techniques that you can use in order to detect whether one of your key servers has been attacked. One very common technique is a file integrity checker. This is a program that runs on your servers and warns you if the contents of a key file has changed.

While document files and other data might be expected to change frequently, system files should not. So the integrity checker, when first installed on a known-clean system, calculates a checksum for every file. This is a unique number that is derived by a mathematical formula that takes into account every byte in the file. Each time the checksum is calculated for a given file, the checksum should remain the same. If it doesn't, the file has changed.

As to how often you run the integrity checker, that is entirely up to you. Typically it's done every few days, depending on the importance of the machine being monitored. File integrity checkers are widely available for Windows and Unix systems, including in freeware and open-source varieties. You'll find them available on the internet in places such as download.com, and they are well worth using as a poor-man's IDS.

If you use a file integrity checker, it's important to have an understanding of why the contents of a file might, or might not, change. Sometimes a change happens for a legitimate reason, such as an application altering an entry in one of its data files. Even executable program files sometimes change after installation, such as when they update themselves via the internet.

Sometimes things might not be what they seem. You might expect a system access log file to change often (i.e. every time the system is accessed). But maybe the change is actually caused by the hacker deleting a few lines in order to cover his tracks (this is a common technique, and one which I actively practised during my time as a hacker). Another common hacker technique is to replace system files with hacked versions. For example, the hacker might replace the program that handles logins with one that contains a pre-programmed 'back door'. The amended login system will continue to consult its database of valid usernames and passwords whenever someone attempts to log into the system, but will also allow immediate entry to anyone who uses a password of, say, 'open-sesame' even if that password does not appear in the list of accepted accounts.

Management Responsibilities

An IDS or IPS alerts you instantly to what might be a real hacker in the process of trying to cause real damage to your IT resources. So what are you going to do about it? Before you buy and install the IDS, start by doing some managerial planning:

- If the IDS alarm sounds, what will you do?

- Who will the alert be sent to?

- How will that person react, and who else will that person tell?

- What actions will each person take, and how will those actions affect the company? Will you simply pull the plug on the affected server while you wait for the expert to arrive? If so, does that mean that no one can do any work while this happens?

- How will you preserve the evidence of the attack?

- What happens if the alarm happens in the middle of the night? Will anyone be in the right place to notice it?

- If you don't have the expertise to appreciate the content of the alert, is there someone on the end of a telephone who will be able to help, day or night? Will they be able to diagnose the problem remotely or will they need access to your premises?

- Do you have an emergency backup procedure that will allow staff to perform basic functions such as answering telephones and responding to urgent emails even if the entire corporate network is unavailable, in such as way as not to divulge to customers (or to hackers) that something is very wrong?

Most of these questions are fairly simple to answer with a little planning and foresight. Plus a heavy dose of good management, including co-operation between senior managers and the technical staff on the ground. It is of the utmost importance that you consider these questions, and answer them, before you even consider buying and installing any form of intrusion detection/prevention system.

FUNDAMENTAL FIVE

Your action points for this chapter:

1. If you don't have an IDS, consider whether your business could benefit from some sort of automated system that could warn of attacks in progress. ☐

2. As an alternative to an IDS, consider the use of other techniques such as a file integrity checker. ☐

3. Ensure that your management and technical team are aware of their immediate roles and responsibilities should the IDS detect an attack in progress. ☐

4. If you prefer to examine server log files rather than obtain warnings in real time, invest in some software that makes it easier to detect anomalies in those logs. ☐

5. Do some research on the Web to gather unbiased opinions as to which IDS might be the best for your particular situation. ☐

Outsourcing

By now you're probably thinking that keeping on top of IT security is just too much trouble. Go on, admit it. You're secretly hoping that there's someone out there who can do it all for you. Well, there is. There are companies to whom you can outsource some or all of your IT security. They are generally known as MSSPs (Managed Security Services Providers), and they certainly have their advantages over doing everything yourself.

But before you write out the cheque and prepare to put your feet up, you need to know that it's not quite as easy as that. It pays to understand the advantages and disadvantages before you make any decisions.

Much of the daily life of an IT security department involves doing routine things such as resetting forgotten passwords and installing patches on servers, as well as mundane tasks like checking the firewall logs for evidence of attempted hacks while keeping a watching eye for alerts from the Intrusion Detection System. MSSPs can do all this for you. Just set up the necessary accounts and passwords to allow the MSSP staff to access your servers and firewall logs, and configure the IDS to send its alerts to your MSSP's operations centre rather than your own email address. They will then take over your responsibilities, patching servers as required and taking immediate action if the IDS suggests that they should. They will also perform regular analysis on the firewall logs and work with you to investigate any entry that arouses their suspicion.

Benefits

Handing over some of your IT security work to outsiders is, in many ways, a great idea. Those outsiders are specialists in their field and they know what they're doing. They almost certainly have more combined experience among their staff than exists in your department. They have the time and the motivation to develop their own software that helps them do their job better. And because they have multiple clients in many different lines of business, you get the benefit of all their experience gained while protecting those clients.

Outsourcing security to an MSSP also brings rapid response to major problems. If a virus or hacker is detected in your systems, action to locate the source of the attack and prevent it from spreading will generally begin in minutes, regardless of whether the incident occurs at 3pm on a normal Thursday afternoon or at 9pm on Christmas Day. And when the MSSP staff aren't actively solving problems they will use their 'free time' to continually scan your log files to ensure that evidence of past attacks has not been overlooked.

Communication between you and your MSSP will normally happen by email or the Web. Email will generally be used for routine requests and reports, such as when you need to request that they set up a new user account or reset a forgotten password. Dedicated Web-based reports, usually generated automatically by the MSSP's own systems, will keep you continually up to date with the status of your systems and of any outstanding problems or requests that have yet to be dealt with.

Drawbacks

The decision on whether to outsource your IT security is a difficult one, and you're not going to find a definitive answer in a book such as this one. You will, of course, find the answer on the Web sites of all MSSPs within the pages of their very impressive online brochures. One particular company, Counterpane, spends a full 17 pages extolling the virtues of its service and explaining why you'd be mad to do it any other way.

But there are plenty of good reasons why signing up with a managed security service provider or similar organization (Counterpane prefers MSM, or Managed Security Monitoring) might not be the best option for your company. Or, indeed, for any company. For a start, the reason we're all here is security. And one key factor in security is not to hand over the keys to your most private electronic resources. Yet your MSSP will need these keys if it's to do the job properly. They won't be able to add new user accounts to your network, or install security patches on your servers, or indeed do anything else, unless you entrust them with your administrator-level passwords.

Remember that the majority of security breaches are inside jobs. MSSPs like to point out that handing over your security to another company prevents your own staff carrying out attacks. If this really is true, surely you're just shifting the potential problem from your own premises to someone else's. After all, you can't guarantee the honesty of every employee who works for the MSSP.

If this is a concern to you (and it really should be) but you're still keen to outsource some of your IT security efforts, remember that some functions are safer to outsource than others. It's quite common for large companies to allow external organizations to handle their email spam filtering, for example. All incoming email is diverted to the external company, where the spam is removed or merely marked as suspect, before being allowed to carry on its journey to the intended recipients. Allowing an external company to handle this operation is less risky than a full outsource of all IT security, but it does still mean that the filtering company gets to read all of your company's incoming messages and attachments.

Another option is to outsource key elements of security monitoring during specific time periods, such as overnight and during national public holidays. If this provides cover at a time when otherwise your servers would remain unmonitored, the benefits will generally outweigh the potential problems. You could even configure your IDS, for example, so that it is only accessible by the MSSP during the times at which they are on duty.

Evaluating Security Service Providers

Choosing the wrong MSSP is one of the worst mistakes you can make in business. It might just turn out to be the last mistake you ever make, too. Ultimately it often comes down to personal relationships, and choosing the company that you think you can most comfortably work with. But there are many other considerations that you should bear in mind too.

Look for a proven track record. Make sure that the company has been trading for a while and that its financial position is healthy. The prospect of your MSSP going out of business is truly frightening, yet it does happen. Once you have picked a short list of potential candidates, research them thoroughly on the Web. Don't simply look at the companies' own Web sites – check out online discussion forums and news sites too. If there are some unhappy customers out there, you need to know about them while you still have the chance. Ensure that your MSSP has $24 \times 7 \times 365$ availability. Hackers don't stick to office hours and neither should those who aim to defeat them. Ask to see copies of the standards and procedures that the companies work to.

A satisfactory contract and SLA (Service Level Agreement) between you and the MSSP is vital. Make sure you know what you're getting, and not getting, for your money. If the standard terms specify a two-hour response to an IDS trigger and you'd prefer 30 minutes, don't be afraid to say so. Remember, the risks here are all yours rather than theirs, so insist on the level of service that gives you the confidence promised in the brochure. Discuss how the MSSP trains, manages and disciplines its staff, and the procedures that it uses to ensure that staff don't misuse customers' confidential information.

Don't deal with MSSPs that also sell consultancy services or security products, because there's a conflict of interest. Any problems that the MSSP discovers should be solved quickly, not used as a reason to persuade you to invest in more products or services that the MSSP just happens to have available on special offer this month.

Once the contract is up and running, test it. For example, get a friend to run a port-scan against your company from their home PC and time how long it takes for the MSSP to inform you that something is amiss. If the MSSP fails your test, think very carefully before agreeing to give them a second chance.

Healthy Paranoia

There are few things more important to a company than the security of its IT systems. Without a network that is continually available, reliable and secure, you can't carry on in business. If you lack the in-house skills to maintain the security of your key systems an MSSP will take over for you, albeit at a price. But no one knows as much about your business as you do, and no other company will have your interests at heart to such an extent. I therefore always advise against outsourcing security unless there really is no alternative.

Maybe the temptation to consider employing an MSSP is actually an indication of a greater problem in your company, such as poor training or lack of IT security staff. In which case, spending the money on addressing those issues will frequently provide greater benefits than going down the outsourcing route. Handing over your administrator passwords to a third-party organization requires a huge leap of faith. If they are misusing your information, how will you find out? If they simply take your money and fail to respond adequately and quickly to problems, how will you know?

Perhaps the ultimate irony is that, if you have all the necessary skills that enable to you to know how well your MSSP is performing, you probably don't need an MSSP at all.

FUNDAMENTAL FIVE

Your action points for this chapter:

1. Use the Web to thoroughly investigate possible service providers thoroughly before making any decisions. ☐

2. Ask potential MSSP partners for reference sites, and make appointments to talk to those sites rather than taking the recommendation on trust. ☐

3. Don't take up MSSP services from a company that also sells security consultancy or products, as there is a definite conflict of interest. ☐

4. Ensure that your MSSP gives you a detailed SLA so you know exactly what level of service and response times you can expect. ☐

5. If you outsource any of your security monitoring, test the service occasionally by initiating a port scan or some other hacker-like activity. ☐

Securing your Premises

Most people assume that the typical hacker rarely ventures onto the premises of the company whose systems he wishes to attack. He prefers instead the anonymity of the internet and the freedom that it gives him to attack targets all over the world regardless of time zones. Consequently, most companies put all their IT security effort into protecting their servers from internet-based attack and fail to give adequate consideration to the activities that a hacker could carry out in person. Such neglect is at best unwise and at worst highly dangerous.

The successful and wise IT security person understands that there is no such thing as the typical hacker. Sure, most of them operate via the internet at weird hours of the night and don't have the social skills to inveigle their way into buildings. But not all hackers fit the typical mould. While the curious student might not wish to attempt to enter your building, someone who's carrying out some industrial espionage on behalf of your competitors just might. And modern technology means that the unwelcome visitor needs just a couple of minutes alone in an unmonitored part of your building to do what he has to do.

Unauthorized Actions

Once the intruder has entered your building, he has a number of options at his disposal. If he can find his way into an empty meeting room and find a spare network socket, he might plug a wireless access point into it. He can then continue to probe and attack your network at his leisure from anywhere within a few hundred feet. If he manages to gain access to an employee's PC, he might install a keystroke logger that he can then interrogate remotely via email in order to read private correspondence or steal passwords.

If he has a USB flash drive, he might use some social engineering skills to copy information from a PC onto the drive. Such as posing as an IT technician who needs to install an updated network driver on the PC to cope with a forthcoming system upgrade, and he just happens to have a copy of the driver on his flash drive.

Remember that all MP3 music players can also be used as portable disk drives, to which can be copied any type of data file. A visitor who asks permission to plug his mobile phone into the USB port of one of your PCs in order to charge a flat battery might actually be running a program that silently copies documents to the phone's memory. Programs to do this are widely available on the internet, including one for the iPod called 'Slurp'. Install the software on your iPod music player, plug it into any handy PC, and no one is aware that you are not listening to music but that you are simply watching the device grab copies of all the files on the computer.

If the hacker can't find a handy PC or network socket, all is not lost. The paperless office was first mooted many decades ago but has failed to materialize, so hackers can be fairly confident that they will find a plethora of printouts lying around, some of which might be of particular interest. Most mobile phones and PDAs nowadays include megapixel cameras that are quite capable of producing a readable image of a printed sheet of paper. Waste bins are a particularly good source of interesting printouts, and sheets that have been torn in half are always bound to contain particularly interesting data (go on, admit it, you do that too).

The Danger of a Stranger

Those on your premises at any time can be divided into one of two categories, namely staff and strangers. In this case, we define staff as those who are governed by your employment contracts by virtue of having signed them, which makes it relatively easy (and lawful) for you to monitor them, dictate where they can and can't go, and discipline them if they deviate from the behaviour that is expected of them. Everyone else should be regarded as a stranger and as a potential unwelcome visitor unless they are explicitly known and trusted. If you don't have sole use of your building, employees of other companies with whom you share the building should be put in the stranger category.

To help reduce risks posed by strangers on your premises, ensure that visitors are escorted at all times while they're on your premises. A favourite trick of the hacker is to gain access to a building by setting up a sales appointment and then to roam freely into other rooms under the pretence of needing to visit the toilet or make an urgent call on his mobile phone.

Review the security of your publicly accessible areas, i.e. those that can be entered by someone who has not yet reported to the reception desk and possibly has no intention of doing so. For example, if your reception desk is on the first floor, the unmanned ground floor entrance lobby and the stairs are publicly accessible areas, as might be a lift or elevator if one is installed. Don't install PCs or network sockets in public areas. If you have no option but to do so, ensure that they are adequately protected. While it might impress clients if you have a PC in the public area from which they can check their email or read more about your organization, there are obvious dangers if that computer is part of your company's internal network.

A hacker can often break out of a locked-down software environment in seconds. For example, I once used a public access internet terminal which had been supposedly locked down so that it was impossible to use any other program apart from the Web browser. I typed `file:///\cmd.exe` into the browser's address bar and got myself a command prompt, from which I had full control of the computer.

Incidentally, those old 'careless talk costs lives' posters from the war still have their place in corporate life today. Ensure that staff know not to discuss confidential matters in any public place. You never know who might be listening. One particularly embarrassing example of this concerns a team of executives from a PR agency, travelling on a train to meet a new client that they had recently signed up. As they rehearsed their presentation, they were unaware that the person sitting in the adjacent row of seats worked for the new client. When the truth came to light later that morning, the team of PR executives were immediately sent back to the train station, having been dismissed for breaching the confidentiality clause in their contract.

Who Goes There?

Ensure that rooms containing important computer equipment such as servers, or confidential information, are locked whenever they are empty, even if just for a few minutes. Don't unnecessarily highlight the location of server rooms – most staff don't need to know where they are, and casual visitors or passers-by certainly don't. When Microsoft built its new UK headquarters, its server rooms were on the first floor, clearly visible behind a huge glass pane by anyone who happened to arrive in the reception area and raise their head to admire the atrium. I took the trouble to point this out to the company. By the time of my next visit, the glass pane had been replaced with an enormous advertising hoarding.

If you don't already use them, consider the deployment of proximity badges or some other device that allows you to control access to discrete locations. Although relatively expensive to implement, proximity badges allow you to program each door within a controlled area so that it can only be opened by members of a specific group. Most systems also keep a record of each time a card is used, thus providing you with a log of everyone who has entered a particular area during a given time period. Tailgating and other techniques mean that such logs are not 100% reliable, but they do provide an instant short-list of initial suspects in the event that unauthorized activity has taken place within a protected room. A cheaper alternative to a full installation of a badge-controlled secure area is to install keypad combination locks on, for example, the server room door. Ensure that the code is changed regularly, and if someone who knows the code leaves the company.

Check fire doors and emergency exits to ensure that they cannot be used as a point of entry by hackers. There's little to be gained from employing uniformed security personnel and a fierce receptionist at the front door of your premises if there's a group of staff who congregate around a wedged–open fire door every hour for a nicotine fix. The hacker will simply take the path of least resistance and your data will be not far behind.

FUNDAMENTAL FIVE

Your action points for this chapter:

1. Staff who man your reception desk are your first line of defence against intruders. Ensure that they are trained to look out for suspicious behaviour. ☐

2. Ensure that network sockets in publicly accessible places, such as meeting rooms, are disabled if not required. You should be able to do this via your network switch equipment. ☐

3. Ensure that all possible points of ingress, such as fire doors, can not be opened from the outside without triggering some form of alarm. ☐

4. Unoccupied rooms which contain computer equipment, especially servers, should be kept locked and, ideally, alarmed too. ☐

5. Take extra care if your share your building with other companies, as it becomes harder to spot uninvited visitors. ☐

Forensics

I T security within a company environment is largely about policy-making and fire-fighting. The former involves ensuring that the company and its employees adopt best practice with regard to areas such as passwords, access controls, encryption and so on, in a way that satisfies the requirements of the business, its customers, and any regulations or laws that apply. The latter means dealing with episodes such as forgotten passwords, corrupted data that needs restoring from backups, and so on. In addition, there are occasional routine checks that need to be carried out to ensure that staff are not misusing your systems. This involves checking firewall logs, the security logs on your servers that Windows keeps as a matter of course, as well as any other records that you retain. You might, for example, keep automatic copies of all email sent and/or received, or all documents printed,

or all Web sites accessed (if you don't log all Web site accesses, you could always look through the cache files on each user's PC, as Web browsers tend to keep these things).

In almost every case the log files and all your other activities will lead you to conclude that all is well. But very occasionally, your suspicions will be aroused. Maybe it's an entry in a log file that doesn't seem quite right, or perhaps someone has been behaving oddly (such as working very early or late when no one else is about). Or another member of staff might consult you in confidence to say that they suspect employee X of copying confidential files without permission, accessing legally-dubious Web sites, moonlighting for the competition, or fiddling expenses claims. It's now time to play the detective and to enter the world of computer forensics.

Investigating an employee who is suspected of misusing your company's computers is a difficult game. If you manage to prove that the abuse did take place, there's the distinct possibility for dismissal or prosecution of the offender. Therefore the repercussions can be severe if you get it wrong – it's quite possible that you could find yourself on the wrong end of a lawsuit for wrongful dismissal or libel if you incorrectly accuse someone of accessing child porn Web sites. It's not unknown for someone accused of such offences to commit suicide – definitely not something that you want on your conscience. For all these reasons, it makes sense to involve the police at the earliest opportunity if you have strong suspicions about someone and the nature of the offence is serious enough to warrant prosecution.

Thankfully, the vast majority of cases of computer misuse are not sufficiently serious that the police need to be involved from the start. Typical cases might involve someone copying confidential files without permission, or sending abusive or offensive emails (or emails with abusive or offensive attachments) to colleagues. In one case that I am aware of, an employee used his company email account to send phishing emails to thousands of people. In instances such as this it will probably fall on you, perhaps at the request of your personnel or HR department, to provide evidence that the alleged incidents did indeed take place and to discover whodunnit.

Evidence of computer misuse exists in many places, and not just within the misused computer itself. Before the investigation starts, you should identify these places and isolate the evidence. For example, examine your firewall logs, email server logs, Web proxy logs, domain server security logs, door entry system logs, CCTV footage, and so on. If anything is found which relates to the computer that is about to be investigated, or its user, copy it to a reliable source so that there is no chance of this potential evidence being overwritten in the normal course of operations.

When to Show Your Hand

An investigation will normally follow one of two paths, depending on whether there is already sufficient evidence of the misuse, whether immediate action needs to be taken to stop it continuing, and whether you're prepared to divulge to the offender that you are aware of his actions. If all of these answers are "yes", then you can seize the computer(s) from which the offences are thought to have been undertaken. You can then examine the machines in detail to locate as much evidence as you think is necessary. The offender might admit his guilt as soon as you confront him, in which case any further action is probably unnecessary, but this is not always the case.

Conversely, if you are not 100% sure of your facts, you may not wish to show your hand quite yet. In which case the investigation will need to begin covertly. This is especially true if you suspect that the alleged offender is keeping encrypted files on the hard disk and you suspect that he or she will be unwilling to divulge the passwords. In this case, you might want to quietly install a keystroke logger or similar utility on the system to find out what passwords are being used.

Let's start by discussing the situation where a computer needs to be seized and subsequently examined. We'll then cover in-place covert investigation, which has many similarities but also some important differences.

Seizing a PC

When you're seizing a PC with the intention of gathering evidence from it, golden rule number one is to avoid doing anything that could allow the offender to claim that the evidence you have gathered is unreliable and therefore inadmissible. When you turn on a computer and Windows starts up, dozens of files are accessed and altered. Even something as simple as moving a window around on the screen will alter a file – in this case, the registry entry which stores details of the window's position on screen so that it can automatically open in the same place next time.

When you seize a computer, you therefore need to preserve its state as far as possible. If the suspected offence is sufficiently serious, you might even wish to wear gloves and take the necessary precautions so as not to disturb any fingerprints. However, offences of such seriousness are generally best handled by the police, rather than being carried out in-house.

If the computer is turned off, leave it turned off. If it's turned on, turn it off. Don't do this via the Windows shutdown facility – just pull the power cord out of the wall. Turning off a modern computer by pressing its "On" button will still take it through the clean Windows shutdown process, which will change lots of files and might additionally run any programs such as cache cleaners that are configured to execute each time the computer is turned off, so don't go for this approach.

With the machine shut down, it can be taken away for examination. This is always best done by two people rather than just one, in case the situation becomes unpleasant or there are subsequent disputes as to how the process was handled. If at all possible, get the user to sign in writing that he or she is aware that the computer has been taken away for investigation, and ensure that the document is timed, dated and witnessed. You might also consider using a camcorder to record the entire process, though this can be intimidating to the subject of the seizure so might be best avoided, depending on particular circumstances.

If there's a program running at the time of the seizure, take a photograph of the screen before you turn off the computer. This will be your only opportunity to preserve this information, and it might be relevant in the future.

If the investigation involves a dispute about the origin of printed information, consider seizing any local printer too. By establishing a link between the make and model of the printer, and the printer-related information contained in metadata within documents held on the seized computer, you can prove or disprove that the particular computer was ever used to print documents to the printer.

While you are on scene, look for any other supporting evidence such as note pads, printouts, photographs and so on.

Golden rule number two is never to examine the master copy of your suspect's hard disk. Create a copy of the drive (known as an image) and work from there, otherwise you risk destroying evidence. Should the offender's lawyer subsequently claim that your image is not a true copy, you can power up the original drive in the presence of the lawyer to prove otherwise.

Creating an image of a drive is not as easy as it sounds because, for reasons covered earlier, you can't start up Windows or indeed any other general-purpose operating system in order to access it. You will therefore need to use a specialist program, running on a specially configured PC, which can read the suspect hard disk and copy its contents to another hard disk, a DVD, or whatever other medium the system supports. Used with care, a general-purpose drive imaging product such as Norton Ghost, produced by Symantec, will do the job admirably. Beware of simply copying files rather than taking an image – the latter means that you'll also include parts of the drive that are occupied by files that have been deleted.

Once you have your image you can start to examine it. Standard Windows tools will let you examine the contents of browser caches, the recycle bin, and the regular document files. But to the trained investigator there's a lot more on a hard disk (or an image of one) than meets the eye. With the right software you can examine the contents of deleted files, and fragments of current files which have been deleted from documents by the user but which haven't yet been permanently expunged from the drive by Windows.

By looking inside document files using specialist software you will find much more information than is normally shown by the program that created that document. For example, as you page through the unintelligible commands and control characters in a Word document you'll find, in among the text, the name of the owner of that copy of Word. You'll also find the make and model of the printer that was used to print that document. If you're trying to trace the origin of a printed document and you need to know which computer was used to create it, such techniques are invaluable.

The market leader in forensic examination software is EnCase, from Guidance Software (`www.guidancesoftware.com`), but at some $2,500 it's not cheap. It is, though, the tool recognized by law enforcement agencies on both sides of the Atlantic and evidence produced from it is often trusted more than that produced by other software. It handles both the imaging and investigation aspects of a case, and will even trawl the depths of handheld computers such as the Palm as well as conventional Windows, Mac and Linux machines. But if you can't justify the price, a

Web search for computer forensics software will bring up many cheaper solutions.

Check out the Guidance Software Web site for a useful collection of white papers and other advice on computer forensics. And if you sign up for a Web-based briefing on the product you can download the Encase user manual, which, at some 400 pages, contains lots of useful advice in addition to explaining how to use the software.

The third and final golden rule of forensics is to create and maintain an accurate audit trail of your actions. Throughout the process of seizing and examining a computer, keep a written record of everything that takes place. Don't be afraid to go into intricate detail. This record will be of immense value if there is every any dispute or doubt as to how the investigation was carried out.

Covert Monitoring

If you're not ready to pounce on your suspect, but you need to monitor the activity on a PC without the knowledge or permission of its regular user, there are software products that can help you. However, undertaking such activity puts you in a legal grey area so it's always worth taking legal advice before doing this. While monitoring all activity on a shared server is generally permitted under computer misuse and privacy legislation, singling out a particular user is harder to justify. It certainly helps if all staff are advised beforehand, in your computer usage policy, that the company reserves the right to do this if serious misuse is suspected. Make it clear that such monitoring will only undertaken if authorized by a senior manager, and that logs will be seen only by those who need to see them.

My covert monitoring software of choice is TrueActive (**www. winwhatwhere.com**). Once installed on a computer, it hides its presence and does not appear on the system tray or in the Task Manager's list of applications. Although it appears in the list of running processes, it changes the name of its process regularly to avoid arousing any suspicion. The program can log all keystrokes, Internet activity, chat room and Instant Messaging, remote data retrieval, the clipboard, any typed passwords, and much more besides. It can also record images of the screen display at timed intervals or upon certain trigger actions, such as when a particular file is accessed or a Web site visited. It can store its logs on the suspect's PC in a hidden file, or can send the log to the investigator covertly by ftp or email. Covert monitoring using software such as TrueActive also avoids the problem of having to crack any passwords that your suspect has used to encrypt files on the computer. You simply record him accessing the files, and therefore watch as he types the required password.

Encounters

A word is in order at this point about the sort of material that you may encounter during an investigation of the contents of someone's computer. By its very nature, your work may possibly involve you seeing material and images that you'd rather not see and, in some cases, material which is illegal to possess. Child pornography is the most obvious example, but other types include racially offensive material or images of sexual violence.

In most cases, computer misuse, pornography and child protection legislation allows for this, and someone who encounters such material during the course of investigative work will not be regarded as having committed an offence. You must, however, store the material securely and not transmit it anywhere by public networks such as email. You would also be strongly advised to contact the police at the earliest opportunity, or at least to take legal advice. The sooner you do this, the less the risk of you or your company being subsequently accused of ignoring or covering up a serious problem.

Hiding the Evidence

Dishonest employees who use their company-supplied computers for nefarious purposes have a variety of techniques at their disposal and as the investigator you need to be aware of them. While software such as EnCase provides all the tools you need for carrying out an investigation, it won't do your job for you.

Some of the ways that perpetrators try to cover their tracks and hide evidence of their activities include:

■ To create space for storing pirated software or music, or a collection of pornography, the user creates a hidden partition on his hard disk that is not normally visible if the machine is booted in the standard way.

■ They store files not on their office computer but on an external system such as a public email server (Hotmail, Gmail and so on). They can then retrieve the files when they are required, either from the office or from home. Free software is available which allows the 2 GB of space in a Gmail account to be accessed as a standard network drive from within Windows.

■ They copy files or folders to removable media such as external hard disks or a USB stick and then delete the information, with the intention of recovering it with an 'undelete' program at a later date. An investigator who casually examines the media will assume that it is blank, but a closer look with the necessary software will reveal its contents.

■ They use steganography. This is a technique for electronically hiding information inside an innocent-looking file. To the untrained eye, the file might appear to be a high-resolution image of a sunset or a farm animal. And indeed the image will display quite correctly if viewed with any expected program such as Paintbrush, Photoshop, Internet Explorer and so on. But unbeknown to the viewer, a special program has been used to hide other information inside the file by scattering it in tiny fragments throughout the image. The fragments are so widespread that the image looks normal when viewed on screen or paper, but the hidden data can be extracted by means of the special program and a password. This technique is often used by criminals to send stolen credit card information or even child pornography images over the internet, because it arouses less suspicion than sending data files which are clearly identified as being encrypted.

■ They use misleading filenames or file extensions. At first glance, a file called giraffe.jpg is probably a picture of a giraffe. But there's no guarantee that it does contain anything to do with giraffes or that it really is a jpg image file – it might be a stolen Excel spreadsheet containing your personnel file that has been renamed. Most forensic investigation software packages will automatically detect such adjustments.

■ They modify file creation dates/times, file metadata, or the contents of log files, to cover their tracks. Programs to do this are freely downloadable from the internet. By modifying file creation times to suggest that the computer was being used at a time when the suspect was not in the office, for example, the suspect can introduce a degree of doubt as to whether someone else might have been responsible for those actions that you are investigating.

Hackers go to all sorts of lengths to ensure that, if they get caught, investigators will have a hard time uncovering the true extent of their activities. My favourite example involved a hacker who wired the computer in his bedroom to a pressure pad under the carpet. During the normal course of events he avoided walking over the pad. But when the police knocked at his door because they suspected him of being a hacker he innocently stepped on the pad as he made his way to the computer, which triggered into action a program that he had written. When the police searched his hard drive it was totally blank.

Caught On The Net

While the techniques mentioned above are frequently used to hide or disguise information held on computers without permission, the reality nowadays is that most computer misuse in the workplace doesn't involve storing files but misuse of the internet. This includes sending and receiving offensive or pornographic images and movies, sending or receiving pirated software, and attempting to use the internet to commit fraud or to steal goods, services or information.

Detecting such activity, therefore, is not going to be as easy as looking for renamed files or apparently-empty partitions. The act will have been committed some time ago and the incriminating material long since removed to a safer place, so you need to look much more carefully for clues. This generally means looking in log and cache files on the user's PC, as well as on any email servers that the person might have used. Specialist forensic software such as EnCase will help you, but basic investigations can be undertaken with much simpler software if you know how, including freeware utilities that are widely available from the Internet.

Start by examining the user's Web browser cache. In the case of Windows and Internet Explorer, which is the most popular combination, the browser cache contains details of all recent Web sites that have been visited and, in many cases, copies of the pages themselves including all text and graphics. The browser uses this cache so that the page can be displayed more quickly if the user revisits it at a later date, but it's also extremely useful to the forensic investigator. For this reason, you should always configure your company's computers with large browser caches and a long (30-days or more) expiry date on the Web access history file. Although this requires additional disk space when compared with the default settings, this is unlikely to be a problem on all but the oldest computers within your company. And by ensuring that staff don't have access to Administrator-level accounts, you can prevent these settings from being reduced in the future.

You can examine the internet cache files manually by looking in the correct folder (directory). By default, for a user called john, you need to look in three separate locations:

- **C:\Documents and Settings\john\Local Settings \Temporary Internet Files\Content.IE5**

- **C:\Documents and Settings\john\Local Settings\History \History.IE5**

- **C:\Documents and Settings\john\Cookies**

The folder name of Content.IE5 is correct for both Internet Explorer versions 5 and 6 – there's no Content.IE6 on a computer that uses IE version 6.

Internet Explorer's log files are hard to decipher. You can't simply look at a file in a Content.IE5 folder and reconstruct a user's Web browsing session. But thankfully there are some handy free programs that can help you do just that. One is Pasco (**sourceforge.net/projects/Odessa**), which interprets the encoded data in a Content.IE5 file and turns it into a list of URLs that the user has been looking at recently. Pasco is a command-line program that produces a text file that can easily be loaded into Excel.

A more friendly and useful utility, again available free of charge, is Web Historian. It will automatically extract data from log files created by many of the most popular browsers including Internet Explorer, Firefox and Safari, and produce an XML file as a report that can be viewed in Excel. You can download it from **www.red-cliff.com**.

Next, look at deleted files. Programs to undelete files are widely available (see **www.diskeeper.com**, for example) and, even if the file can't be fully reinstated, you may be able to gather sufficient clues from the file's name. For example, someone who denies having stolen a copy of the personnel database but who appears to have a copy of personnel.xls among the deleted files on his computer probably has some explaining to do.

Deleted files can be recovered because, when Windows deletes a file, the information in that file is not wiped from the hard disk. The file is simply marked as no longer being required, so that Windows can re-use its space on the hard disk at a later date if it needs to. Until that space gets re-used, it's possible to view data in deleted files if you use special software. Of course, a good place to find deleted files in an easily digestible form is the recycle bin. So check to see whether the user has forgotten to empty the recycle bin recently.

Check the Most Recently Used (MRU) files lists of all installed Windows applications. The easiest way is to load each application and click on the File (or File, Open) menu. You'll often be presented with a list of recently-opened files for instant opening, which will provide some reliable clues as to which documents have been recently accessed on that computer. Alternatively, search the registry for entries containing the acronym MRU.

If you think you know what you're looking for (e.g. a person's name or telephone number) and you suspect that it might be somewhere on the hard disk, but you've no idea what file it might be in, there are some useful tools that can search the entire drive. One such is FileLocator Pro (**www.mythicsoft.com**), which can search an entire hard disk including PDF and Zip files. Another is Ztree (**www.ztree.com**). You can also use free products such as Google Desktop Search (**desktop.google.com**). But remember that installing software on a computer will overwrite space that currently contains information contained in deleted files, so you are destroying potential evidence whenever you do this. This is why you should always work on image files, and these should be made available on the investigator's computer in such a way that the image is not altered when the investigator installs or runs software.

Don't forget metadata. Many files include metadata that contains additional information not normally viewable. Microsoft Office data files (Word documents, Excel spreadsheets and so on) contain embedded information which tells you the name of the person who created the file, the name of the printer that was last used to output the file, the full path name of the file's location on the hard disk, and much more besides.

Music files such as MP3s have metadata fields that can tell you which album a track was copied from, and the name of the track and the performer. Very handy if you suspect that someone has renamed copyrighted music files to innocent-sounding names such as my-lecture.mp3. Image files use the EXIF specification to add data such as the make and model of the camera or scanner used, and the exposure settings. All of which can be of potentially immense help to the IT forensic investigator.

If you suspect that the user of the seized PC has been chatting to an accomplice via an instant messaging network, there may be log files available that can be used as evidence. Recent versions of Microsoft's Windows Messenger program have an option that allows the user to log the text of all conversations to a file on the hard disk.

Don't Wait

Almost by definition, forensic investigations are usually reactive. They take place in response to an event, such as a server being hacked or some illegal image files being discovered on someone's computer. But this need not always be the case. Don't be afraid to instigate forensic processes proactively. For example, if you suspect that someone is misusing your network or copying your confidential files to an external location, it strengthens your hand if you gather the evidence in advance.

Your forensic investigations begin to skate on thin legal ice if they are mere 'fishing expeditions'. Although it is not generally illegal to carry out an investigation if you believe that someone has been misusing your systems, wholesale investigation of one or more people in the hope that you might uncover incriminating evidence is at least unwise. Investigations should only be carried out in response to a specific incident, or if you have a genuine suspicion that an incident is about to take place.

Useful Resources

There are two excellent online resources that should be considered essential reading for anyone who thinks that they might be involved in seizing a computer or responding to high-tech crime. They are designed for use by the police and can be found online at `www.centrex.police.uk/hightechcrime/resources.html`. The titles are 'Good Practice Guide for Computer Based Electronic Evidence' and the 'European Guide to the Seizure of E–Evidence'.

▶ FUNDAMENTAL FIVE

Your action points for this chapter:

1. Evaluate the various software products that allow in-depth analysis of the contents of a hard disk, so that you have the necessary tools to hand should you require them in the future. ☐

2. Don't embark on fishing trips. You must not investigate a user's computer unless they are suspected of misusing it. ☐

3. Make it clear to all staff, in your employment contracts, that the company reserves the right to monitor computer usage if the staff member is suspected of committing an offence. ☐

4. If your investigations uncover material or activity that is clearly illegal, consult your lawyers and/or the police as soon as possible. ☐

5. Ensure that you are aware of the various ways in which hackers can cover their tracks and hide information on a computer. ☐

40

Planning
for the Worst

Occasionally, maybe once or twice in your entire career, things go Very Badly Wrong Indeed. Not merely a forgotten password or an infected file or a crashed server, but something much more serious which results in some or all of your company becoming unable to continue operating normally.

Such disasters include flood, fire, terrorism, a lightning strike, vandalism, earthquakes, a car crashing into your building, a gas explosion, an infestation of insects, the discovery of asbestos or a dangerous gas in the area, or a workman cutting through a major cable which leaves your premises without the prospect of any power or telecoms for a month.

By their very nature, disasters are hard to predict. Unlike traditional fire-fighting events that are pretty much guaranteed to happen on a regular basis, there's no certainty that you'll ever encounter a major disaster at all. But because the consequences of such an incident for a business are so severe, you need to do some basic preparation just in case the worst does happen.

Incidentally, of all the disasters that could render your IT systems beyond repair, industry colleagues tell me that flooding is by far the most common. Not the sort caused by heavy rain or overflowing rivers, but flooding caused by damaged water pipes in the ceiling above computer rooms or in the ducts that they share with network and power cables. So, now might be a good time to check out the plumbing situation around your server rooms.

DRP and BCP

Security experts refer to activities called Disaster Recovery Planning or Business Continuity Planning. A Web search for either of these terms will lead you to much in-depth information on how to go about it, but such advice is generally aimed at international corporations with large numbers of specialist personnel and the budgets to match.

For example, I was once involved in providing some security aware-ness training to a bank based in London, and we used the bank's own Disaster Recovery Centre as a venue. The centre turned out to be a huge office suite with computers and telephones, capable of seating many hundreds of staff, sitting completely unused in an expensive part of London, ready to be pressed into instant service in the case of a major incident at the main offices a few miles down the road. Such a facility costs millions of pounds to buy and maintain, and is well beyond the means of most companies. But for the typical bank, not having such a facility is simply a risk that is not worth taking.

This chapter will help you put together a basic DRP, or Disaster Recovery Plan, so that you can be confident that some semblance of business can continue if something major were to happen. Although a complete set of duplicate offices is assumed to be beyond your budget, there are still plenty of things that you can do to provide some cost-effective protection.

Insurance

DRP is about managing risk, and the best way to manage risk is to make it someone else's problem. Make sure that your insurance policy is up to date, and look into additional insurance that might help to protect you from IT-related disasters such as data loss. Although it's not cost-effective for most companies to have empty offices standing by, you may find that your insurance policy will cover the rental of additional short-term office space if it is needed in a hurry. However, if the disaster which triggers the policy claim is widespread, e.g. serious flooding of your entire town, any additional office space in nearby locations will be in short supply and very expensive, so ensure that the policy allows for this.

Many policies include cover for data recovery in the event that a disaster leads to loss of information. When most companies kept their data in filing cabinets and could hire a bunch of typists to re-enter it into the computer if required, such cover was a useful option. Nowadays, things are different and it's likely that no amount of money would enable you to re-create all of your data files if your central file stores were lost in a disaster. The only way to protect against such loss is to make regular backups.

Recovering from a disaster involves bringing together a quartet of essentials: priorities, places, people and facilities. We will cover each in turn.

Priorities

In the minutes and hours after the disaster, your first task is to decide what needs doing. Your DRP should spell out who will make these decisions, and what sort of questions they should ask. For example, if you're going to have to rebuild all your systems from scratch, do the employee systems come first or should the public Web site be top of the list? What about the telephone system? And should all of this happen before you start to arrange any temporary office space and before you call your insurers to make a claim? Where will this initial decision-making session take place, and how will the members of the decision-making panel be notified if the disaster happens in the middle of the night?

Places

An early decision that you have to make, once the scale of the event becomes apparent, is how much of the normal place of work can continue to be used. Possible answers to this question are 'all of it', 'some of it', or 'none of it'. It's impossible to cover every possible disaster and to give precise details of what you should do in each case, because everyone's disaster is different. But you should have some pre-prepared actions that cover each of these eventualities.

If all of the current premises can be used, then the impact is minimal. If only some of the space is inhabitable, then you need to decide who should inhabit it. For example, draw up plans in advance that deal with 25%, 50%, and 75% availability. For each category, document which staff members or departments should be given space, and how much. Then, if a disaster occurs and you calculate that your usable office space is down to 50% of capacity, it's merely a case of consulting the pre-prepared list to decide who will report for duty and who should stay at home for the time being. By simply notifying all staff that 'the 50% plan is now in operation', everyone will know what they are expected to do.

Deciding on whether your premises are capable of being occupied is not always easy and won't always be your decision to make. If everything looks normal but only half the power sockets are working, does that count as 100% or 50% availability? Equally, if nearby builders discover that your building is full of asbestos and needs to be closed down right away while the material is removed, you will have no say as to whether staff can continue to work.

If your current office location is rendered less than 100% usable, it's likely that you will need to find some additional space for a period of time. Renting or buying office space and leaving it empty just in case you need it is uneconomical for most companies, so another solution is called for. This can involve staff working at home for a while, perhaps even teaming them up so that two or three people share a room at one employee's house if that employee happens to have sufficient space and facilities. Again, your Disaster Recovery Plan should spell this out. Make sure you know in advance who will be going where, and that everyone knows how to access a central location from which they can find out whether the Disaster Plan is in operation and, if so, which part of it applies (i.e. the full-scale emergency where everyone works from home or the less-disastrous one in which everyone reports to the nearby hotel to decide what to do next).

There are companies that rent office space by the hour, which are useful when they're required at short notice. Hotel rooms are handy too, and most have wireless internet access. However, if the emergency is widespread then shortages of such places will rapidly occur, so taking advantage of employees' homes is often a better bet unless you can arrange in advance that a hotel or other location will permanently guarantee you first refusal on some short-notice space in return for a regular fee.

One sensible idea is to arrange a reciprocal agreement with a company of a similar size, local (but not too local) to your business, such that you can use a small amount of each other's office space and facilities in the event that either company suffers a major problem. Even a meeting room with three or four computers and telephones, which can be your base for a few days or weeks, is better than nothing. This works best if the other company is not a direct competitor.

If your company operates from more than one site then you are at a distinct advantage. However this isn't 100% reliable, especially if the sites are situated close together. For example, a terrorist incident could render all sites inaccessible.

People

Make sure you have home addresses, mobile phone numbers and external email addresses for all staff and that these are kept safely and securely, accessible at any time from any location. In the immediate aftermath of the event, you need to be able to contact key staff and tell them where to report. Bear in mind that this exercise might have to be carried out from an unfamiliar location such as a hotel room rather than your normal office.

You should also keep a record of any staff who have the necessary capabilities to work from home and, if so, for how long. For example, someone who requires relatively little supervision (such as a travelling sales person) and who has internet access at home can happily work from there for a while.

Facilities

A company needs more than a collection of desks and some people in order to do business. You also need computers, power, telephone lines and internet access. Your DRP needs to consider how you would cope if, in the space of a few minutes, all your existing computer equipment and everything else in your premises were rendered useless by, say, a fire or flood.

Obtaining computers isn't difficult. Many staff will probably have their own, which can be pressed into service in an emergency. Additional hardware can easily be bought or rented quite cheaply. But what about your data? Is there a backup of all your important information, stored securely off-site? And even if there is, how often is it updated and do all the relevant people know how to access it? How easy would it be to copy the contents of your backups onto a new network file server, once you've bought the hardware?

Do you have records of the passwords etc required to access external systems such as those operated by your Web-hosting supplier? What about all the important phone numbers such as those of suppliers and insurers? Do you have diagrams of all your key IT components, to aid in rebuilding them?

Do you rely on any specialist hardware that can't be easily purchased on the high street and, if so, do you have details of suppliers to hand? Is there a supply of cheques and purchase orders, or some way of getting cash out of the bank, so that you can actually buy things to start the recovery process? Who will arrange to redirect your telephones to a new location? If you run your own mail server, will incoming email need to be forwarded to a new system and, if so, who will arrange this? Can incoming snail-mail also be redirected and, if so, where to?

Maintaining and Testing the DRP

Your Disaster Recovery Plan needs to provide answers to all of the above questions, so that you are as prepared as you could possibly be for any emergency that strikes. In an ideal world you would also test the plan by putting it into full operation. But while such exercises might be within the realms of possibility at the typical bank or Government, any small or medium company is almost certainly unwilling to do this. The alternative is to do regular walk-throughs.

A walk-through involves a group of people sitting round a table, pretending that a disaster has taken place, asking all the necessary questions that might arise and checking that the plan contains all the answers. If, as is almost certainly the case, there are gaps in the plan, immediate steps should be taken to make a note of these omissions and to update the plan as soon as possible. The plan should also be reviewed as a matter of routine every year or so, to take account of staff arrivals and departures and other important changes.

Incident Response

Not all events which can befall corporate IT can be classified as disasters. A virus outbreak is one such example, as might be the discovery that a hacker has managed to deface your Web site or that your office has been broken into and some computers stolen. While not true disasters, such events do require immediate action by people who have the necessary training and planning under their belt in order to do the right thing at the right time. All of which comes under the heading of Incident Response.

Your plan for dealing with security incidents such as these should, like your DRP, be prepared in advance and reviewed regularly. It can be part of the DRP or a separate document, depending on whether the team or person responsible for both documents is the same.

Make sure everyone knows what constitutes an incident, and what they should do if an incident occurs. For example, a single user who accidentally deletes an important document can probably deal with it on their own, or perhaps by contacting the help desk. But if someone on the help desk is informed that the main hard disk on the server appears to have died, this should trigger the incident response plan, which probably involves notifying certain key people.

British Standard 18044 (see **www.bsi-global.com**) is a useful guide to incident and disaster recovery planning, dealing extensively with management and reporting issues rather than the technical side of things.

Don't Panic

While planning for disaster should be part of the job of everyone responsible for overall IT security within an organization, it's essential to keep things in perspective. The odds of ever having to initiate the full-scale disaster plan are minuscule. However, the chances of having to implement one particular part of the plan, perhaps to deal with a major hardware failure on a key server, are not insignificant. The benefits of having such plans arranged and considered in advance of the incident are enormous, and more than justify the relatively small cost of doing so.

Sadly, many companies put together a DRP not for their own benefit but merely because their auditors or some regulatory body decrees that there must be such a document. It is therefore prepared with little enthusiasm and rarely updated. And then, when it is actually required, its content is simply not reliable. Beware of falling into this trap – an unreliable DRP is worse than not having a DRP at all.

Record Everything

Public sources of information such as the Web are a great way to find solutions to problems. If a software product throws up an error message such as DEV_9 or INTERNET_31, typing that message into a search engine will help you find other people who have encountered it previously and, hopefully, will also include details of how they fixed the problem. If you have to look up such an error message once, copy the answer to a database in case you need to do it again. This will allow you to build up a knowledge base of problems and how to solve them. You should also keep your own records of any problems that arise, and the action that was taken in order to solve the problem. Just as importantly, if certain actions fail to fix the problem or actually exacerbate it, record this too. If your help desk or technical support department uses a dedicated package to manage jobs, the program will have such a facility built in. Otherwise, a shared document on a network server or on your intranet will suffice.

In the case of a disaster, whether major or minor, this collection will be incredibly useful in helping to track down the cause of the problem.

▶ FUNDAMENTAL FIVE

Your action points for this chapter:

1. Prepare a basic Disaster Recovery Plan. Ensure that each member of the DR team knows their roles and responsibilities. ☐

2. Store the DR plan in multiple locations so that it can be retrieved from off-site by all those who need it. ☐

3. Arrange some temporary office space to be used in an emergency, perhaps in employees' homes or by making a reciprocal arrangement with another company. ☐

4. Update your plan regularly, to take account of new systems and technology that you may have introduced. ☐

5. Ensure that you know which systems are most critical and therefore must be restored first. ☐

41

Hardware Theft

The majority of this book has so far been about how to prevent the loss of, or damage to, your company's information. This chapter is different because it's all about preventing the theft of computer hardware.

You might be wondering why this highly important topic has been left almost until last. Surely the consequences of someone walking off with an expensive laptop or desktop computer are severe? Actually, no. This topic has been left until now for a good reason: in today's business environment your hardware isn't important. At least, it's nowhere near as important as your data. A new laptop to replace one that gets lost or stolen can be picked up for a few hundred pounds. A desktop machine or an entry-level server can be had from just about any high-street store nowadays, including your local late-night supermarket, for the price of a few trolleys of groceries.

Hardware is simply a commodity item, frequently chosen on price rather than performance. While it is obviously a good idea to protect that hardware from loss and theft, such efforts should not be at the expense of protecting data. The consequences of losing a couple of laptops from the back of your sales manager's car are insignificant when compared to the loss of your customer database that was probably stored on each of them in an unencrypted format.

If those two laptops contained the only copies of said database, and there were no other backups, the problem has just become 10 times worse and could well mean the end of your company. Therefore, while it makes sense to protect hardware, put things into perspective. If time and money are limited when it comes to your overall IT security strategy, put hardware at the bottom of the list and data at the top. Never be tempted to do things the other way round because it just doesn't make sense.

Protecting Laptops

Of all the IT hardware that might ever be lost or stolen, laptop computers are top of the thieves' shopping lists. Consequently there are a few essential precautions that you must take to ensure that your company's laptops don't fall prey to opportunists.

First, if you or your staff need to carry a laptop in public, don't make it obvious to everyone else. Manufacturers of laptops are keen that you spend additional money on expensive padded shoulder bags that clearly identify you to any mugger who happens to be around. Ditch the smart bags in favour of a standard briefcase (the cheaper the better). A laptop computer is a business tool, not a status symbol with which to impress fellow commuters.

Next, make sure that laptops are not left unsecured on office desks overnight. Implement a rule that compels all staff to lock their laptop in a drawer or a central cupboard before they leave the office, if they don't intend to take the machine home. If you go for the central cupboard approach, ensure that the cupboard is securely locked and that the location of the key is not obvious, otherwise you are merely helping the burglar rather than hindering.

If staff take laptops off the company premises, perhaps to use at a conference or sales meeting, remind them to hide the machine out of sight whenever it's left in a car or a hotel room. Although it is legally difficult to make staff financially responsible for company equipment if they take it out of the office, that's no reason not to remind them that they could be subject to disciplinary action if their negligence leads to a loss.

Thieves often resort to devious tactics to steal hardware. A good friend of mine once attended a sales conference with some colleagues, which took place in the function room of a large hotel. Midway during a session, the fire alarms sounded. The hotel staff sprung into action and arrived to usher the delegates out of the room, but my friend insisted that no one would be leaving until the door of the function room could be locked. After a full and frank discussion, the hotel staff eventually went to locate a key and my friend's request was satisfied. Everyone left the room and assembled in the car park. It was a false alarm. There was no fire. When the delegates unlocked the door of the function room and returned to their conference, all was as they had left it. Unlike the next-door room in which another company was holding a similar event. They hadn't insisted on their door being locked, and every delegate's laptop was missing.

Another technique is for the thief to position himself in front of the laptop's owner in the queue for an airport security check. The thief walks through the metal detector as normal, then hangs around for a few seconds before continuing his journey. While he's hanging around, the laptop owner places his laptop on the conveyor belt for scanning and then walks through the metal detector. By the time he's out the other side, the thief has already picked up the laptop from the belt and walked quickly away from the scene.

So what can you do to help prevent laptops being stolen, especially when they are away from base? You insurance might well cover such eventualities, but it will probably require an addition to your policy and the premium that you pay. Sadly, in my experience, those increased premiums are sufficiently high as to persuade most organizations that it is easier and cheaper to bear any losses and not to insure the machines at all. So your best bet is a combination of protection and deterrence.

Every laptop comes with a universal slot into which you can secure a locking cable to tie the machine to the nearest desk. A Web search for 'Kensington Lock' will lead you to the parts you need. To attach other devices, such as expensive flat-screen displays, to those cables where a Kensington slot is not available, metal loops attached to self-adhesive pads are available. Just glue the pad to the equipment and then fit the cable and padlock as normal.

You should also invest in a set of asset labels. These are thin self-adhesive metal labels, each bearing your company logo and phone number plus a unique serial number. Attach a label to each of your laptops and other similar devices. They're a good deterrent and a great way to help the police identify any stolen property that they recover. Just make sure you keep a secure record of each label's serial number and details of the equipment to which it is attached.

For a more high-tech anti-theft solution, it's possible to buy transmitter devices that can be installed in equipment and which will trigger an alarm if someone attempts to carry the equipment off the premises. Installation of such systems is expensive, as receivers need to be fitted to all exits. A cheaper option, though still relatively high-tech, is to install some special software onto the computer so that, if it is stolen, it will attempt to 'phone home' as soon as the eventual recipient or thief connects it to the internet. Once it has made contact with the central server, police can track it by tracing the phone number or IP address. Check out www.winlocate.com and www.pcphonehome.com, for example.

Labels and cables are a highly visible deterrent that have been proved to reduce instances of theft. Less visible, but highly effective, are techniques such as Smart Water (see www.smartwater.com). Each bottle of Smart Water has chemicals added in order to give it a unique forensic identity, which can be verified by anyone with the correct equipment. Just put a few drops of the water on each item that you want to protect and, if it is stolen and later recovered, the police will know whom to contact to arrange its safe return.

Yet another option is a smoke-based system, whereby someone who breaks into your office triggers a machine that instantly fills the room with a thick white vapour that makes it impossible to see anything. Hopefully they will have the good sense to fumble their way out before the police arrive.

Protecting computer equipment isn't just about technology and locks. It's also about effective management, especially to deter employees and other trusted people from stealing it. Keep a good record of all equipment, and be seen to do so. Send out regular reminders to all staff that details of newly-purchased kit must be reported to the security department so that it can be tagged and a record made of the employee to whom the kit has been assigned. This will ensure that everyone is kept aware that, should they walk off with the equipment in question, its loss will be noticed and can be traced.

Above all, use encryption to mitigate your losses. A stolen computer containing encrypted information is merely the loss of a computer. A stolen computer containing the same information in unencrypted form is a far greater loss.

▶ FUNDAMENTAL FIVE

Your action points for this chapter:

1. Remember that data is almost always more valuable than the hardware on which it is stored. ☐

2. Never leave laptops visible and unattended in cars, hotel rooms and so on. Ensure that all staff are aware of this fundamental rule, and that failing to abide by it may invalidate any insurance policy. ☐

3. Never transport laptops in identifiable bags or cases. Use anonymous briefcases rather than branded bags. ☐

4. Attach non-removable labels to all hardware assets that bear your company's name and a unique reference number. ☐

5. Implement a policy that says that any person who carries hardware off the premises should have written authority permitting them to do so. ☐

42

Let's Be Careful Out There

I T security is a complex topic. Keeping up to date with the latest hacker techniques is a difficult job. Ensuring that your company's systems remain safe from hackers, viruses, spyware, malware, phishers, social engineers, denials of service and myriad other disasters is no easy task. Security product vendors continue to claim that installing their products will bring you peace of mind, but that's just not true. There's no silver bullet or universal panacea. If you want a job in which you can relax and not be in a continual state of panic that something terrible is about to happen, IT security is not it.

Thankfully, there are a lot of ways that you can help to make your life easier. Hopefully this book has provided you with some useful ideas. You should also put aside some regular time to keep up to date with developments in the industry. Consider block-booking half an hour in your diary every Wednesday afternoon, say, to browse the Web for interesting security news, as well as for critical patches that might affect products upon which your company depends. If you don't keep up to date with the hackers, you can't defend yourself from them.

You might also wish to re-read the set of action points at the end of each of the preceding chapters. I call them my Fundamental Five because, if you stick to those, you're well on your way to being your company's IT security guru.

Most criminals, whether in-house or external, are opportunistic by nature. Effective IT security is not about being totally impenetrable, because achieving such a state is unfeasibly expensive and restrictive. So long as you can keep your systems sufficiently unattractive to hackers so that they simply give up and decide to try somewhere else, you can consider yourself as being in control of the problem. You'll never defeat the hacker, but you can certainly frustrate him. And in this game, that's normally good enough.

Index